What is Islamophobia?

T0150474

What is Islamophobia?

Racism, Social Movements and the State

Edited by
Narzanin Massoumi,
Tom Mills and David Miller

www.plutobooks.com

First published 2017 by Pluto Press
345 Archway Road, London N6 5AA

www.plutobooks.com

Copyright © Narzanin Massoumi, Tom Mills and David Miller 2017

The right of the individual contributors to be identified as the author of
this work has been asserted by him in accordance with the Copyright,
Designs and Patents Act 1988.

British Library Cataloguing in Publication Data
A catalogue record for this book is available from the British Library

ISBN   978 0 7453 9958 4   Hardback
ISBN   978 0 7453 9957 7   Paperback
ISBN   978 1 7868 0068 8   PDF eBook
ISBN   978 1 7868 0070 1   Kindle eBook
ISBN   978 1 7868 0069 5   EPUB eBook

Typeset by Stanford DTP Services, Northampton, England

Simultaneously printed in the United Kingdom and United States of America

Contents

List of Tables

List of Figures

List of Acronyms

ADL – Anti-Defamation League
AfD – Alternative für Deutschland (Alternative for Germany)
AJC – American Jewish Committee
BBC – British Broadcasting Corporation
BMSD – British Muslims for Secular Democracy
CAMERA – Committee for Accuracy in Middle East Reporting in America
CEO – Chief Executive Officer
CIA – Central Intelligence Agency
CMPs – Closed Material Proceedings
CND – Campaign for Nuclear Disarmament
CPS – Crown Prosecution Service
CSC – Centre for Social Cohesion
CSP – Center for Security Policy
CSS – Centre for Secular Space
EDL – English Defence League
EHRC – Equality and Human Rights Commission
ESMOs – Elite Social Movement Organisations
EU – European Union
FBI – Federal Bureau of Investigation
FDD – Foundation for Defense of Democracies
FN – Front National (France)
FPÖ – Freiheitliche Partei Österreichs (Austrian Freedom Party)
GCSE – General Certificate of Secondary Education
GOP – Grand Old Party (US Republican Party)
HJS – Henry Jackson Society
IAM – Islamophobia Awareness Month
ICSR – International Centre for the Study of Radicalisation
ICT – International Institute for Counter-Terrorism (Israel)
IDC – Interdisciplinary Center (Herzliya, Israel)
IPT – Investigative Project on Terrorism
ISIL – Islamic State of Iraq and the Levant

ISIS – Islamic State of Iraq and Syria
JNF – Jewish National Fund
JRCT – Joseph Rowntree Charitable Trust
KH – Keren Hayesod
KTCO – Kentish Town Community Organisation
MAB – Muslim Association of Britain
MCB – Muslim Council of Britain
MEF – Middle East Forum
MEMRI – Middle East Media Research Institute
MEND – Muslim Engagement and Development
NATO – North Atlantic Treaty Organization
NGO – Non-Governmental Organisation
NUS – National Union of Students
NUT – National Union of Teachers
PII – Public Interest Investigations
OLFA – One Law For All
OWAAD – Organisation of Women of Asian and African Descent
PEGIDA – Patriotische Europäer Gegen die Islamisierung des
    Abendlandes (Patriotic Europeans Against Islamisation of the West)
PIRA – Provisional Irish Republican Army
PVV – Partij voor de Vrijheid (Party for Freedom, the Netherlands)
RDR – Race Disproportionality Ratio
RICU – Research, Information and Communications Unit, Home
    Office
RJC – Republican Jewish Coalition
SANE – Society of Americans for National Existence
SBS – Southall Black Sisters
SIOA – Stop Islamization of America
StWC – Stop the War Coalition
TA – Terrorism Act
UCU – University and College Union
UIA – United Israel Appeal
UJIA – United Jewish Israel Appeal
UK – United Kingdom
UKACIA – UK Action Committee on Islamic Affairs
UKIP – UK Independence Party
US – United States
VOICE – Victims Of Islamic Cultural Extremism (UK)

WAF – Women Against Fundamentalism
WINEP – Washington Institute for Middle East Policy
WLUML – Women Living Under Muslim Laws
WZO – World Zionist Organization

Acknowledgements

This book is one of the products of the Understanding Conflict conference that we organised at the University of Bath in June 2015. We thank all those who helped make that event possible including the Economic and Social Research Council (ESRC) and the University of Bath as well as all participants. At the time, we wrote about the difficulties of putting on events like that, noting that the police had shown an interest, as relayed to us by the security office of the University of Bath (Miller and Massoumi, 2015).

The ideas expressed in this book have been rehearsed and developed via a number of articles on *Open Democracy* and we thank the editors there for offering us the space to develop these ideas that are sometimes seen as controversial. We have also presented versions of the ideas at a wide variety of seminars and meetings throughout the UK, which have included both formal academic and more engaged events.

The academic events are:

- 'Terrorism expertise and the "radicalisation" thought collective', Seminar presentation, École des hautes études en sciences sociales, Paris (17 April 2015). Thanks to Sylvain Laurens and Francis Chateauraynaud.
- Keynote address at the Critical Studies on Terrorism Annual Conference 2015: Beyond Critique, BISA Critical Studies on Terrorism Working Group, University of Leeds (3–4 September 2015).
- 'Contesting racialisation: Islamophobic social movements and the battle of ideas', 12th Annual Historical Materialism Conference, SOAS, London (5–8 November 2015).
- Five Pillars of Islamophobia Seminar, Canterbury Christ Church University, Kent (19 November 2015). Thanks to Fahid Qurashi.
- 'The state and social movements from above as the driving forces of anti-Muslim "racism"', Centre for Citizenship and Ethnicity seminar series, University of Bristol (3 December 2015). Thanks to Tariq Modood.

- Islamophobia and Eroding Civil Society, Paris (11 December 2015). Thanks to Hatem Bazian.
- The State, Civil Society and Islamophobia, European Institute of the Mediterranean, Barcelona (15–16 December 2015). Thanks to Elisabetta Ciuccarelli.
- 'Women, racism and war: Gaza and the global "War on Terror"', Social Science in the City, Watershed, Bristol (24 March 2016). Thanks to Michal Nahman and Smadar Lavie.
- New Racisms II: Neoliberalism and its Others, University of Sussex (9–10 June 2016). Thanks to Naaz Rashid and Malcolm James.
- State Crime Seminar: The State, Islamophobia and the Problems of Researching Terrorism and Extremism, Queen Mary University of London (24 November 2016). Thanks to Tom McManus and Penny Green.
- Racisms and Political Mobilisations Conference, University of East London (19–20 January 2017). Thanks to Gargi Bhattacharyya, Satnam Virdee and Aaron Winter.

We should also mention the Racism and Islamophobia event at the University of Huddersfield, which was due to be held on 12 July 2016, to which one of us was invited as a keynote speaker. It was cancelled at the last minute as a direct result of the effect of the Prevent duty, an indication of the way the duty undermines both freedom of speech and academic freedom. Some of the saga is recorded in Amrit Singh's (2016) valuable report on Prevent.

We thank the organisers and participants of the following more engaged events, at which one or other of us has spoken:

- Radical Independence Conference, Glasgow (22 November 2014).
- Critical Platform: Islam, Extremism, Terrorism, organised by the Cordoba Foundation, Queen Mary University of London (20 January 2015).
- Five Pillars of Islamophobia tour, organised by Mend, Manchester, Leeds, Leicester, Ilford (September 2015). Thanks to Sufyan Ismail and all at Mend.
- Bristol University (12 October 2015).
- Islamophobia Awareness Month: Muslims, Civil Liberties and the West, Bristol University (26 November 2015).

- Constructing the 'Other': The Framework of Islamophobia in Britain, SOAS Islamic Society, London (11 November 2015).
- The Environment of Hate: The New Normal for Muslims in the UK, Islamic Human Rights Commission, P21 Galler, London (17 November 2015).
- Students not Suspects, Nottingham University (18 November 2015).
- Students not Suspects, Bristol University (17 March 2016).
- 'How expert are the terrorism experts?', Bath Royal Literary & Scientific Institution, 19 April 2016.
- Youth Radicalisation Conference, Bristol Somali Forum, City Academy Bristol (9 April 2016).
- Prevent, Islamophobia and Civil Liberties National Conference, Goldsmiths, London (4 June 2016).
- Challenging Islamophobia, Launch of Interculture, Trinity Centre, Bristol (11 June 2016).
- Islamophobia Conference 2016, Islamic and Human Rights Commission, P21 Gallery, London (10 December 2016).

We would also like to thank a range of people who have supported us in our work, for example, by providing information or identifying sources, offering their time and other resources as well as giving constructive feedback and a stimulating environment in which to develop our arguments. We are grateful to Ismael Patel, Asim Qureshi, Muhammad Rabbani, Ibrahim Mohamod, Solenne Jouanneau and Sylvain Laurens (in Paris and Strasbourg), Hatem Bazian, Nariman Massoumi, Hilary Aked, Tom Griffin, Sarah Marusek, Piers Robinson, Tariq Modood, Naima Bouteldja, Ed Augustin, Rizwaan Sabir, Shenaz Bunglawala, Deepa Kumar, Arun Kundnani, Waqas Tufail, Hannah Dee, Shelley Asquith and Malia Bouattia.

Bibliography

Miller, D. and Massoumi, N. (2015), 'University research on terrorism may never be free from interference', *Guardian*, 15 June.

Singh, A. (2016), *Eroding Trust: The UK's PREVENT Counter-Extremism Strategy in Health and Education*. Open Society Justice Initiative. New York: Open Society Foundations. www.opensocietyfoundations.org/sites/default/files/eroding-trust-20161017_0.pdf. Accessed 2 March 2017.

PART 1

Introduction: What is Islamophobia?

1

Islamophobia, Social Movements and the State: For a Movement-centred Approach

Narzanin Massoumi, Tom Mills and David Miller

Despite a considerable growth in writing on Islamophobia in recent years there is still no clear agreement as to what it is, where it comes from and how it relates to other forms of racism. Indeed, two decades after the term entered into common usage in the English-speaking world, Islamophobia is still not universally recognised as a form of racism. This remains the case even in academia, where the literature on racism is still largely separate from work on Islamophobia. The relative inattention Islamophobia has received from sociologists of racism is surprising given the considerable growth in hostility towards Muslims in recent years, which could hardly have gone unnoticed. And it is all the more surprising given that one of the great insights of this subfield of sociology has been to recognise 'race' as a social construct arising in particular historical and political contexts, rather than a property of the victims of racism.

In this introductory chapter we offer a theoretically grounded, empirically rich, sociological conception of Islamophobia which focuses not on the characteristics of Muslim people, but rather on *political practices*. In this sense, our approach differs from much of the existing work on Islamophobia, which has tended to focus on the conflicting discourses around citizenship, identity, belonging and nationhood (Bulmer and Solomos, 2015; Esposito and Ibrahim, 2013; Modood, 2007). By contrast, we set out an argument that conceives of Islamophobia not simply as a product of abstract discursive or ideological processes, but of concrete social action undertaken in the pursuit of certain interests.

'In our view, solely focusing on the religious, cultural or even political identities of Muslim people only offers a partial view of Islamophobia. A more satisfactory approach than starting with how the meaning of Muslim identities are constructed and contested, for example, is to focus on the set of institutions and policies that disproportionately impact upon Muslims. This is an empirical question which can be investigated through conventional social scientific methods. Doing so should draw our attention not only to the structures, agents and practices that produce racist outcomes, but also to the social, political and cultural action undertaken which puts the infrastructure of subordination in place.

In this chapter, and others in this collection, we discuss these agents and institutions under the rubric of the 'five pillars of Islamophobia'. By this we mean that there are specific social actors (pillars) that produce the ideas and practices that result in disadvantage for Muslims. We argue that the state is the foremost of these, in particular as a result of the activities of the counter-terrorism apparatus. We suggest that there are four other collective social actors (or social movements) that are important in supporting and extending anti-Muslim racism. These are the neoconservative movement, (parts of) the Zionist movement, the counterjihad movement (and the far right) and elements of liberal, left, secular and feminist movements. Before discussing the state and these various social movements, we turn first to the question of why we should theorise Islamophobia as a form of racism.

Theorising Islamophobia

A key reference point for accounts of Islamophobia has been the late Fred Halliday's article, '"Islamophobia" reconsidered' (1999). This is the most highly cited article on Islamophobia on Google Scholar and after nearly two decades still has political purchase for those on the left and right who oppose mobilisations against Islamophobia. In the article, Halliday argued against using the term Islamophobia; a position rooted in his critique of 'communalist' identity politics. Unlike some other Islamophobia deniers (e.g. Malik, 2005), Halliday acknowledges the existence of anti-Muslim racism. But he argues that since such racism targets 'a people' rather than a religion, 'anti-Muslimism' is a more fitting term. For Halliday, and others, the concept of Islamophobia inevitably conflates legitimate or honest criticisms of reactionary religious practices (particularly those based around gender) with racism, thus silencing progressive critics of Islam. This is an argument commonly made by liberals, and some leftists (as well as, more recently, the far right), and we deal with it and similar arguments in Chapter 11. For now though, it is worth considering in more detail the relationship between Islam and what Halliday calls 'anti-Muslimism' and what we prefer to call Islamophobia.

One response to Islamophobia from anti-racist campaigners – and one broadly in keeping with the Halliday thesis – has been to point out that while it may appear to target a religion rather than an ethnic group, in reality it overwhelmingly impacts upon ethnic minorities. Islamophobia is therefore *in effect* racist, even if as a set of ideas it might seem (or be presented as) unconnected to any particular ethnic group. But while it is certainly true that Islamophobia overwhelmingly impacts on people of colour, and this is an important point to bear in mind, in analytical terms this is nevertheless a very limited and limiting position to take, leading to the view that a policy, practice or set of ideas can only be considered racist insofar as it relates to a specific ethnicity. It is a position that implicitly assumes that 'race' is somehow more 'real' than religious identity, or at least that the latter is a more legitimate basis for discrimination and oppression. This is not a position we think politically acceptable or intellectually sustainable.

The anti-essentialist concept of 'racialisation' – which was developed by sociologists to emphasise the dynamic and historically contingent nature of 'race' – offers a clear solution to the unnecessary analytical confusion which still surrounds questions of Islamophobia and 'race', as well as offering a definitive rebuttal to those who argue, one way or another, that Islamophobia, by definition, cannot be a form of racism. If 'race' is a fiction created when certain ethnic heritage or cultural practices attach to social advantage or disadvantage, it is hard to see religious identity as ontologically distinct from 'race'. For good reason then, racial-isation is increasingly used to explain Islamophobia as a form of racism (e.g. Garner and Selod, 2015). For some time though Islamophobia was somewhat neglected in the racialisation literature. The edited collection on racialisation by Murji and Solomos (2005), for example, contains no chapters examining Islamophobia directly, and a review of the literature on the bibliographic database, Scopus, shows that until recently there was very little work utilising both concepts. In response to this gap in the literature, a relatively small number of scholars in recent years have begun to use the concept of racialisation to situate Islamophobia within the trajectory of contemporary racisms (Garner and Selod, 2015; Meer, 2013; Meer and Modood, 2009, 2011a; Vakil, 2011). These scholars directly challenge the position taken by Halliday and others by attempting to show that the anti-'religion' element of Islamophobia is in fact a form of racism in that it devalues the culture of a minority group (Meer and Modood, 2009, 2011a; Vakil, 2011). 'Cultural racism', according to these scholars, is not just a proxy for biological racism; the anti-Islam element of anti-Muslim racism is itself racist. (For an empirical explication of this position, see Khattab and Modood, 2015 on the 'Muslim penalty' in the employment market.)

These scholars have made an important contribution to the ways we understand race, religion and culture, and have rightly drawn attention to the neglect of Islamophobia within current sociological understandings of racism. But their strong focus on cultural recognition turns attention away from the agents and interests behind racism. This is a problem in the literature on racialisation and racism more generally, which has often placed too much emphasis on how the 'meaning of race' is negotiated and in different times and contexts, without sufficient attention to the practical action taken to put in place the infrastructure of disadvantage and subordination.

At this stage, it is perhaps worth stating that an empirical focus on political practices does not mean ignoring ideas. On the contrary, one cannot separate ideas and practices since they inform each other. But it is important to recognise the limitations of idealist explanations of racism. Ideas do not 'float freely', they are materially produced and disseminated by particular social actors with particular interests in the particular circumstances in which they find themselves. In the case of Islamophobia, ideas about Muslims of course play an important role in the political action we consider to be of central importance, but it is quite wrong to see the issue here as simply being a set of wrong ideas circulating in society.

In contrast to ideas-based approaches, we offer a materialist or realist account of Islamophobia which understands it as a structural phenomenon. But while we conceive of Islamophobia as – like other forms of racism – a product of social structures, we think it crucial to recognise the social action that not only takes place in relation to structures, but also remakes or transforms them. Thus, we endeavour to provide an account which recognises the role of agency more than is often found in radical scholarly accounts of racism. The earlier work of Robert Miles (1982), for example, who in his updated book on racism (2003) offers only a very brief discussion of Islamophobia, exemplifies some of the problems with how racism has been understood in the historical materialist tradition, with racism treated in an overly determinist or reductionist manner, and seen as an instrumental ideology to divide the working class.[1] Similarly, Middle Eastern Studies scholar Stephen Sheehi (2011: 32) conceives of Islamophobia as an 'ideological phenomenon which exists to promote political and economic goals, both domestically and abroad', arguing that it is 'institutionalized by the US government ranging from war to programmatic torture to extrajudicial kidnappings, incarceration and executions to surveillance and entrapment'. Sheehi's book offers a much more developed account of Islamophobia, and one which commendably recognises the key roles of ideas, and indeed the vast range of think tanks and lobby groups spreading Islamophobic ideas and practices. But it does not focus on the practical action that is involved in the production of Islamophobia and seems to regard Islamophobic acts as the consequences of ideology, as opposed to the acts themselves being Islamophobic. Thus, Sheehi (2011: 32) writes that the 'effects of Islamophobia' include a series of acts such as those carried out by governments (war, torture, extrajudicial killings) or in the daily lives of Muslims (harassment, discrimination, hate speech). But in our view these actions are themselves Islamophobic, as opposed to being simply the result of a racist ideology.

Another significant intellectual current in studies of racism, and one that has commendably paid far more attention to the problem of Islamophobia, is work influenced by poststructuralism, which views Islamophobia through the lens of Orientalism and 'othering', taking inspiration from Said (1977) and Fanon (1967 [2008]) (Grosfoguel, 2012; Samman, 2012; Skenderovic et al., 2014). These scholars break radically from liberal, and indeed Marxist, accounts of racism, and effectively situate racist ideas historically and geopolitically. But in our view there are serious limitations to this body of work also, in that it similarly fails to illuminate the social forces involved in producing racism, with interests collapsed into the hopelessly vague concepts of discourse or culture.

We can, and should, be far more precise, focusing on the specific agents and institutions implicated in racist practices and in the production of Islamophobic ideas, policies and structures. Islamophobia is a form of 'structural racism'. But it does not flow intrinsically and mysteriously from culture, colonialism or imperialism, nor equally vaguely from a capitalist or neoliberal 'racial order'. For reasons we have already outlined, we agree with Kapoor and Kalra on the need to move beyond 'the plethora of identity [based] work' (Kapoor and Kalra, 2013: 6) in favour of an 'account of the destructive and disruptive operations of state power' (Kapoor, 2013: 228).

The Islamophobic state

We regard the state, and more specifically the sprawling official 'counter-terrorism' apparatus, to be absolutely central to the production of contemporary Islamophobia – it is the backbone of anti-Muslim racism. An increasingly powerful and largely unaccountable set of institutions, with close relations with multinational technology and security companies, targets 'extremists' and those said to have been 'radicalised', focusing on Muslims in particular. These concepts are imprecisely defined in official discourse. Consequently, the way they are operationalised in the state bureaucracy, together with the routine practices of the police and other public servants, means that many thousands of people in the UK, including non-Muslims, are now regarded as legitimate targets for suspicion, surveillance and intelligence-gathering. In this section we examine the range of powers deployed by the state, and illustrate how they systematically disadvantage Muslims (and some others).

The extraordinary powers of the UK counter-terrorism apparatus are partly a legacy of the prevention of terrorism powers introduced in response to the conflict over the British presence in Northern Ireland as 'temporary provisions'. These were put on a permanent footing by the Blair government in the shape of the Terrorism Act 2000.

Under Section 44 of that Act, the police were entitled to stop and search any person or vehicle without any requirement for 'reasonable suspicion'. Due to the draconian nature of this power, Section 44 was originally intended to be restricted to specified areas, and for limited periods. But in the event, the Metropolitan Police were granted rolling authorisation, meaning that for almost a decade this power was in operation throughout the whole of the Greater London area. Guidance on Section 44 published by the Home Office in 2004 stated that:

> There may be circumstances where it is appropriate for officers to take account of a person's ethnic background when they decide who to stop in response to a specific terrorist threat (for example, some international terrorist groups are associated with particular ethnic groups, such as Muslims). (quoted in Kundnani, 2006)

Comparing the self-identified ethnicity of those stopped and searched under Section 44 with that of the population of England and Wales as a whole, Quinlan and Derfoufi note that Asians and Blacks were disproportionately targeted compared to Whites, with Asians in 2009/10 on average over six times more likely to be stopped and searched, and black people on average almost eight times more likely (the respective average disproportionality ratios for each group being 6.2 and 7.86) (Quinlan and Derfoufi, 2015: 136). Parmar's examination of the impact of Section 44 stop and searches in London concluded that minorities had been 'criminalised' on the basis of their religious background, and that this had deepened intra-ethnic tensions (Parmar, 2011: 369). Section 44 was declared unlawful by the European Court of Human Rights in January 2010, which noted in its judgment that 'none of the many thousands of searches has ever resulted in conviction of a terrorism offence' (Gillan and Quinton v UK, para.148).

Schedule 7 of the Terrorism Act 2000 is a similarly draconian power which applies to port and border controls. Described by the civil liberties group Liberty (2017) as 'a breathtakingly broad and intrusive power', it allows police to detain people at ports and airports for up to nine hours, to conduct searches of their person and to seize their belongings for up to seven days. Those detained under Schedule 7 are not entitled to a publicly funded lawyer, are obliged to answer questions and, if detained at a police station, provide biometric data, including fingerprints and DNA. All this can be done without any requirement for 'reasonable suspicion', meaning that those detained under this power need not be suspected of any crime, yet have less legal rights than criminal suspects.

The religion of those detained under Schedule 7 is not recorded in official statistics, but there are figures on the ethnicity of those examined or detained. Hurrell (2013) has examined disproportionality in the use of Schedule 7 powers for the period 2010/11 to 2012/13 by comparing Home Office statistics on its use with demographic data from the 2011 Census and passenger data from the Civil Aviation Authority and the Department of Transport. Like Quinlan and Derfoufi, she uses the race disproportionality ratio (RDR), which has been used by the Equality and Human Rights Commission (EHRC) as a measure of disproportionality in police stop and searches. The RDR can be calculated by (1) dividing the proportion of the total individuals targeted by the authorities who identify with a particular minority by the proportion of white people targeted; (2) dividing the proportion of that ethnic minority in the population by the proportion of white people in the population; and then (3) dividing the former figure by the latter. A value of 1.0 indicates no disproportionality. Anything above this value indicates that that minority is being disproportionally targeted. Hurrell's calculations comparing 2011 Census data with the use of Schedule 7 power at airports in 2010/11 suggested that travellers identifying as Pakistani, African or a member of 'any other' ethnic group (a category which includes Arabs) have experienced extremely high levels of disproportional targeting under Schedule 7. Pakistani people in particular stood out. The RDRs for Pakistani travellers were 52.6 for total examinations, 135.9 for over the hour examinations and 154.5 for detentions (Hurrell, 2013: 28). What this means is that someone with Pakistani ethnicity is over 150 times more likely to be detained under Schedule 7 than a white person. By way of comparison, the headline figure for the EHRC's 2010 report *Stop and Think*, which revealed the continuing discriminatory use of police stop and search powers, was based on a black/white RDR finding of 6.5 (Equalities and Human Rights Commission, 2010).

We can utilise a similar method to examine referrals to 'Channel', the UK government's 'pre-criminal diversionary programme', which it claims 'provide[s] support for people vulnerable to being drawn into any form of terrorism'. While the government does not publish figures on referrals, some data has been released under the Freedom of Information Act by the National Police Chief's Council. A 2013 disclosure stated that between April 2007 and December 2011, 67 per cent of those referred to the programme were Muslim. No data on the religion of persons referred was then recorded between January 2011 and March 2012, and the proportion recorded as Muslims from April 2012 to March 2013 fell to 57.4 per cent. These figures, however, are somewhat misleading since they include a substantial proportion of individuals whose religion is not known, a different category to those of no religion, or who preferred not to state their religion. Excluding this unknown category suggests that in the earlier period of the programme over 90 per cent of those referred (whose religion was known) were Muslims. Then from April 2012 to March 2013, it would suggest that Muslims made up approximately 78 per cent of those referred. Over the whole of that period, according to the same disclosure, 14 per cent of referrals were categorised as being related to far-right extremism. Figures disclosed for 2013/14 state that 689 of the 1,252 individuals referred were categorised as Muslims, which again excluding those whose religion is not known (388), suggests that Muslims made up over 79 per cent of referrals in that more recent period.

In short, the available data on Channel reveals that Muslims certainly make up the majority of referrals, and likely make up the great majority, with the far right making up the remainder. While the proportion of Muslims making up the referrals to the Channel programme is remarkable enough in itself, to appreciate the significance of these figures they should be compared to the proportion of the population as a whole which Muslims make up, which according to the 2011 England and Wales Census is 4.8 per cent. If being Muslim had no significant impact on the probability of referral to the programme, therefore, we would expect Muslims to make up roughly the same proportion of persons referred to the Channel programme. This is obviously not the case and even taking the lowest proportion of referrals suggested by these somewhat patchy official figures (78 per cent) would suggest Muslims are overrepresented by a factor of 16.25, and that a Muslim is over 70 times more likely to be referred to the Channel programme than a non-Muslim.

The most recent figures released under the Freedom of Information Act show that there has been a sharp increase in Channel referrals following the Counter Terrorism and Security Act 2015, which introduced a statutory duty for designated public institutions to pay 'due regard' to 'prevent people from being drawn into terrorism'. While there were a total of 6,306 individuals referred in the eight years between April 2007 (when Channel was established) and May 2015, between July 2015 and June 2016 there were 4,611 referrals, a 75 per cent increase on the previous year. Notably, of these some 2,311 were children (including 352 under nine years old). At the time of writing, the youngest person known to have been referred to Channel was three years old.

The introduction of the Counter Terrorism and Security Act 2015 inaugurated a new phrase of the 'War on Terror'. This has meant that the counter-terrorism apparatus has spread from its traditional home in the police and intelligence services, to occupy almost every branch of the state, from schools and universities, to GP surgeries, social care, opticians, libraries and even nurseries. It has meanwhile become increasingly difficult for Muslims to engage in politics or public life. Between 5 December 2012 and 8 May 2014 the Charity Commission marked 55 British charities with the new code, 'extremism and radicalisation' without the organisations' knowledge, while Freedom of Information requests made by the *Guardian* have shown that more than a quarter of live investigations by the Commission concern Muslim charities (Ramesh, 2014). In October 2014, David Cameron awarded extra powers and £8 million to the Charity Commission to 'confront the menace of extremism'. The Charity Commission intervened to choke off future funding to advocacy group Cage, which works with victims of the 'War on Terror'. Charitable donors, including the Joseph Rowntree Charitable Trust (JRCT), came under what JRCT called 'acute regulatory pressure' to cut off future funding, and acceded. A subsequent Judicial Review brought by Cage was withdrawn when the Charity Commission conceded that 'it does not aim to restrict trustees exercising their discretion in advancing their objects, including around funding decisions' (Ritchie, 2015).

Theorising state racism

Given the above, it is surprising how little critical attention is given to the state in discussions of Islamophobia. In various liberal accounts, scholars have focused not on how citizens should respond to racist state practices, but rather how the authorities can best ameliorate racism in society. Such research tends to examine how the state and its citizens should respond to the challenge of cultural and religious diversity, examining the status of Muslims within liberal democracies and considering how liberal citizenship frameworks should be adapted to accommodate the challenge of 'difference' posed by Muslim migration (e.g. Cesari, 2004, 2013). Multiculturalists – in a variation on this liberal theme – go further in thinking through how states should respond to the cultural diversity of their citizenry. Meer and Modood (2009, 2011a), who, as outlined above, focus on the racialisation of Muslims to emphasise the importance and prevalence of cultural racism, argue that the disrespect of Muslim identity (or misrecognition) is in itself a form of harm and the source of grievance for many Muslims. The solution for them is a form of cultural pluralism within the public sphere, with a particular emphasis on religious diversity, for example, through legislation against religious discrimination and the introduction of religious pluralism into political and educational institutions.

Meer and Modood have argued that without recognising the racial- isation of Muslims, Muslims in the UK will not enjoy the same civil rights as other groups. A good example of this is the failure of the UK race relations legislation which until 2003 significantly disadvantaged Muslims. So while the 1976 Race Relations Act, and the legislation that followed, recognised the principle of 'racial equality', introducing measures against discrimination on the basis of 'race, colour or national origins' (Race Relations Act 1976), there was a disparity in the ways that different groups were treated. Jews and Sikhs were included as members of ethnic and racial groups, whereas Muslims were not (Meer and Modood, 2011b: 65). So, until 2003, Muslims were afforded no legal protection against discrimination *as Muslims*, meaning that up until that time if you were denied a job on the basis of wearing a hijab, or showing some other visible signs of being Muslim, you would have no legal recourse.

We certainly recognise the great importance of civil rights. But it is precisely these protections that are being eroded by the executive in the name of counter-terrorism. The state is certainly not a homogeneous structure, but a complex set of institutions, sections of which reflect, or can be pressured by, movements 'from below' and perform valuable social functions. We should not imagine that the state is neutral on the question of Islamophobia, and can therefore be appealed to as an effective arbitrator on questions of Islam and cultural difference. Government counter-terrorism policy significantly disadvantages Muslims (and others) through exceptional legislation, pre-emptive incapacitation and intelligence and surveillance. Both liberal and multiculturalist approaches turn the problem on its head, starting with Muslims and then working 'upwards' towards the institutions of the state. In opposition to this approach, we advance an analysis which rather than asking how the state can accommodate Muslim difference, examines the ways in which the state has disadvantaged Muslims, and asks how we should respond to this.

The racial state?

Other authors share our less sanguine conception of the state, but tend to overemphasise the importance of ideas or to decouple their analysis from any concrete interrogation of state practices. David Goldberg, for example, who rejects the term racialisation, focuses on racial formations as an intrinsic feature of the state.

In *The Racial State*, Goldberg argues that 'race is integral to the emergence, development, and transformations (conceptually, philo-sophically, materially) of the modern nation-state. Race marks and orders the modern nation-state, and so state projects, more or less from its point of conceptual and institutional emergence' (Goldberg, 2002a: 4). The 'socio-cultural embeddedness of race – its form and contents, modes and effects of routinization and penetration into state formation and order,' Goldberg writes elsewhere, 'has been basic to fashioning the personality of the modern state' (Goldberg, 2009: 109, 52). It is not always clear in Goldberg's dense writings whether he is advancing a historically contingent argument about the racist character of European nation-states, or making broader theoretical claims about the essentially racialising character of modern state bureaucracies. In general, he seems to be adopting the latter theoretical position, while pointing empirically to the former. Race, for Goldberg, is 'more than simply threaded through the fabric of modern and modernizing racial states' (Goldberg, 2002b: 240). What he terms the 'racial state'

> is racial not *merely* or reductively because of the racial composition of its personnel or the racial implications of its policies – though clearly both play a part. States are racial more deeply because of the structural position they occupy in producing and reproducing, constituting and effecting racially shaped spaces and places, groups and events, life worlds and possibilities, accesses and restrictions, inclusions and exclusions, conceptions and modes of representation. They are *racial*, in short, in virtue of their modes of population definition, determi-

nation, and structuration. (Goldberg, 2002b: 239, emphases in the original)

For Goldberg, race and racism, it would seem, are inherent in the ratio-nalising and homogenising impulse of the modern state, especially its territorial regulation of human populations. The trouble with this totalising account is unwittingly revealed in an earlier passage in *The Racial State* in which Goldberg notes that his 'racial state could be said to be everywhere – and simultaneously seen nowhere. It (more or less invisibly) defines almost every relation, shapes all but every interaction, contours virtually all intercourse' (Goldberg, 2002b: 235). This incredibly broad sweep is precisely the problem. If something can be said to be everywhere, and yet is seen nowhere, what does its theorisation add to our understanding? More specifically, we might ask of the preceding quoted passage: if particular policies have no 'racial implications', in what meaningful sense can the state responsible for said policies be said to be 'racial'? Goldberg's insistence on the centrality of race and racism to the emergence of the modern nation-state perhaps serves as a useful counterpoint to 'colour-blind' liberal accounts (on which see also Mills, 1997), or to those with an unrealistic faith in the state's intentions in the field of racial politics. But his approach ends up with exactly the opposite problem, envisaging the state as an undifferentiated oppressive structure, and seeing racism as inherent in the classification processes and disciplinary mechanisms of governmentality that define membership of the nation. According to Goldberg:

> Racial states oversee a range of institutional, definitive and disciplinary practices. They are engaged in definition, regulation, governance, management, and mediation of racial matters they at once help fashion and facilitate. For one, racial states *define* populations into racially identified groups, and they do so more or less formally through census taking, law, and policy, in and through bureaucratic forms, and administrative practices. (Goldberg, 2002a: 109–10, emphasis in the original)

This is all true of course. But it ignores the fact that laws, policies and census data are not inherently racist. On the contrary, the inclusion of 'racial' categories in the census have been amongst the demands of anti-racist movements in order that racial disadvantage can be made visible and countered, though such arguments have not been uncontroversial (Emigh et al., 2016: 132–44). It is simply not clear in Goldberg's work specifically what claims are being made about the state, or its role in reproducing racial disadvantage. While he distinguishes between different types of racial states, thereby acknowledging different degrees of state racism, his 'deep' theory of the racial state remains ill-suited to an empirical investigation of racism and racial politics.

A more focused and concrete rendering of the concept of 'the racial state' can be found in Omi and Winant's classic account of racial politics in the US, which Goldberg draws on in *The Racial State*. From the early period of European colonisation of the Americas, Omi and Winant note in *Racial Formation in the United States*, race served as 'multi-levelled organizing principle' linking 'the corporeal/visible characteristics of different social groups to different sociopolitical statuses' and providing 'various religious and political principles for inclusion and exclusion'. Race thus served to 'fuel and justify first the colonial impulse and later the nation-building process', providing the rationale for exclusion from the imagined community of the nation (Omi and Winant, 2015: 76).

The racial state, in Omi and Winant's account, lies at 'the core of a given racial regime'. It manages the 'racial system', which is 'encoded in law, organized through policy-making, and enforced by a repressive apparatus' (2015: 148) making 'use of ideology ... to "glue" together contradictory practices and structures' (2015: 138).

Omi and Winant seem to have moved away from some of the more deterministic elements visible in the first edition of *Racial Formation* (1986). Introducing a recent collection entitled *State of White Supremacy*, Jung concurs with Omi and Winant's original claim that the US state is 'inherently racial', adding that 'in all likelihood, [it] will always be racial' (Jung et al., 2011: 2). The former claim, however, does not appear in the most recent edition of *Racial Formation* (2015), and Omi and Winant have always emphasised that 'racial systems' are 'unstable', noting that 'the great variety of conflicting interests encapsulated in racial meanings and identities can be no more than pacified by the state' (2015: 148). Any racial order, according to Omi and Winant, is always open to contestation by subordinate groups and the racial state in the US 'has been transformed over and over in unending efforts to deal with its fundamental contradictions' (2015: 147).

While Goldberg is influenced by structural Marxism, and to some extent also by Foucault, the Gramscian influence on Omi and Winant lends itself to a greater emphasis on historical contingency and political contestation. For Omi and Winant, the racial state is, along with anti-racist social movements, one of 'the two central actors in the drama' of US racial politics (2015: 149), and it is the interaction over time between these two central actors that has determined the 'trajectories of racial politics' (2015: 140). This seems more useful than Goldberg's totalising and politically fatalistic theory, but we would go further than Omi and Winant in emphasising the role of broader social actors in shaping and reshaping what they term 'the racial state'. To this end we now turn to the discussion of social movements from above.

The state and social movements from above

Though the state is identified here as the 'backbone' of Islamophobia, this is not a product, as we have already noted, of the inalienable nature of the 'capitalist' or 'racial' state, and nor is it simply an effect of 'structure'. Rather, it is produced in the contest between social movements from below and their opponents: social movements from above. We define social movements in a broad way following Barker (2013: 66):

> A process in which a specific social group develops a collective project of skilled activities centred on a rationality ... that tries to change or maintain a dominant structure of entrenched needs and capacities, in part or whole.

It is a critical part of our argument that the shape and extent of Islamophobia are shaped not just by the relationship between the state and social movements from below, but also in contest with their counterparts from above. It is to outlining our understanding of such movements that we now turn.

Elite social movements

Cahill (2004) adopts the concept of elite social movements in his Gramscian account of the rise of the 'radical neoliberal movement' in Australia. Elite social movements, Cahill suggests, are similar to the 'new social movements' in that they are 'dynamic social actors who seek not only to influence state policies, but, very often, to bring about broad based social, cultural and political change in accordance with the ideologies around which they cohere' (Cahill, 2004: 50). But whereas new social movements are rooted 'in popular protest by groups and individuals from a more diverse range of class locations', elite social movements, according to Cahill, are comprised primarily of elites 'and thus enjoy a privileged position in symbol manipulation, access to political decision makers and financial resources' (2004: 50). Cahill notes that very few 'commentators have suggested the idea of elite social movements ... [and] none of these provide a comprehensive framework' (2004: 50). He points to a passing reference in Jessop's theorising of the capitalist state, in which he refers to 'popular or elite movements organized around extra-economic institutional orders, with their own modes of domination and exclusion and their own politics of identity and difference' (Jessop, 2002: 32). But the concept is not further developed by Jessop. The major antecedents to Cahill's use of the concept are to be found in Boies and Pichardo (1990, 1993–94) and Sklair (1997).

Boies and Pichardo argue that what they called elite social movement organisations (ESMOs), while neglected in social movement and state theory, 'are probably important casual agents in setting the course of social change in capitalist societies' (Boies and Pichardo, 1990: 23). They develop their analysis through an examination of the Committee on the Present Danger, a propagandistic outfit which in various iterations has pushed for higher levels of military spending in the US (and which had an important role in the genesis of the neoconservative movement which we discuss below and in Chapter 10). Boies and Pichardo note that according to the assumptions of various branches of state theory, as well as 'resource mobilisation' theories of social movements, it would seem to make little sense for elites to form an organisation like the Committee on the Present Danger, since it already possesses the power necessary to advance its interests within existing institutional networks (Boies and Pichardo, 1990: 2–3). With regard to state theory, they note that neither structuralist nor instrumentalist approaches allow much room for the agency of EMSOs, since in the case of the former the state is viewed as (relatively) autonomous from particularist interests and its actions determined by structural forces, and in the case of the latter elite interests are secured by the power that the capitalist class wields through the state. They also identify a third theoretical school they term 'class-dialectical theorists' – noting especially the work of Domhoff (e.g. 1990, 2006) – which places greater emphasis on contestation within the state, and pays more attention to elite organisations such as the Trilateral Commission. However, they argue that in such accounts, EMSOs tend to be seen as existing more for the development of consensus than the mobilisation of resources towards accomplishing social change (Boies and Pichardo, 1990: 4). In their critique of social movement theory, they acknowledge that EMSOs are covered in the literature, but argue that their characterisation as 'counter-movements' arbitrarily restricts analysis to reactive elite behaviour, overlooking the possibility of proactive elite mobilisation. They argue that EMSOs potentially play an important role not only in elite cohesion and planning, and in responding to challenges to elites from below, but also in intra-elite competition, the advancement of elite interests in circumstances where rules constrain certain actions, and in the proactive pursuit of elite interests.

As Sara Diamond notes of social movement studies, 'even the best scholarly research has tended to focus disproportionately on social movements opposed to the status quo' (Diamond, 1995: 6). A review of the geographical literature on Latin American social movements in 2008, for example, 'revealed almost no work on rightwing or elite social movements, in spite of their continued – and growing – importance throughout the region' (Perreault, 2008).

Most work that does focus on social movements from above focuses on the 'social movement for global capitalism', as Leslie Sklair describes it, or associated elite clubs, policy planning and lobby groups (Carroll and Carson, 2003a, 2003b; Carroll and Sapinski, 2010; Domhoff, 1975; Gill, 1986; Sklar, 1980). The work of Boies and Pichardo (above) is one of the few to examine elite social agency in relation to issues of foreign policy and conflict. Though not conceptualised in terms of social movements, there is of course, significant literature on elite think tanks and intellectual movements, as Chapter 10 of this book on the neoconservative movement, makes clear. Cox and Nilsen (2014: vi) do, however, specifically note that 'massively powerful' movements from above include 'racist mobilisations', which have tended to be conceptualised in the literature under the rubric of 'counter-movements'.

Social movements from above and Islamophobia

Turning to the role of social movements in Islamophobia, we prefer the concept of social movements from above over 'elite social movements' on the grounds that it is not the social location of the individuals involved that is the critical question, but rather the orientation of the movement to power and inequality. We propose here an analytical framework for social movements that might allow us to usefully delineate movements from above from movements from below.

1. Emergence: From what milieu, social and political struggles, and crises did the movement emerge?
2. Organisational form and political location: Where in the system do they operate? A movement on the streets, or in the corridors of power? Are their movement organisations membership organisations, or think tanks and policy groups? With which other groups or movements do they form alliances or develop antagonisms?
3. Strategy and goals: What ideas and political demands or policy prescriptions do they advance? What specific campaigns have they mobilised on?
4. Outcomes: What have been the intended or unintended outcomes of the movement?

Such a range of questions is necessary in part because we, and the movements and societies of which we are part, are always in flux; partly because movements from below can be defeated, or partially successful, in which case their leaders are able to obtain roles within elite institutions, or as participants in movements from above; and partly because movements from above (or indeed the state itself) can employ third party techniques, fostering or manufacturing radical or popular movements that in fact serve dominant interests. The well-known phenomena of co-option, incorporation, capture, compromise or 'sell out' means that the precise orientation of social movements at any given moment in time will sometimes be difficult to determine, and will be a politically contested question (Bumiller, 2009; Chasin, 2001; Sklair, 2001; Sklair and Miller, 2010). Moreover, in any of these cases, and at any particular point on the curve of the rise and fall of a particular movement, those with genuine or recent connections 'below' can objectively, perhaps unwittingly, play a role which effectively serves the interests of power, and/or can become part of movements from above. It can also obviously be the case that individuals can change sides, or find themselves on opposite sides in relation to differing issues or struggles. In what follows, we set out the main elements of each of our 'pillars' of Islamohobia, focusing on the interactions of these different movements.

We have identified four main Islamophobic currents that can be said to be analytically separate, if overlapping, social movements, which together are the main social movement drivers of Islamophobia. It is obvious that each of these overlap with the others in significant enduring, if dynamic and specific ways (Griffin, 2009). The four social movements from above that we identify are: (1) the neoconservative movement; (2) parts of the Zionist movement; (3) the counterjihad movement and the far right; (4) the pro-war left, New Atheists, New Secularists, some feminist currents.

(1) The neoconservative movement

Neoconservatism originated in the US and is a militaristic movement preoccupied with foreign policy issues, but also having strong commitments to social and domestic issues, including issues related to race and racism. Many of the adherents or progenitors of the movement were former leftists (often Trotskyists – such as Albert Wohlstetter of the Rand Corporation, Sidney Hook of the Hoover Institution, Melvin Lasky of the CIA-funded *Encounter* magazine or Irving Kristol of the CIA's Congress for Cultural Freedom, then the American Enterprise Institute) and most had, or developed, strong support for Israel as an important principle, while at the same time being concerned to protect the pre-eminence of the US in the global system. The neocons emerged in US politics 'in opposition to the New Left of the 1960s, fears over a return to US isolationism during the Vietnam War and the progressive international isolation of Israel in the wake of wars with its Arab neighbours in 1967 and 1973' (Lobe, 2003).

The neocons are most well known for the role they are said to have played in authoring the attack on Iraq, in part via the Project for a New American Century (PNAC). Nevertheless, the movement also has adherents in most European countries. They came together at the Democracy & Security International Conference in Prague on 5–6 June 2007 an event dubbed the 'Neoconservative International' (Lobe,

2007). That event was organised by the Prague-based Prague Security Studies Institute, the Adelson Institute for Strategic Studies at the Shalem Center in Jerusalem and Jose Maria Aznar's Madrid-based Foundation for Social Analysis and Studies (FAES). Other European-based neocon outfits include groups and think tanks set up by US parent organisations. We use three examples that illustrate well the intertwined nature of the neoconservative movement and other social movements we discuss here.

Firstly, the European Foundation for Democracy, which originates from a hard right Washington-based neocon think tank, the Foundation for Defense of Democracies (Cronin et al., 2016). Yet its EU offshoot amongst its anti-Muslim hardliners includes a UK member from the secularist movement Tehmina Kazi, the director of British Muslims for Secular Democracy (BMSD) (Powerbase, 2016).

Secondly, UN Watch and the Transatlantic Institute. While the latter is open about its link to the parent, UN Watch has claimed to be independent (Powerbase, 2015a). Both were in fact set up by the American Jewish Committee, a US Zionist group that has been a stalwart of the neocon scene. It is the publisher of *Commentary* magazine that refers to itself as the 'flagship' and 'intellectual home' of the neoconservative movement (Commentary, 2017).

The third example is Counterjihad Europa which was central to the creation of the counterjihad movement. It was a project of the Center for Vigilant Freedom, a US-based think tank set up in 2006, the director of which, Christine Brim, was later Chief Operating Officer of the Center for Security Policy, a well-connected neocon think tank in Washington, DC. Counterjihad Europa hosted the Counterjihad Brussels Conference in 2007, which inaugurated a coalition of counterjihad groupings that formed the kernel of the counterjihad movement including groups from Germany, Denmark, Belgium and the UK (Powerbase, 2015b).

Many other neoconservative organisations have US advisers, money or affinities but are organisationally independent, such as the UK-based think tanks, the Policy Exchange and the Henry Jackson Society (named after the hawkish Democratic Senator Henry 'scoop' Jackson). Neoconservative think tanks have been at the forefront of pressuring governments to take more direct action against Muslim communities and have tended to do this by operating at an elite (as opposed to street) level.

(2) Parts of the Zionist movement

The Zionist movement is a transnational social movement and has been since its beginnings at the first Zionist congress in 1897 – at which the intent to create the state of Israel was declared (Cohen, 1946). After the achievement of this goal in 1948, the movement did not cease but entered a period of reorganisation in which the avowedly Zionist elements declined as Lee O'Brien (1986) shows. 'It was not,' she writes (1986: 17–18) of the US experience, 'until the 1967 war and emergence of pro-Israelism as a mass phenomena among American Jews that an expanded and more flexible definition of Zionism was accepted by Israel and the world Zionist movement.' This occurred at the 1968 World Zionist Organization (WZO) conference where the Jerusalem Programme was set out that 'delineates the ideological framework within which the Zionist establishment is willing to co-exist with the pro-Israelism of American Jews'. Co-existence meant a recognition that *Aliyah* (immigration to Israel) was no longer the primary component of the movement and set the course for the plethora of pro-Israel groups seen today in the US, UK and elsewhere which do not necessarily have direct and formal ties with the official Zionist movement.

Nonetheless, the formal relationship between the Israeli state and the movement provides an important structure for the movement as a whole. At the centre are the National Institutions, quasi-governmental or para-statal institutions in Israel that have significant powers but which are also constituted in part by Zionist organisations outside Israel. Each of the organisations pre-dated the creation of the state of Israel in 1948 but they still form the core of the transnational Zionist movement and retain branches and affiliates in many countries around the world. They include the following organisations, all of which are based in the same building complex in Jerusalem:

- World Zionist Organization (created 1897, added 'World' to its title in 1960)
- Jewish National Fund (JNF) (founded at the Fifth Zionist Congress in Basel in 1901)
- Keren Hayesod – United Israel Appeal (KH-UIA) (created at the World Zionist Conference in London on 7–24 July 1920)

- Jewish Agency for Israel (created at the 16th Zionist Congress, held in Zurich, Switzerland in 1929).

Each of these organisations has offices (affiliated organisations in the case of the first three) in a range of countries across the world including in the UK and US. The National Institutions form a structural link between the Israel lobby in the diaspora and the Israeli state. It should also be noted that the WZO, the JNF and KH-UIA are all intimately involved in supporting or legitimating the occupation, and in some cases support ongoing settlement activity, which is also supported by some funders of Islamophobic organisations, as detailed in Chapter 9.

Various parts of the Zionist movement have contributed to Islamophobia in a number of ways. There are some connections between the far right and the counterjihad movement and the radical settler movement in Israel, but more important are a range of pro-Israel think tanks, lobby groups and public relations organisations which have targeted Muslims and Muslim civil society organisations. In the US these include, for example, the Committee for Accuracy in Middle East Reporting in America (CAMERA) and the Middle East Media Research Institute (MEMRI). A range of pro-Israel charitable foundations and philanthropic business operatives have directed resources towards neo-conservative and Islamophobic think tanks and lobby groups. These take the alleged threat from Islam or 'Islamism' as their primary focus, and in addition to the groups just mentioned, form the core of what has been dubbed the Islamophobia network by the Center for American Progress (Ali et al., 2011). These groups include: Act! For America, The Clarion Project, Center for Security Policy, David Horowitz Freedom Center, Jihad Watch, Stop Islamization of America (SIOA), Investigative Project on Terrorism (IPT), the Society of Americans for National Existence (SANE) and the Middle East Forum.

Of the eight largest funders of the Islamophobia/counterjihad networks in the US, four of the funders (the Abstraction Fund and associated Rosenwald family foundations, Fairbrook Foundation, Newton and Rochelle Becker Foundation, Russel Berrie Foundation) also gave significant resources to more than one Zionist or pro-Israel group (Aked, 2015; Bulkin and Nevel, 2014). The picture in the US is to some extent replicated in the UK in the sense that Zionist foundations have been amongst the largest donors to the neoconservative think tanks that have dealt in Islamophobia (Griffin et al., 2015; Mills et al., 2011). We discuss this further in Chapter 10.

In Chapter 9, Sarah Marusek unearths new data on the extent of pro-Israel interests' involvement in funding the transatlantic Islamophobia. We should note, though, that significant elements of the Zionist movement in the UK and US, while retaining a Zionist self-identity, are not in general involved in such activities. This is true of some mainstream Zionist/pro-Israel groupings, as well as most of the left of the movement; organisations such as Peace Now or J Street do not feature in the networks referred to here.

(3) The counterjihad movement and the far right

The far right is the most obvious social movement engaged in racism politics targeting Muslims. The traditional far right, meaning neo-fascists and neo-Nazi groups, has increasingly come to target Muslims as the enemy *du jour*. In some cases this has meant disavowing or at least claiming to disavow anti-Semitism, and in some cases it has meant an attempted rapprochement with some elements of the Zionist movement (Hafez, 2015). The counterjihad movement is a new addition to the pantheon of anti-Muslim groups on the far right, and it self-identifies as a movement specifically targeting Muslims. The counterjihad movement has been important in developing anti-Muslim politics on the streets, and in fostering racist violence against Muslims (for example, the English Defence League and PEGIDA), but it also has elements which are interested in electoral politics (as in Belgium's Vlaams Belang, the Netherlands' Partij voor de Vrijheid, headed by Geert Wilders, Sweden's Democrats and Britain's UKIP) as well as think tanks and campaign groups such as the International Free Press Society, Stop the Islamisation of Europe and others). Security analyst Toby Archer (2008) has noted of the counterjihad movement: 'As with any forming of political ideology or cultural phenomenon, the actors identified with counter-jihad are heterogeneous. There are differences and even conflicts between the many characters involved. Overall, however, they all agree that Islam as an ideology is a threat to non-Muslims and to Western culture.'

We can discern various currents in the counterjihad coalition in the organisations and individuals taking part in its known activities. These include neoconservatives, the Christian right, the far right, the populist right and Revisionist Zionism, which is on the far right of Israeli politics (Powerbase, 2015a). This is an indication of the range of the coalition and also the important sense in which the social movements we discuss here are heterogeneous and to some extent porous.

(4) The pro-war left/New Atheists/New Secularists/some feminist currents

The left and liberal movements engaged in supporting discrimination against Muslims are in general united by a form of secularist politics which has come to view radical Islam as a threat to democracy or progressive values. In this it shares something quite important with the other currents discussed above. Like the neocons, some conservative Zionists and the far right, the characterisation of 'Radical Islam' or 'Islamism' is often expansive, including forms of Muslim religious observance or practice, and failing to make a clear distinction between what are often termed 'fundamentalists' and ordinary Muslims, or in practice using the term 'Islamist' loosely such that it includes most Muslims active in public life. We noted above that some elements of the secularist movement have collaborated with the Christian and neo-conservative right in their anti-Islam activities and we can see a similar trajectory in, for example, the pro-war left as that seen in the journey made by those Trotskyists that became the neoconservative movement. In Chapter 11 we examine the various left/liberal and secularist currents and demonstrate the Islamophobic nature of their ideas and activities.

Each of these four movements is treated as analytically and empirically separable from the other, but in practice, as should be clear already, there are many overlaps, connections, alliances and common interests between them. We examine each in subsequent chapters.

The organisation of this book

The chapters in this book are organised into the following parts. Following our conception of the importance of the state and social movements, Parts 2 and 3 deal with those actors. The fourth concluding part deals with the question of how to resist Islamophobia.

Part 2: Islamophobia, Counter-terrorism and the State

The chapters in Part 2 develop our understanding of how Islamophobia is produced in relation to counter-terrorism and the state. In Chapter 2 Arun Kundnani advances the concept of Islamophobia as a form of racial ideology that serves to legitimise US empire. He argues that US Islamophobia in both legitimising violence and driving to depoliticise opposition needs to be understood beyond identity or discursive processes, as driven directly by the political activities and the interests of ruling elites. Such processes are analysed in Chapters 4 and 5. In Chapter 3 Deepa Kumar offers what she calls an 'intermestic' analysis of Islamophobia. Such an approach overcomes the limitations of focusing separately on domestic or international, offering a more holistic analysis of the production of Islamophobia. Asim Qureshi (Chapter 4) details the racism that lies at the heart of the counter-terrorism matrix in his discussion of case studies of torture and detention victims. Shenaz Bunglawala (Chapter 5) recounts the drive to push out Muslims from public life by targeting Muslim charities and civil society organisations.

Part 3: Social Movements from Above

Part 3 examines the movements and actors responsible for pushing Islamophobia practices. We begin with an account from the US, where Nathan Lean (Chapter 6) traces some key elements of the mainstreaming of anti-Muslim views in politics, especially in the context of the election of Donald Trump. Scott Poynting and Linda Briskman (Chapter 7) describe the politics of Islamophobia in Australia and highlight in particular the role of the state in circulating and promoting information about Muslims with little factual basis. Hilary Aked (Chapter 8) examines the counterjihad movement and its attempts to harness the counter-extremism language of the state. In Chapter 9 Sarah Marusek explores the transatlantic network funding Islamophobia and uncovers significant funding of Israeli settlements and the infrastructure of occupation. Tom Griffin, David Miller and Tom Mills (Chapter 10) discuss the history of the neoconservative movement, focusing on the role of elite think tanks as a particular strategy of what they term a social movement from above. Lastly in this part, Narzanin Massoumi, David Miller and Tom Mills examine what we call the fifth pillar of Islamophobia: the left and secular movements which we argue have contributed significantly to the rise of Islamophobia.

Part 4: Fighting Back

In Part 4, we examine what we have learned about Islamophobia and what consequences this has for combating it. This concluding chapter argues for the importance of solidarity with Muslim communities and civil society organisations, a key focus on the state in anti-racist struggles, and a clear separation between anti-racist groups and the state in terms of funding relationships and counter-terrorism policies. Lastly, the chapter suggests it is important for left, civil liberties and human rights groups to come together to defend the rights of Muslims and other citizens to engage in politics and to oppose state violence both overseas and at home.

Note

1. He later renounced this determinist view (Ashe and McGeever, 2011).

Bibliography

Aked, H. (2015), 'The undeniable overlap: right-wing Zionism and Islamophobia', 29 September. www.opendemocracy.net/mirrorracisms/hilary-aked/undeniable-overlap-right-wing-zionism-and-islamophobia. Accessed 10 February 2017.

Ali, W., Clifton, E., Duss, M., Fang, L., Keyes, S. and Shakir, F. (2011), *Fear Inc.: The Roots of the Islamophobia Network in America*. Washington, DC: Center for American Progress.

Archer, T. (2008), 'Countering the "counter-jihad"', *RUSI Monitor*, 15 August.

Ashe, S. and McGeever, B. (2011), 'Marxism, racism and the construction of "race" as a social and political relation: an interview with Professor Robert Miles', *Ethnic and Racial Studies*, 34 (12), 1–29.

Barker, C. (2013), 'Class struggle and social movements', in C. Barker, L. Cox, J. Krinsky and A.G. Nilsen (eds), *Marxism and Social Movements*. Leiden: Brill, pp. 63–81.

Boies, J. and Pichardo, N.A. (1990), 'Elite social movements and the state: a case study of the Committee on the Present Danger', CRSO Working Paper No. 416.

——(1993–94), 'The Committee on the Present Danger: a case for the importance of elite social movement organisations to theories of social movements and the state', *Berkeley Journal of Sociology*, 38, 57–87.

Bulkin, E. and Nevel, D. (2014), *Islamophobia & Israel*. New York: Route Books.

Bulmer, M. and Solomos, J. (2015), *Muslims, Migration and Citizenship Processes of Inclusion and Exclusion*. London: Routledge.

Bumiller, K. (2009), *In an Abusive State: How Neoliberalism Appropriated the Feminist Movement Against Sexual Violence*. Durham, NC: Duke University Press.

Cahill, D.C. (2004), 'The radical neo-liberal movement as a hegemonic force in Australia, 1976–1996', PhD thesis, History and Politics Program, University of Wollongong. http://ro.uow.edu.au/theses/193. Accessed March 2017.

Carroll, W.K. and Carson, C. (2003a), 'The network of global corporations and elite policy groups: a structure for transnational capitalist class formation?', *Global Networks*, 3 (1), 29–57.

—— (2003b), 'Forging a new hegemony? The role of transnational policy groups in the network and discourses of global corporate governance', *Journal of World-Systems Research*, 9 (1), 67–102.

Carroll, W.K. and Sapinski, J.P. (2010), 'The global corporate elite and the transnational policy-planning network, 1996–2006: a structural analysis', *International Sociology*, 25 (4), 501–38.

Cesari, J. (2004), *When Islam and Democracy Meet: Muslims in Europe and the United States*. New York: Palgrave Macmillan.

—— (2013), *Why the West Fears Islam: An Exploration of Muslims in Liberal Democracy*. New York: Palgrave Macmillan

Chasin, A. (2001), *Selling Out: The Gay and Lesbian Movement Goes to Market*. Houndmills, Basingstoke: Palgrave Macmillan.

Cohen, I. (1946), *The Zionist Movement*. New York: Zionist Organization of America.

Commentary (2017), 'About us'. www.commentarymagazine.com/about/. Accessed 10 February 2017.

Cox, L. and Nilsen, A.G. (2014), *We Make Our Own History: Marxism and Social Movements in the Twilight of Neoliberalism*. London: Pluto Press.

Cronin, D., Marusek, S. and Miller, D. (2016), *The Israel Lobby and the European Union*. Glasgow: Spinwatch and Europal.

Diamond, S. (1995), *Roads to Dominion: Right-wing Movements and Political Power in the United States*. New York: Guilford Press.

Domhoff, G.W. (1975), *The Bohemian Grove and Other Retreats*. New York: Harper and Row.

—— (1990), *The Power Elite and the State: How Policy is Made in America*. New Brunswick, NJ: Transaction Publishers.

—— (2006), *Who Rules America?: Power and Politics, and Social Change*. New York: McGraw-Hill.

Emigh, R.J., Riley, D. and Ahmed, P. (2016), *Changes in Censuses from Imperialist to Welfare States*. Houndmills, Basingstoke: Palgrave Macmillan.

Equalities and Human Rights Commission (2010), *Stop and Think: A Critical Review of the Use of Stop and Search Powers in England and Wales*. London: Equality and Human Rights Commission.

Esposito, J.L. and Ibrahim, K. (eds) (2013), *Islamophobia: The Challenge of Pluralism in the 21st Century*. New York: Oxford University Press.

Fanon, F. (1967), *Black Skin, White Masks*. Reprinted in 2008. London: Pluto Press.

Garner, S. and Selod, S. (eds) (2015), 'The racialization of Muslims: empirical studies of Islamophobia' (Special Issue), *Critical Sociology*, 41 (1), 9–19.

Gill, S. (1986), 'Hegemony, consensus and trilateralism', *Review of International Studies*, 12 (3), 205–22.

Goldberg, D.T. (2002a), *The Racial State*. Malden, MA and Oxford: Blackwell.

—— (2002b), 'Racial states', in D.T. Goldberg and J.S. (eds), *A Companion to Racial and Ethnic Studies*. Malden, MA and Oxford: Blackwell, pp. 233–58.

——(2009), *The Threat of Race: Reflections on Racial Neoliberalism*. Malden, MA and Oxford: Blackwell.

Griffin, T. (2009), 'The Neocons, the BNP and the Islamophobia network', Spinwatch, 17 September. www.spinwatch.org/index.php/pete-roche/item/5419-the-neocons-the-bnp-and-the-islamophobia-network. Accessed 10 February 2017.

Griffin, T., Aked, H., Miller, D. and Marusek, S. (2015), *The Henry Jackson Society and the Degeneration of British Neoconservatism*. Glasgow: Public Interest Investigations.

Grosfoguel, R. (2012), 'The multiple faces of Islamophobia', *Islamophobia Studies Journal*, 1 (1), 10–33.

Hafez, F. (2015), 'From anti-Semitism to Islamophobia: the European far right's strategic shift', *Discover Society*, 22, 1 July. http://discoversociety.org/2015/07/01/from-anti-semitism-to-islamophobia-the-european-far-rights-strategic-shift/. Accessed 30 March 2017.

Halliday, F. (1999), '"Islamophobia" reconsidered', *Ethnic and Racial Studies*, 22 (5), 892–902.

Hurrell, K. (2013), *An Experimental Analysis of Examinations and Detentions under Schedule 7 of the Terrorism Act 2000*. London: Equality and Human Rights Commission.

Jessop, B. (2002), *The Future of the Capitalist State*. Cambridge: Polity.

Jung, M.-K., Vargas, J., Costa, H. and Bonilla-Silva, E. (2011), *State of White Supremacy: Racism, Governance, and the United States*. Stanford, CA: Stanford University Press.

Kapoor, N. and Kalra, V. (2013), 'Introduction: the state of race', in N. Kapoor, V. Kalra and J. Rhodes (eds), *The State of Race*. Basingstoke: Palgrave Macmillan, pp. 1–12.

Kapoor, N. (2013), 'Afterword: racial futures', in N. Kapoor, V. Kalra and J. Rhodes (eds), *The State of Race*. Basingstoke: Palgrave Macmillan, pp. 223–8.

Khattab, N. and Modood, T. (2015), 'Both ethnic and religious: explaining employment penalties across 14 ethno-religious groups in the UK', *Journal of the Scientific Study of Religion*, 54 (3), 501–22.

Kundnani, A. (2006), 'Racial profiling and anti-terror stop and search', Institute for Race Relations. www.irr.org.uk/news/racial-profiling-and-anti-terror-stop-and-search/. Accessed 21 January 2017.

Liberty (2017), 'Schedule 7'. www.liberty-human-rights.org.uk/human-rights/countering-terrorism/schedule-7. Accessed 14 February 2017.

Lobe, J. (2003), 'What is a neo-conservative anyway?', Inter Press Service, 11 August. www.ipsnews.net/2003/08/politics-what-is-a-neo-conservative-anyway/. Accessed 10 February 2017.

—— (2007), 'A neo-conservative international targets Iran', Lobelog.com, 9 June. https://web.archive.org/web/20070703020904/http://www.ips.org/blog/jimlobe/?p=27. Accessed 15 February 2017.

Malik, K. (2005), 'Islamophobia myth', *Prospect*, 20 February.

Meer, N. (2013), 'Racialisation and religion: race, culture and difference in the study of antisemitism and Islamophobia', *Ethnic and Racial Studies*, 36 (3), 385–98.

Meer, N. and Modood, T. (2009), 'Refutations on the Muslim question', *Patterns of Prejudice*, 41 (5), 61–81.

—— (2011a), 'The racialisation of Muslims', in S. Sayyid and A. Vakil (eds), *Thinking Through Islamophobia: Global Perspectives*. London: Hurst, pp. 69–84.

—— (2011b), 'The multicultural states we're in', in A. Triandafyllidou, T. Modood and N. Meer (eds), *European Multiculturalisms: Cultural, Religious and Ethnic Challenges*. Edinburgh: Edinburgh University Press, pp. 61–87.

Miles, R. (1982), *Racism and Migrant Labour*. London: Routledge.

Miles, R. and Brown, M. (2003), *Racism*. London: Routledge.

Mills, C.W. (1997), *The Racial Contract*. Ithaca, NY: Cornell University Press.

Mills, T., Griffin, T. and Miller, D. (2011), *The Cold War on British Muslims: An Examination of Policy Exchange and the Centre for Social Cohesion*. Glasgow: Public Interest Investigations.

Modood, T. (2007), *Multiculturalism: A Civic Idea*. Cambridge: Polity Press.

Murji, K. and Solomos, J. (eds) (2005), *Racialization: Studies in Theory and Practice*. Oxford: Oxford University Press.

O'Brien, L. (1986), *American Jewish Organizations & Israel*. Washington, DC: Institute for Palestine Studies.

Omi, M. and Winant, H. (1986), *Racial Formation in the United States*, 1st edn. New York: Routledge.

—— (2015), *Racial Formation in the United States*, 3rd edn. New York and Abingdon: Routledge.

Parmar, A. (2011), 'Stop and search in London: counter-terrorist or counter-productive?', *Policing and Society*, 21 (4) 369–82.

Perreault, T. (2008), 'Latin American social movements: a review and critique of the geographical literature', *Geography Compass*, 2 (5), 1363–85.

Powerbase (2015a), 'Counterjihad movement', last modified 21 December. http://powerbase.info/index.php/Counterjihad_movement. Accessed 10 February 2017.

—— (2015b), 'Counterjihad Europa', last modified 14 December. http://powerbase.info/index.php/CounterJihad_Europa. Accessed 10 February 2017.

—— (2016), 'Tehmina Kazi', last modified 8 August. http://powerbase.info/index.php/Tehmina_Kazi. Accessed 10 February 2017.

Quinlan, T.L. and Derfoufi, Z. (2015), 'Counter-terrorism policing', in R. Delsol and M. Shiner (eds), *Stop and Search: The Anatomy of a Police Power.* Basingstoke and New York: Palgrave Macmillan, pp. 123–45.

Race Relations Act (1976) (Repealed). www.legislation.gov.uk/ukpga/1976/74/pdfs/ukpga_19760074_en.pdf. Accessed 30 March 2017.

Ramesh, R. (2014), 'Quarter of Charity Commision inquiries target Muslim groups', *Guardian*, September. www.theguardian.com/society/2014/nov/16/charity-commission-inquiries-muslim-groups. Accessed 30 March 2017.

Ritchie, M. (2015), 'Cage's judicial review of Charity Commission funding approaches withdrawn', *Charity Times*, 22 October. www.charitytimes.com/ct/cages-judicial-review-of-charity-commission-funding-approaches-withdrawn.php. Accessed 4 February 2017.

Said, E. (1977), *Orientalism.* London: Penguin.

Samman, K. (2012), 'Islamophobia and the time and space of the Muslim other', *Islamophobia Studies Journal*, 1 (1), 107–30.

Sheehi, S. (2011), *Islamophobia: The Ideological Campaign Against Muslims.* Atlanta, GA: Clarity Press.

Skenderovic, S., Wildmann, D. and Spaeti, C. (eds) (2014), 'Special Issue: Imaginaries of the Other: past and present expressions of Islamophobia', *Patterns of Prejudice*, 48 (5).

Sklair, L. (1997), 'Social movements for global capitalism: the transnational capitalist class in action', *Review of International Political Economy*, 4 (3), 514–38.

—— (2001), *The Transnational Capitalist Class.* Oxford: Blackwell.

Sklair, L. and Miller, D. (2010), 'Capitalist globalization, corporate social responsibility and social policy', *Critical Social Policy*, 30 (4), 472–95.

Sklar, H. (1980), *Trilateralism: The Trilateral Commission and Elite Planning for World Management.* Boston, MA: South End Press.

Vakil, A. (2011), 'Who's afraid of Islamophobia?', in S. Sayyid and A. Vakil (eds), *Thinking Through Islamophobia: Global Perspectives.* London: Hurst, pp. 271–8.

PART 2

Islamophobia, Counter-Terrorism and the State

2

Islamophobia as Ideology of US Empire

Arun Kundnani

All empires require violence to sustain themselves. And the violence perpetrated by imperial powers at the periphery always flows back, in one form or another, to the centre. In modern times, that violence always takes on a racial character.

Since at least the 1979 Iranian revolution, the US foreign policy establishment has regarded the Middle East as the most troublesome territory in its mental map of the world, a region where resistance to empire seems to be especially strongly felt, particularly against the US key regional ally, Israel. As such, a belief in an 'Islamic threat' has become a kind of collective unconscious of the US ruling elite. In the final years of the Cold War and its aftermath, the European colonial legacies of Orientalism were drawn on as a repository of myths to construct a new ideological enemy (Said, 1978). Rather than see the Palestinian national movement as rooted in a struggle against military occupation, it has been more convenient to think that Arabs are inherently fanatical: in other words, the problem is 'their' culture, not 'our' politics. With the War on Terror, that rhetoric was applied to Muslims as a whole: their religion seen as somehow especially prone to violence. The vocabulary of 'terrorism', 'extremism' and 'radicalisation' is selectively applied in order to systematically associate Muslims with fanatical violence. The US government's own violence – torture, drone strikes, military occupations and so on – could then be more easily normalised. The US Islamophobia thus involves, among other things, the depoliticisation of Muslim opposition to empire, a culturalist naturalising of conflict between 'Islam' and the 'West', and a dehumanising legitimisation of violence against Muslims, producing a vast death toll in Afghanistan, Iraq, Pakistan, Palestine, Somalia, Yemen and elsewhere.

The US academy has generally paid little attention to the historical connections between racism and empire; the interaction of Islamophobia and the War on Terror is even less frequently analysed. Critical academic analysis of foreign policy in the US is heavily circumscribed by the mechanisms of academic funding, prestige and informal censorship. An additional challenge is that the study of US empire takes place, if at all, within the disciplinary boundaries of international relations, history or area studies, where the interactions with domestic racial factors tend not to be considered. Alfred W. McCoy's *Policing America's Empire* (2009) and Robert Vitalis's *White World Order, Black Power Politics* (2015) are noteworthy exceptions. Equally, most scholarship on race and ethnicity in the US academy constrains itself to the borders of the US – indeed, the constitution of those borders through settler colonialism is itself understudied (Mamdani, 2015). Over the last decade, though, an incipient body of scholarship has emerged that seeks to trace the connections between race and empire, including that of Sohail Daulatzai (2012), Keith Feldman (2015), Deepa Kumar (2012), Alex Lubin (2014), Nadine Suleiman Naber (2014), Junaid Rana (2011), Steven Salaita (2006) and Nikhil Singh (2006).

Racialising Islam

The concept of Islamophobia itself, though, has received a level of academic attention. Indeed, in 2012 the philosopher Brian Klug described Islamophobia as a concept that had come of age in academia. Those such as Halliday (1999) and Malik (2005) who argued that the term was merely a smokescreen to block criticisms of Islam or to protect Islamic political movements from scrutiny were increasingly marginalised.

Broadly and roughly speaking, there are two approaches that scholars of Islamophobia have adopted, which can be labelled 'personal' and 'structural'. In the personal approach, Islamophobia is understood largely as a phenomenon of individual psychology: it is driven by fear and hatred of cultural difference; it has been provoked by events such as 9/11; and it is associated cognitively with stereotyping (Byers and Jones, 2007; Croucher et al., 2013; Lee et al., 2009). From this perspective, tackling Islamophobia requires practices such as interfaith work to overcome fear through personal interaction. In the structural approach, Islamophobia is a phenomenon that is: rooted in social processes; connected to, if not generated by, government policies; and tied to wider questions of political ideology and systems of power. It follows from this account that tackling Islamophobia requires a movement able to address broader political and social processes. Of course, the distinction between the personal and structural is not absolute: most personal approaches acknowledge the role of wider social factors in shaping the psychology of individual prejudice, while most structural approaches recognise the need to comprehend how individuals experience and internalise Islamophobia. The structural approach, which constitutes the majority of scholarship on Islamophobia, can itself be divided into work which only emphasises the *imaginary* and work which also emphasises *interests*. In the first, larger, category, scholars are most concerned to understand Islamophobia as a cultural process of othering whose operation can be examined in the law, media, politics and so on. The emphasis is on the role of discourse in the construction of exclusionary notions of identity and difference. There is a reluctance to systematically relate identity-producing discursive processes to broader social structures (Ali, 2012; Ibrahim, 2008/09; Love, 2009; Meer and Modood, 2009; Modood, 2003; Werbner, 2013). In the second category, the cultural processes that construct identities and differences are further related to social interests and strategies of securing power on the part of particular groups in society; Islamophobia is grounded, ultimately, in the political projects of ruling elites (Kumar, 2012; Kundnani, 2014).

Within the structural approaches, Islamophobia is increasingly seen as, wholly or partly, a form of racism. As Bayoumi (2006: 270) put it, Islamophobia 'in effect, turned a religion, namely Islam, into a race'. To recognise this does not imply critiques of Islamic belief are automatically to be condemned as racially motivated; it does mean opposing the social and political processes by which antipathy to Islam is acted out in violent attacks on the street or institutionalised in state structures as profiling, violations of civil rights and mass violence.

One advantage of this kind of analysis is that the substantial body of research on race can be drawn on to enrich our understanding of the conceptually thinner notion of Islamophobia. For example, Weberian scholars within the British 'race relations' paradigm have been exploring the sociology of race since the 1970s (Rex, 1970); Marxian scholars and those working within the black cultural studies paradigm have developed an equally extensive body of research on racism (Gilroy,

1987; Hall, 1980; Hall et al., 1978; Sivanandan, 1976). In the US, critical race theorists and historians of whiteness have produced sophisticated accounts of the American racial formation and racial state (Allen, 1993; Goldberg, 2002; Omi and Winant, 1986; Roediger, 1991). A central concept in these bodies of scholarship is racialisation, which refers to the process by which racial meanings are attached to social groups or actions (Miles, 1993).

Analysing Islamophobia as a form of structural racism also has the advantage of countering reductive identitarian formulae, which tend to see 'Islam' and the 'West' as deep, stable, ongoing cultural entities rooted in distinctive moral principles. While academics and commentators nowadays usually open their texts with a ritual rejection of the simplistic 'clash of civilisations' approach, they often go on to implicitly draw on various forms of culturalism when they come to their own analysis. Emphasising that Islamophobia, like all racisms, is socially and politically constructed usefully calls attention to the ways in which it is produced and reproduced.

However, a number of challenges immediately present themselves when attempting to understand Islamophobia as a form of structural racism. First is the question of whether Islam, however defined, can actually be turned into the basis of a process of racialisation. There is no neat alignment between the identity of being Muslim and other existing racial identities: Islam has no colour. For example, while the majority of Muslims in Britain are of Asian origin, there is an equal number of Asians who are not Muslim and large numbers of Muslims who are not Asian, including a growing number of white converts.

This connects to the question of whether the concept of racism can be applied beyond bodily difference. For some scholars, Islamophobia is a matter of cultural racism, as opposed to biological racism; it attaches to signs of cultural difference rather than visible bodily differences. Since all racisms are socially and politically constructed, rather than resting on the reality of any biological 'race', it seems possible for markers associated with 'Muslimness' (forms of dress, rituals, languages and so on) to be turned into racial signifiers. But the concept of cultural racism usually retains some link to the body: for cultural racists, cultural differences are thought of as emanations of a different nature, implying that there remains a belief in the body as the essential location of racial identity. However, Islamophobic discourse appears different in this respect; it seems to locate identity not so much in a racialised body but in a set of fixed religious beliefs and practices.

A further set of challenges relates to the demands of applying the concept of Islamophobia to different geographical and historical contexts. In Europe, with its history of racism linked to the continent's colonial histories, there may be some initial plausibility to thinking of Islamophobia alongside racism. But what sense does it make to think of Islamophobia in India as a form of racism? And should Islamophobia be seen as a strictly late twentieth-century and early twenty-first-century phenomenon? Or can it be traced back through colonial history or even earlier to the expulsions of Muslims from Spain in the fifteenth century (Grosfoguel and Mielants, 2006; Kumar, 2012; Meer, 2014; Said, 1978)?

Even in the context of the US since the Cold War, we do not yet have a full picture of the mechanics by which Islam is racialised. Structural accounts of Islamophobia in the US that focus on the cultural imagination of the Other have described how Muslims have been constructed in exclusionary ways through law, the media and politics. These accounts, however, tend to lack explanatory power; they are better at saying how Islamophobia exists than why. By default, these accounts leave an ahistorical impression of Islamophobia as a kind of virus that emerges from the cultural ether at moments of social and political vulnerability. Structural accounts that focus on interests and power relations between social groups are better placed to offer causal explanations for the existence of Islamophobia, relating the cultural process by which Islamophobia emerges to the motivated actions of specific groups.

The danger, though, in this approach is that this process is portrayed in an instrumentalist fashion, as simply the outcome of a conscious propaganda strategy by a section of the ruling elite. On this view, ideas of a Muslim threat have been systematically and consciously circulated by Western ruling elites in order to provide cover for imperialist foreign policies. Prima facie evidence for such an analysis can easily be found in the discourses emanating from neoconservative think tanks and Islamophobic propagandists and their influence on media discourse (Bail, 2012). And it is possible to demonstrate that neoconservatives believe in the need to invent enemies as a way to bind society together, that their alliance with the Israeli right means Islam is a plausible candidate for this role and that their ideas about Islam have been propagated by a US Islamophobia industry funded with at least $40 million between 2001 and 2009 (Ali et al., 2011). (This would be a very small sum with which to buy a new form of American racism.)

But a fuller analysis would have to go beyond the conscious activities of elite political actors and the top-down flow of ideas to look also at the wider social context within which Islamophobia circulates. Islamophobia is only possible because it resonates within the longer trajectories of racisms that are embedded in the social structures of the US. To illustrate, consider a poster created by a Texan restaurant owner and hung on the wall of his business in Katy, a suburb of Houston, while I was there in 2011. It consists of a large photograph of a lynching that had taken place in the early twentieth century. Where in the original image one would have seen the black face of the victim, in the restaurant's version a stereo-typical Middle Eastern face has been superimposed. The poster's caption read: 'Let's play cowboys and Iranians'. It is disturbing to see a poster explicitly glorifying racist violence displayed on the wall of a restaurant. All the more so because, in the same neighbourhood, I was told of teenagers beaten up at school simply for being Arab, of harassment of mosque congregations and of death threats against Muslims aired on local radio stations.

But the image is also revealing for another reason: it points to the ways in which anti-Muslim sentiment is best understood as part of a longer racial history in the US. The poster's caption, with its play on the phrase 'cowboys and Indians', is an implicit celebration of the genocide of America's Indigenous peoples by European settlers, the first act in the racial history of the continent and one that continues to haunt a culture preoccupied with enemies at its frontiers. Likewise, the poster's use of a photo of a lynching ties its meaning to the history of racial segregation after the abolition of plantation slavery and the way that racist violence was used to maintain white supremacy. Anti-Muslim racism appears, then, as the most recent layer in this longer history, a reworking and recycling of older logics of oppression. By visually connecting anti-Muslim sentiment to other US racisms, the restaurant owner made explicit the racial subtext to elite Islamophobic discourse that claims to be post-racial, and highlighted Islamophobia's relationship to settler colonialism.

This racialisation of 'Muslimness' is also analogous in important ways to modern anti-Semitism, which, like Islamophobia, can be seen as racialising a religious identity (Klug, 2014; Meer, 2013). At the heart of modern anti-Semitism is a conspiratorial conception of power in which racial enemies are seen as able to direct world history through the secret control of the media and high finance. Anti-Semites view Jews as constituting an outcast subclass threatening the purity of the social body from below and also as a secret class above society able to manipulate events to maintain its power. All racist discourse has this double aspect: racialised immigrants, for example, are perceived simultaneously to be lazy and also stealing our jobs; they are accused of both refusing to integrate into the 'host' society and also secretly infiltrating it. But anti-Semitism was historically unique in positioning Jews as both a cosmopolitan superpower standing above the social body and as a species of sub-humans undermining it from below. In the twenty-first century, Islamophobes have begun to think of Muslims in a parallel way: Islam is seen as secretly controlling Western governments while at the same time being a backward, seventh-century ideology whose followers constitute a dangerous under-class. For Islamophobes, President Obama is secretly a Muslim and used his control of the White House to advance the Muslim Brotherhood's planned takeover of the US, while the European Union is no more than a front organisation to enable the Arab colonisation of Europe. At the same time, Islamophobes see Muslims as a dangerous under-class locked in a medieval belief system. Islamophobia has thus inherited the same ideological template as modern anti-Semitism.

Liberalism and empire

Accounts of Islamophobia that overly focus on its origins in neoconservative propaganda tend to neglect the ways that versions of liberalism have been ideologically central to it. Liberal intellectuals play more than just a secondary enabling role. The broader ideological contours of the War on Terror that cover liberal as well as conservative terrain need to be taken more seriously.

The advocacy of mass violence against racialised populations in the name of defending liberal values is not new – it is a tradition that stretches from Napoleon to Tony Blair. Liberalism has long had a problem of only seeing the violence of racial others, while its own violence is hidden from view. In the abstract, there is no reason why liberal principles of individual freedom cannot be applied consistently. And principled liberals have been essential to many struggles against racism and imperialism. But liberalism is not just a body of ideas; it is also the ideology of a social system – capitalism – that sustains itself through marginalising racial groups, through class exploitation and through the drive to imperial expansion; thus, the cultures of racialised groups and exploited classes inevitably become politically insurgent. The liberal demand to depoliticise culture – to abandon 'dangerous ideas', to deradicalise and to integrate to 'Western' values – is therefore highly political and leads liberals to consider all manner of coercive initiatives to engineer the liberal subjects they feel are missing among oppressed groups. Liberalism then becomes a peculiarly cultural project that aims at upholding a 'way of life', if necessary through what writers like Sam Harris call a 'war of ideas' – and he does not use the word 'war' metaphorically (Harris, 2005: 53).

In the Obama era, the War on Terror was painted in a veneer of liberal values, thereby drawing the US liberal establishment into supporting it and making it a permanent element within the US system of power. Neo-conservatives invented the War on Terror but Obama liberals normalised it. For this to happen, there needed to be an underlying consensus among both establishment liberals and conservatives; at the root of that consensus is a shared commitment to defending the US empire and the belief that there is a 'Muslim problem' that threatens it. Like any other ideological process, the reproduction of Islamophobia cannot simply be seen as an elite conjuring trick, deployed consciously and strategically by well-funded propaganda organisations. It is also about the unconscious disavowal and displacement of real political conflicts. It is not simply the fear of individual acts of terrorism that lies behind the vocabulary of radicalisation and extremism. It is also an anxiety at the emergence of a politically engaged Muslim population that is opposed to US hegemony and the emergence of a public space in which racialised populations are able to articulate a knowledge of empire.

The categorisation of Muslims into 'moderate' and 'extremist' reflects this anxiety:

To be classed as 'moderate', Muslims must forget what they know about Palestine, Iraq, and Afghanistan, and instead align themselves with the fantasies of the War on Terror; they are expected to constrain their religion to the private sphere but also to speak out publicly against extremists' misinterpretations of Islam; they are supposed to see themselves as liberal individuals but also declare an allegiance to the national collective; they are meant to put their capacity for reason above blind faith but not let it lead to criticisms of the West; and they have to publicly condemn using violence to achieve political ends – except when their own governments do so. No wonder moderate Muslims are said to be hard to find. (Kundnani, 2014: 110)

The state surveillance gaze that tries to sift the moderate from the extremist among Muslim populations is where the racialisation of Islam in the US is perhaps most clearly evident. From the 1980s, but especially after 9/11, a process was underway in which law enforcement, national security and military agencies began to read Muslim bodies for the signs of 'radicalisation' – such supposed indicators as growing a beard, starting to wear 'Islamic' clothing or speech expressing specific forms of religio-political ideology (Federal Bureau of Investigation, 2006; Silber and Bhatt, 2007). These signifiers of 'Muslimness', such as facial hair, dress and expressive activity, are taken to be markers of suspicion for a surveillance gaze that is also a racial gaze; it is through such routine bureaucratic mechanisms that counter-terrorism practices involve the social construction of racial others. This points to the way that anti-Muslim racism is not just a set of ideas but also inheres in state practices, both domestically and internationally.

The infrastructure of this surveillance gaze is deeply entangled with the global project of empire. It integrates military and commercial networks, from the visual and wi-fi surveillance conducted by military drones to the databases of US tech corporations, from homeland security profiling at airports to the interrogation of detainees at CIA black sites. It blurs the boundaries between state and industry, between military and civilian policing, and between internal and external security. It is legitimised by the global racialised War on Terror, on drugs and on unauthorised immigration. The production of Muslims as objects of surveillance is thus analogous to and overlaps with other systems of security surveillance that feed the deportation of immigrants and the mass incarceration of the prison-industrial complex.

How are we to conceptualise the intertwining of surveillance practices and race in the War on Terror? Paddy Hillyard's concept of 'suspect communities' provides a model in which processes of racialisation can be seen as central to surveillance (Hillyard, 1993). Hillyard studied the experience of the Irish population in Britain under the anti-terrorist legislation introduced in the early 1970s, which was part of the state's attempt to maintain control in the North of Ireland in the context of an armed insurgency by the Provisional Irish Republican Army (PIRA). What Hillyard documents is the police practice of arresting those suspected of involvement with the PIRA and interrogating them to identify their friends and family. The police then worked their way through the friends and family and interrogated them in turn, and so on. Eventually, this method of investigation produced in the minds of the police a picture of the 'community' as a network of suspicious persons linked together by various social relationships. By being subjected to this kind of policing, those targeted also came to understand themselves as a community with a shared experience of suspicion at the hands of the police. Hillyard's point is that the Irish 'community' in England does not pre-exist police surveillance but is itself constituted through the interrogation process, both in the minds of the police and their targets. The community is forged in the police cells. The surveillance practices of the police are thus integral to the construction and reproduction of the Irish as a racialised group. In the War on Terror, we can trace similar processes of racialisation (Kundnani, 2014). Generalising, we can say that racialised groupings are reproduced in the very act of collecting information about populations deemed 'threats' by the state.

The concept of 'radicalisation' that organises national security surveillance practices in the War on Terror has become the chief lens through which Western societies now view Muslim populations. This is also one of the points where the question of academic complicity arises, as terrorism studies scholars have produced models of radicalisation for government agencies that then become the basis for surveillance practices and the racisms they generate. The academic discourse on radicalisation has largely operated according to a number of limiting assumptions: that those perpetrating terrorist violence are drawn from a larger pool of extremist sympathisers who share an Islamic ideology that inspires their actions; that entry into this wider pool of extremists can be predicted by individual or group psychological or theological factors; and that knowledge of these factors allows government policies that reduce the risk of terrorism (Laqueur, 2004; Sageman, 2004, 2008; Wiktorowicz, 2005). The study of radicalisation, ostensibly a reflection on the causes of terrorism, is thus in practice limited to a much narrower question: why do some individual Muslims support an extremist inter-pretation of Islam that leads to violence? Terrorist violence is taken a priori to be a product of how Islam is interpreted, rendering irrelevant acts of political violence not carried out by Muslims.

In part, such flawed scholarship on radicalisation is the result of generous government funding for research aligned with the national security state. But it is also a matter of the wider culture of political conformity across academia, entrenched by the neoliberal transfor-mation of the university. Young critical scholars of national security disproportionately find themselves in the most precarious sectors of the academic job market while war criminals like David Petraeus can walk into well-paid posts. Meanwhile Steven Salaita, one of the leading scholars of anti-Arab racism in the US, was removed from an academic post for supposedly 'uncivil' Twitter posts critical of Israel.

Genuine scholarly critique of racism and empire is thus constrained by institutional as much as intellectual challenges. For those on the receiving end of imperialist violence, the questions posed by an editorial in the first issue of the journal *Race & Class* are as relevant as when they were first written in 1974:

What good is your knowledge to us? Do you in your analyses of our social realities tell us what we can do to transform them? Does your apprehension of our reality speak to our experience? Do you convey it in a language that we can understand? If you do none of these things, should we not only reject your 'knowledge' but, in the interests of our own liberation, consider you a friend to our enemies and a danger to our people? (Sivanandan, 1974: 400)

Bibliography

Ali, W., Clifton, E., Duss, M., Fang, L., Keyes, S. and Shakir, F. (2011), *Fear, Inc.: The Roots of the Islamophobia Network in America*. Washington, DC: Center for American Progress.

Ali, Y (2012), 'Shariah and citizenship – how Islamophobia is creating a second-class citizenry in America', *California Law Review*, 100 (4), August, 1027–68.

Allen, T.W (1993), *The Invention of the White Race: Racial Oppression and Social Control*. London: Verso.

Bail, C.A. (2012), 'The fringe effect: civil society organizations and the evolution of media discourse about Islam since the September 11th attacks', *American Sociological Review*, 77 (6), 855–79.

Bayoumi, M. (2006), 'Racing religion', *New Centennial Review*, 6 (2), 267–93.

Byers, B.D. and Jones, J.A. (2007), 'The impact of the terrorist attacks of 9/11 on anti-Islamic hate crime', *Journal of Ethnicity in Criminal Justice*, 5 (1), 43–56.

Croucher, S.M., Appenrodt, J., Lauwo, G. and Stojcsics, A. (2013), 'Intergroup contact and host culture acceptance: a comparative analysis of Western Europe and the United States', *Human Communication*, 16 (4), 2013), 153–69.

Daulatzai, S. (2012), *Black Star, Crescent Moon: The Muslim International and Black Freedom Beyond America*. Minneapolis, MN: University of Minnesota Press.

Federal Bureau of Investigation Counterterrorism Division (2006), *The Radicalization Process: From Conversion to Jihad*. Washington, DC: Government Printing Office.

Feldman, K.P. (2015), *A Shadow Over Palestine: The Imperial Life of Race in America*. Minneapolis, MN: University of Minnesota Press.

Gilroy, P. (1987), *There Ain't No Black in the Union Jack*. London: Hutchinson.

Goldberg, D.T. (2002), *The Racial State*. Malden, MA: Blackwell.

Grosfoguel, R. and Mielants, E. (2006), 'The long-durée entanglement between Islamophobia and racism in the modern/colonial capitalist/patriarchal world-system: an introduction', *Human Architecture: Journal of the Sociology of Self-Knowledge*, 1, Fall, 1–12.

Hall, S. (1980), 'Race, articulation and societies structured in dominance', in UNESCO (ed.), *Sociological Theories: Race and Colonialism*. Paris: UNESCO, pp. 305–45.

Hall, S., Critcher, C., Jefferson, T., Clarke, J. and Roberts, B. (1978), *Policing the Crisis: Mugging, the State, and Law and Order*. London: Macmillan.

Halliday, F. (1999), 'Islamophobia reconsidered', *Ethnic and Racial Studies*, 22 (5), 892–902.

Harris, S. (2005), *The End of Faith: Religion, Terror, and the Future of Reason*. New York: W.W. Norton & Co.

Hillyard, P. (1993), *Suspect Community: People's Experience of the Prevention of Terrorism Acts in Britain*. London: Pluto Press.

Ibrahim, N. (2008/09), 'The origins of Muslim racialization in US law', *UCLA Journal of Islamic & Near Eastern Law*, 7 (1), 121–55.

Klug, B. (2012), 'Islamophobia: a concept comes of age', *Ethnicities*, 12 (5), 665–81.

—— (2014), 'The limits of analogy: comparing Islamophobia and antisemitism', *Patterns of Prejudice*, 48 (5), 442–59.

Kumar, D. (2012), *Islamophobia and the Politics of Empire*. Chicago, IL: Haymarket Books.

Kundnani, A. (2014), *The Muslims are Coming! Islamophobia, Extremism, and the Domestic War on Terror*. New York: Verso.

Laqueur, W. (2004), 'The terrorism to come', *Policy Review*, August/September, 58–9.

Lee, S.A., Gibbons, J.A., Thompson, J.M. and Timani, H.S. (2009), 'The Islamophobia scale: instrument development and initial validation', *International Journal for the Psychology of Religion*, 19 (2), 92–105.

Love, E. (2009), 'Confronting Islamophobia in the United States: framing civil rights activism among Middle Eastern Americans', *Patterns of Prejudice*, 43 (3/4), 401–25.

Lubin, A. (2014), *Geographies of Liberation: The Making of an Afro-Arab Political Imaginary.* Chapel Hill, NC: University of North Carolina Press.

Malik, K. (2005), 'Are Muslims hated?', *Index on Censorship*, 34 (2), 167–72.

Mamdani, M. (2015), 'Settler colonialism: then and now', *Critical Inquiry*, 41, Spring, 596–614.

McCoy, A.W. (2009), *Policing America's Empire: The United States, the Philippines, and the Rise of the Surveillance State.* Madison, WI: University of Wisconsin Press.

Meer, N. (2013), 'Racialization and religion: race, culture and difference in the study of antisemitism and Islamophobia', *Ethnic and Racial Studies*, 36 (3), 385–98.

—— (2014), 'Islamophobia and postcolonialism: continuity, Orientalism and Muslim consciousness', *Patterns of Prejudice*, 48 (5), 500–15.

Meer, N. and Modood, T. (2009), 'Refutations of racism in the "Muslim question"', *Patterns of Prejudice*, 43 (3/4), 335–54.

Miles, R. (1993), *Racism After 'Race Relations'.* London: Routledge.

Modood, T. (2003), 'Muslims and the politics of difference', *Political Quarterly*, 74 (1), August, 100–15.

Naber, N.S. (2014), 'Imperial whiteness and the diasporas of empire', *American Quarterly*, 66 (4), December, 1107–15.

Omi, M. and Winant, H. (1986), *Racial Formation in the United States.* New York: Routledge.

Rana, J.A. (2011), *Terrifying Muslims: Race and Labor in the South Asian Diaspora.* Durham, NC: Duke University Press.

Rex, J. (1970), *Race Relations in Sociological Theory.* London: Routledge.

Roediger, D.R. (1991), *The Wages of Whiteness: Race and the Making of the American Working Class.* New York: Verso.

Sageman, M. (2004), *Understanding Terror Networks.* Philadelphia, PA: University of Pennsylvania Press.

—— (2008), *Leaderless Jihad: Terror Networks in the Twenty-First Century.* Philadelphia, PA: University of Pennsylvania Press.

Said, E. (1978), *Orientalism.* New York: Vintage Books.

Salaita, S. (2006), *Anti-Arab Racism in the USA: Where it Comes From and What it Means for Politics Today.* London and Ann Arbor, MI: Pluto Press.

Silber, M.D. and Bhatt, A. (2007), *Radicalization in the West: The Homegrown Threat.* New York: New York Police Department Intelligence Division.

Singh, N. (2006), 'The afterlife of fascism', *South Atlantic Quarterly*, 105 (1), Winter, 71–93.

Sivanandan, A. (1974), 'Editorial', *Race & Class*, 15 (4), 399–400.

—— (1976), 'Race, class and the state: the black experience in Britain', *Race & Class*, 17 (4), 347–68.

Vitalis, R. (2015), *White World Order, Black Power Politics: The Birth of American International Relations*. Ithaca, NY: Cornell University Press, 2015.

Werbner, P. (2013), 'Folk devils and racist imaginaries in a global prism: Islamophobia and anti-Semitism in the twenty-first century', *Ethnic and Racial Studies*, 36 (3), 450–67.

Wiktorowicz, Q. (2005), *Radical Islam Rising: Muslim Extremism in the West*. Oxford: Rowman & Littlefield.

3

Islamophobia and Empire: An Intermestic Approach to the Study of Anti-Muslim Racism

Deepa Kumar

The study of Islamophobia has mushroomed since the events of 9/11. A search for scholarly articles in the decade before 9/11 with 'Islamophobia' in the title yields a mere three articles. Of these, one by Fred Halliday, titled '"Islamophobia" reconsidered', argues that the term shields Islamists and Islam from criticism (an argument more typical of the far right these days). In the period after 9/11, however, there were over 1,200 articles and about 20 books by scholars. Almost three quarters of the articles appear after 2011. If we narrow this search and include 'Orientalism' among the subject terms, the result is twelve journal articles. If the term Orientalism is searched in all text, the result is 129 articles, while a search for Orientalism in the title yields almost five thousand scholarly articles. Of these, 19 use Islamophobia as a subject term, and 146 in all text.

I offer three observations from this admittedly rudimentary search. First, the study of Islamophobia has come into its own, particularly in the last half decade, drawing the attention of scholars in Sociology, Religion, Middle East Studies, Media and Cultural Studies, Politics, Ethnic Studies, Postcolonial Studies, English, History, Women's Studies, among others. Second, only a minority, about 1 per cent, draws an explicit connection to Orientalism and about a tenth reference the connection, but not in any substantial way. If Orientalism is understood as a mode of understanding and explaining the 'Muslim world' that comes into being in the context of European colonialism in the late eighteenth and nineteenth centuries, then only a minority see fit to examine either the continuities or discontinuities with this colonial past. This is part of a general trend in scholarship which has eschewed a discussion of empire. Here we see the erasure of empire, particularly US imperialism, as a structuring reality of contemporary anti-Muslim racism. Third, among those who study Orientalism, only a minority discuss Islamophobia (although a larger number do study Islam). It must be noted, however, that the term 'Orientalism' has a variety of meanings which have changed over time and not all definitions are tied to empire. Some scholars use the term to describe an artist or cultural style associated with the East.

Therefore, the above observations are provisional based on the constraints of broad database searches. However, even with these limits, what is evident is the continued need to underscore the relationship between Islamophobia, Orientalism and Empire. It bears repeating that if Orientalism was, among other things, the ideology of European colonialism, then Islamophobia is the ideology of US-led imperialism in the twenty-first century. This is where Edward Said's seminal work *Orientalism* still remains crucial. Despite the ambiguities and pitfalls of his various definitions of Orientalism, Said's work tied knowledge production to imperial contexts. While Said refers to Orientalism as a discourse, it is better understood as an ideology. As I have argued elsewhere, it is best understood as a taken-for-granted framework that offers a 'common sense' hegemonic view of the world (Kumar, 2010). Arun Kundnani has developed further the notion of Islamophobia as ideology, persuasively arguing that it functions as a 'lay ideology'. That is, it 'offers an everyday "common sense" explanatory framework for making sense of mediated crisis events (such as terrorist attacks) in ways that disavow those events' political meanings (rooted in empire, racism and resistance) and instead explain them as products of a reified 'Muslimness'. Thus, Islamophobia involves an ideological displacement of political antagonisms onto the plane of culture, where they can be explained in terms of the fixed nature of the 'Other' (Kundnani, 2016). As ideologies, Orientalism and Islamophobia have features in common, but they also differ with respect to their conditions of production and their modality of operation.

It bears noting that not all Orientalist scholarship was tied to the interests of empire. One of the first critics of Orientalism, Anouar Abdel-Malek made this point forcefully when he argued that many Orientalists produced valuable knowledge (Abdel-Malek, 2000). Hamid Dabashi more recently defends the work of Orientalist scholar

Ignaz Goldziher and draws a distinction between Orientalists who 'heavily invested in producing a particular knowledge of Islam and Muslims compatible with European colonial interests' and those like Goldziher who was an anti-colonial activist in Egypt (Dabashi, 2009: 30). Orientalism is thus a complex and contradictory body of scholarly work. However, as Abdel-Malek also argued, the 'dominant vision' of the East was one produced by 'dons, military men, colonial officials, missionaries, publicists whose only objective was to gather intelligence information in the area to be occupied, to penetrate the consciousness of the people in order to better assure its enslavement to European powers' (Abdel-Malek, 2000: 49). Islamophobia draws from this subset, but as such isn't a scholarly discipline in the manner of Oriental studies. Rather, it is an ideology of racism *tied to practices* that are part of a global project of US-led imperialism. While this form of racism draws on earlier Orientalist stereotypes, and produces (and reproduces) contemporary articulations of Orientalism like the 'clash of civilisations' framework (Kumar, 2010), it is also a product of particular historic conjunctures that are shaped by various national contexts within the global War on Terror.

In this chapter, I offer some thoughts on how we might productively study the international and domestic contexts in which contemporary Islamophobia circulates as a body of ideas and a system of practices. The somewhat inelegant term 'intermestic' has been used to describe this mode of analysis. Here I use the term in a historical materialist sense and suggest that the international and domestic contexts are not wholly separate but rather shape one another dialectically. For instance, British colonisation of Ireland and the practices used in that context such as the deployment of settlers, military conquest, seizure of land and the racialisation of the Irish were used later in the New World (Foner, 2005: 47–9). The 'wild Irish' in Britain became the 'savage Indian' in North America. The same can be said of Spain. Once the project of internal colonisation was complete, and the Moors driven out in 1492, Spain set its sights on New World colonisation using methods that were first developed in the *Reconquista* (Foner, 2005: 47–9). In both the British and Spanish cases either internal colonisation or colonisation of geo-graphically proximate regions would inform external colonisation. At the same time, external conditions inform internal transformations as well. Thomas Bender argues, for instance, that the American revolution was driven by inter-imperialist rivalry on a global scale. In particular, the

Seven Years' War that was conducted on almost every continent on the planet was the precursor to the American War of Independence (Bender, 2016). Nabil Matar argues that the contemporaneous English encounter with Muslims (particularly the Moors and Turks) and with American Indians would lead to parallels being established by English writers between the two, creating an understanding of 'Indians as Muslims' and 'Muslims as Indians' (Matar, 2000). Thus, external and internal contexts dialectically shape one another.

It is generally understood that the modern concept of race arose in the context of European colonisation of the Americas; however, Christian Europe's internal 'Others' – the Jews and Muslims – were prototypes or precursors to racial formations in the New World (Omi and Winant, 1994). Most importantly, for our purposes, what this highlights is that right from the outset, processes of racialisation occurred within the context of empire. And while imperialism during the mercantile stage of the early modern era and the imperialism of the industrial era would have different modalities, 'race' was central to both of these phases of the international political economy.

In what follows, I revisit some of the arguments I made in *Islamophobia and the Politics of Empire* and set out to expand upon them using an intermestic approach. In the next section, I draw on the work of various scholars to outline what such an approach might look like. In the following section, I apply this to the study of Islamophobia in the US context. And finally, I offer some comments and questions that might inform future research.

Empire at home and abroad

It is widely assumed that there has been only one devastating critique of Orientalism, Edward Said's classic *Orientalism*. In fact, however, as Dabashi argues, long before Said's Foucauldian-inspired text, several scholars had studied the production of knowledge in a way that situated it within its broader social and economic context. According to Dabashi, this sociology of knowledge approach can be found a century before Foucault in the work of Karl Marx and Friedrich Engels, Max Scheler and Karl Mannheim. While scholars today draw heavily from Foucault, Dabashi (2009) points to alternative models from which to explain the structural limits placed on the production of knowledge. Also, immediately before Said, Abdel-Malek and Bryan Turner had offered their own searing critiques of Orientalism, not to mention a series of other authors (see Macfie, 2000 for an overview of the various critiques of Orientalism).

The context for this was the successful decolonisation struggles from India to Algeria in the post-World War II era. Although Said's *Orientalism* received the greatest attention, and was one of the most expansive and ambitious critiques, it was far from unique. Various scholars had argued that the Orientalist approach to the study of the Middle East was deeply ideological and served the goals of empire in various ways. If this line of attack on Orientalism opened up new ways of understanding formerly colonised nations, particularly Said's work that inspired the field of postcolonial studies, then a series of developments from the 1970s on have seen the re-emergence of Orientalism (through the 'clash of civilisations' framework) and Islamophobia. Such developments include, among others, the entrenchment of neoliberalism, the corporatisation of the university, the backlash against progressive social movements, and the rise of neoconservatism and the far right, all of which have shaped the contours of knowledge production.

One casualty of these conditions is the slow disappearance of empire and anti-imperialist perspectives in the academy. While the idea of American exceptionalism has a long history, and has influenced scholarly work, the anti-Vietnam War movement as well as the internationalism of the African American struggle opened up spaces to study the US as an empire, akin to previous European empires. However, there has been a slow drift away from this. For instance, in African American studies programmes, which began with internationalist and anti-imperialist commitments, the focus has increasingly shifted to the national context (Vitalis, 2015). Methodological nationalism, seen in many fields, has brought with it at best an elision of empire, and at worst complicity with imperial policies. A few recent books have traced the complicity of scholarship with empire, most notably David Price's *Cold War Anthropology* (2016), George Steinmetz's *Sociology and Empire* (2013) and Robert Vitalis's *White World Order, Black Power Politics* (2015). All these works demonstrate how knowledge production in various disciplines has been tied to imperial aims, building on classic works by Talal Asad, C. Wright Mills and Christopher Simpson, among others, on the role of the academy in aiding imperial white supremacist projects. In

The Racial Contract, Mills (1997) argued that the knowledge produced by Whites based on an 'epistemology of ignorance' was about sustaining slavery and colonisation. According to Mills, 'white misunderstanding, misrepresentation, evasion, and self-deception on matters related to race are among the most pervasive mental phenomena of the past few hundred years, a cognitive and moral economy psychically required for conquest, colonisation, and enslavement' (cited in Steinberg 2016). Decades later, Vitalis's alternative history of the field of International Relations makes a similar case, revealing the depths of white supremacy in the field.

In my study of Islamophobia, I situated contemporary anti-Muslim racism within a longer history of imperial conflict and rivalry, from the Crusades to the War on Terror. While modern racism is of a completely different character than the xenophobic and prejudicial attitudes held in medieval Europe, not least because the modern nation-state has been able to institutionalise racist practices in ways that far exceed those of earlier societies, there are precursors to the current ideological construction of the Muslim as enemy that demonstrate that contemporary Islamophobia is part of a much longer, albeit contradictory, historical lineage. In particular, the idea of Islam as inherently violent, whose origins lie in the Crusades, has been drawn upon quite effectively in the era of the War on Terror.

In the first three chapters of *Islamophobia*, I adopted a global perspective and offered an outline of the relationship between the 'West' and the 'Muslim world' as a way to explain the geopolitical origins of anti-Muslim ideology, particularly from the heyday of colonialism to the current War on Terror. The first chapter set out to debunk the idea of a transhistorical 'clash of civilisations' by using a historical materialist approach. Drawing on various scholars, particularly the work of Maxime Rodison, I showed that the relationship between various European powers and those in the Middle East/North Africa were driven not by an essential, hardwired, hatred between the two, but by political and economic interests. I further demonstrated that the relationship between 'West' and 'East' was complex and contradictory, involving various attitudes towards the East, from positive to downright hostile, both across time and place. In referring to the 'West', I challenged the ways in which both Orientalists and critics of Orientalism have homogenised the

West (I had Said's *Orientalism* in mind, although I didn't explicitly name his work in this way).

Aijaz Ahmed, and before him Sadik Jalal al-Azm, had critiqued Said for homogenising the West, and for presenting all work about the East done in the West as being necessarily tinged by Orientalism. Al-Azm, one of the first to advance this argument, contended that while Said sought to challenge the ways in which Orientalists ascribe an essential nature to the East and West, which make them not only ontologically different but that render one superior to another, Said was himself guilty of essentialising the West (Al-Azm, 2000). By tracing Orientalist attitudes all the way back to Homer, Said seems to suggest that there is something inherent in knowledge production in the West that renders it Orientalist. Additionally, even though one of Said's definitions of Orientalism is as a thoroughly modern phenomenon, his other definitions and his grand sweep of references muddy the historical context and the specificity of Orientalist modes of thought. Such a sweep that compares discourses produced in the capitalist and pre-capitalist eras, Ahmed argued, is one that even Foucault would have objected to (Ahmed, 1994). It leads Said to a place where the explanation for anti-Muslim/Arab caricatures comes out of the 'European mind', which is for Said, as Al-Azm (2000: 218) puts it, 'inherently bent on distorting all human realities other than its own for the sake of its own aggrandisement'. Such a unilinear, essentialist and idealist understanding of Orientalism does not, Al-Azm argues, serve Said well in his attempt to find an approach to how one might study other cultures and peoples in a non-repressive manner. In *Post-Orientalism* (2009) and *Can Non-Europeans Think?* (2015), Dabashi takes on this challenge by offering the 'exilic intellectual' as the agent of counter-hegemonic knowledge production in an era of Terror, and the Arab Spring as the source of new knowledge.

My focus in *Islamophobia* was on anti-Muslim racism in the US and how it emerged from the bowels of imperial America, even while it has also been shaped by Europe and Israel. I drew from Said, but I departed from his method by using a historical and dialectical materialist approach that seeks to root ideologies within their specific contexts, noting not only how knowledge and ideas emerge but how they change as well. I focused on the legal, political and to a lesser extent academic spheres in order to explain how these institutions contribute to the production and reproduction of Islamophobia as an ideology tied to a set of policies and practices. In the last chapter, I offered a 'matrix of Islamophobia' that highlights the various independent, but also interrelated and interdependent, spheres from which anti-Muslim racism emerges and circulates – think tanks, the academy, the political sphere, the national security apparatus, the legal sphere, the media, as well as right-wing social movements. To this, I should have added non-governmental organisations (NGOs) who have become powerful players on the international stage (Kumar, 2016). As such, the matrix was a preliminary attempt to outline the infrastructure of empire as a dynamic system in which each part informs the others. I also argued that left-wing social movements have the ability to counter anti-Muslim racism (this argument was further developed in Kumar, 2014). Building on a Gramscian model of ideological analysis (I also adopted this approach in Kumar, 2007), I suggested that Islamophobia is not a fixed ideology but one that exists as part of a mutually reinforcing system of far right-wing and liberal versions that can be challenged by movements from below. In short, it is important for scholars to study the battle for hegemony as a process for ideological domination in order to unpack the development, retardation and contradictions of anti-Muslim racism within the context of a global capitalist system.

While I examined the global dimensions to the growth of Islamophobia, particularly the Likud-Neocon connection and to a lesser extent the collaboration between various far right-wing groups that call themselves the 'counterjihad' movement, there is considerably more to be done along the lines of what Miller, Massoumi, Mills and Aked have started on the Islamophobic 'movement from above', which they suggest includes not just the far right but liberal groups as well across Europe (see Chapters 1, 8, 10 and 11 in this collection). Lentin and Titley (2011) have told part of that story through their analysis of the crisis of multiculturalism in Europe. Their focus is on 'multiculturalism' as a 'discursive assemblage that is produced and legitimised transnationally'. They draw examples from a range of countries and study the 'networks of exchange and meaning' while also 'paying attention to the specificities of contexts' (Lentin and Titley, 2011: 4). Skillfully weaving together a critique of the far right with the politics of official liberalism, they lay out the contours of cultural racism in the neoliberal era. This work can be productively expanded upon by developing a transnational analysis that goes beyond Europe, examining for instance the role of Israel in the production of cultural racism, as well as the part played by exilic intellectuals such as Ayaan Hirsi Ali and other 'native informants' (e.g. Dabashi, 2011). Such a global intermestic approach would also allow us to see how movements from below counter racism. The most significant moment since 9/11 of such global movements from below came with the Arab Spring of 2011. In a matter of weeks, the idea of 'Oriental Despotism' – that Arabs are incapable of social change and self-rule and are more comfortable with dictatorships than democracy – was challenged more thoroughly than all the scholarly work on the subject. This was particularly so among social movement actors around the globe. In Madison, Wisconsin, protestors carried signs that read 'Fight like an Egyptian', tearing down the idea that only the rational Western subject is interested in and capable of fighting for political representation and against neoliberal austerity. Various social movements, clustered in public spaces, from Tahrir square, Zucotti Park to Puerta Del Sol and Syntagma square, recognised the commonality and universality of their struggle. More recently, when Black Lives Matter came out in support of the Boycott, Divestment and Sanctions campaign against Israel, they underscored similarities between the black and Palestinian struggle, reviving a longer tradition of black-Palestinian solidarity. Implicitly, this plank marks a recognition that the struggle against oppression and the carceral state is a global one. The process of building solidarity therefore involves adopting an intermestic approach to questions of racism.

Finally, an intermestic approach to the study of Islamophobia would examine the ways in which practices developed in one context are transferred to others. The close relationship between the US and Britain leads to counter-terrorism policies that cross the Atlantic in both directions, as Arun Kundnani shows in *The Muslims Are Coming*. Alfred McCoy demonstrated that the practices of surveillance and counter-insurgency deployed by the US in the Philippines in the early twentieth century would come back home to be used on racialised subjects in the US (McCoy, 2009). Thus, domestic and international policy is part of a single dialectic, an integrated process more appropriately referred to as 'intermestic' policy, as stated earlier. For instance, Brian Loveman argues that the while the Monroe doctrine was about asserting US hegemony in Latin America, it was also to a significant degree driven by domestic concerns about the maintenance of slavery in the US. With Spain losing control of its American colonies, US policy makers feared that the abolition of slavery and the emancipation of slaves in those Spanish possessions might foment slave rebellions inside the US and thereby undermine the basic political framework on which the country had been founded. As Loveman writes, 'Domestic tranquility depended increasingly on balancing the conflicting versions of manifest destiny and competing interpretations of American federalism with the maintenance of the slave regime – and preventing slave rebellions. The No Transfer Policy and the Monroe Doctrine … were the foreign policy counterparts to the Missouri Compromise …' (Loveman, 2010: 118). What we can conclude from this is that if domestic and international policies aren't studied together, the ensuing analysis can, at best, offer only a partial explanation for racial formations at various moments.

Robert Vitalis outlines how the logic of white supremacy flows from a fundamental premise that was accepted by scholars of international relations who advocated a system of 'more or less permanent tutelage for darker and inferior people' (Vitalis, 2015: 10), whether the latter were to be found inside the US or outside. He writes that the 'central challenge that defined the new field called international relations was how to ensure the efficient political administration and race development of subject peoples, from the domestic dependencies and backward races at home to the complex race formations found in the new overseas territories and dependencies' (Vitalis, 2015: 25). Even into the 1920s and 1930s, not a single white international relations scholar 'argued on either principled or pragmatic grounds for the restoration of black citizenship rights, the dismantling of Jim Crow in the United States, and self-governance, let alone independence, for the colonies' (Vitalis, 2015: 11). In fact, the denial of voting rights to African Americans due to their 'unfitness' to vote was the basis on which it was determined that the people of the Philippines, Latin America or Africa were incapable of self-rule.

What follows from this is that while the global context is crucial, national histories are also vital to explaining the specific shape of racist ideologies and practices. In short, national peculiarities and the particular experiences of racialisation within nations influence racist articulations of the international 'Other'. Salaita (2006) argues that anti-Arab racism in the US has characteristics that make it 'uniquely American'. He points specifically to the ways in which the logic of settler colonialism and slavery inform contemporary anti-Arab racism. This argument also applies to anti-Muslim racism, which in addition to Arabs includes South Asians (even those who are not Muslims but appear to be Muslims, most notably Sikh men who wear turbans). Salaita further notes that the racialisation of one group interacts with and shapes the racialisation of other groups. As Junaid Rana puts it, 'the category of Muslim in the US is simultaneously a religious category and one that encompasses a broad race concept that connects a history of Native America to Black America to immigrant America in the consolidation of anti-Muslim racism' (Rana, 2007: 151).

Thus, if we set out to analyse the current anti-Muslim phenomenon in the UK, we would see it as a product of the complex interaction of colonialism, immigration and neoliberalism. Kundnani traces post-9/11 anti-Muslim racism to the 'mythology surrounding asylum seekers that emerged in the 1990s' (Kundnani, 2007: 5). He notes that the media and politicians

> blamed asylum seekers for the spread of TB, AIDS and SARS; for failing schools and hospitals; for falling house prices and for rising house prices; for low wages, rising crime, prostitution and road accidents. They were even to blame for the dwindling number of fish in Britain's rivers, the declining number of swans and the disappearance of donkeys. (Kundnani, 2007: 5)

According to Kundnani, this politics of scapegoating served multiple interests – for the Conservative Party it was a means of gaining popularity, for newspapers it made for a good front page story, and for local authorities it was a means to explain the housing shortage. In Denmark, Yilmaz (2016) roots the current anti-Muslim racism within a process spanning three decades, during which immigrants went from being seen as workers to being viewed as 'Muslims'. In France, Delphy (2015) asserts that the contemporary idea of Islam as a problem goes back 40 years to the responses to immigrants from former French colonies. She forcefully argues that France's particular attitude towards race, and its denial of the existence of systematic racism, means that the mere presence of religious symbols or clothing is seen as an attack on French identity. Since multiculturalism has been all but absent in the French context, some of the most blatant forms of Islamophobia are to be found there, forms that in the US would be frowned upon in polite society.

In short, particular national contexts and internal dynamics are crucial to the actual shape and form of racist ideologies and practices. In what follows, I outline the ideology of Islamophobia in the US as a product of both particular national histories and processes of racialisation, as well as an amalgam of transnational influences. By no means is this a comprehensive accounting. It is rather a preliminary outline of what a historical materialist intermestic approach to Islamophobia might look like.

Islamophobia and terrorism

In the US, anti-Muslim racist ideology in the twenty-first century cannot be traced to the decades-long history of anti-immigrant rhetoric in ways one might in Europe. While immigrants have been scapegoated in the neoliberal era, the typical target was Latino immigrants, particularly those from Mexico. This is why Donald Trump had to attack both Latino and Muslim immigrants and citizens. Anti-immigrant hysteria does not line up as neatly in the US with the 'Muslim' outsider as it does in Europe (where it includes Arabs, non-Arab North Africans, South Asians or people from Turkey), given its location and specific imperial relations with its neighbours, as well the significant presence of black Muslims. The geographic context of US imperialism shapes anti-immigrant discourses in different ways from Europe given the latter's proximity to the Middle East, North Africa and South Asia and the differences in the geographic patterns of their domination of different regions of the globe. Migration from economically less developed to advanced industrialised countries often reflects historic patterns of colonisation, settlement, foreign investment and other types of intervention. As A. Sivanandan put it, 'we are here, because you were there'. All that said, the idea of the Muslim outsider as a threat to national culture has become more prevalent in the US despite repeated liberal assertions of multicultural-ism as the hallmark of American national identity.

The more immediate and relevant context for the development of Islamophobia after 9/11 in the US is the development of the notion of the 'terrorist' starting in the 1970s. Two events, the Munich incident of 1972 and the Iran hostage crisis of 1979–80, would inform the process by which first the 'Arab' and later the 'Muslim' race would be produced. While past processes of racialisation do inform the present, Micheal Omi and Howard Winant argue that 'race is continually in formation'.

It is in that sense that the two aforementioned events are pivotal. Put another way, it is only by situating the production of races, or the process of racial formation, within their specific historic context that we might understand both the continuities with the past and the structuring reality of the present (Omi and Winant, 1994: x). Omi and Winant state that their theory of racial formation suggests that society is suffused with racial projects, large and small, to which all are subjected. This racial 'subjection' is quintessentially ideological. Everybody learns some combination, some version, of the rules of racial classification and of racial identity, often without obvious teaching or conscious inculcation. Thus are we inserted in a comprehensively racialised social structure. Race becomes 'common sense' – a way of comprehending, explaining and acting in the world. A vast web of racial projects mediates between the discursive or representational means in which race is identified and signified, on the one hand, and the institutional and organisational forms in which it is routinised and standardized, on the other. These projects are the heart of racial formation processes (Omi and Winant, 1994: 60).

Scholars familiar with the work of Terry Eagelton, Raymond Williams, E.P. Thompson, Stuart Hall and others within the British cultural studies tradition, or the work of the Chilean scholar Jorge Larrain on ideology, would immediately recognise Omi and Winant's discussion of racist ideologies as being consistent with those in the Marxist tradition. While Omi and Winant only cite Stuart Hall among the aforementioned intellectuals, their work nevertheless offers an important method by which to study the formation of races. In a forthcoming essay, I draw on their work, which I use along with Barbara and Karen Fields's notion of 'racecraft' to discuss 'terrorcraft' (Fields and Fields, 2012). By terrorcraft, I mean a system of meaning-making that draws both from witchcraft as well as 'racecraft'. Terrorcraft is like witchcraft in that it fabricates a fictitious being, the 'terrorist', an actor ostensibly responsible for widespread 'evil' and death, despite the reality that only a tiny number of Americans are killed each year by jihadists. While such groups as al Qaeda and ISIS or the Islamic State consciously employ tactics that are today considered acts of 'terrorism', that term was not applied to similar acts in the past. As Lisa Stampnitzky has shown, those who participated in plane hijacking or kidnappings in the period before the 1970s, for example, were not called terrorists, but instead were identified as 'bandits, rebels, guerillas, or later, urban guerrillas, revolutionaries, or insurgents' (Stampnitzky,

2014: 2). Similarly, Brulin (2011) argues that when US presidents prior to the 1970s discussed hijackings or bombings of commercial aircraft, they described the perpetrators as 'air pirates', 'sky pirates' or 'hijackers'. Thus, 'terrorism' is an ideological system similar to witchcraft which served as a means of explaining bad things in the medieval world. Further, like 'racecraft' the terrorist is, from the very start, both raced and gendered. The Arab/Muslim male becomes the personification of terrorism (even if the occasional 'Jihadi Jane' does enter the picture).

The threat of the Arab terrorist took root in the US after the Munich incident, when members of the Palestinian group Black September murdered several Israeli athletes whom they had taken hostage at the 1972 Olympics. The Nixon administration, having strengthened its strategic ties to Israel after the 1967 war, responded by launching Operation Boulder, a system of racial profiling that involved scrutinising the activities of Arab Americans and profiling Arab visa applicants. Without a moment's hesitation, the Nixon administration took the actions of a handful of Palestinians at Munich as representative of tens of millions of Arabs. This is an instance of what Albert Memmi called the 'mark of the plural' in *The Colonizer and the Colonized*, in which he observed that acts of individual non-Whites are seen as generalisable to an entire group, while those of Whites are limited to the individual. After the bombing of Pearl Harbor, for example, all Japanese Americans were viewed as members of a suspect community that had to be locked up in internment camps. Racialised Others are thus denied the individuality afforded to Whites, even while in some cases (Arabs and Muslims today and Native Americans in the past) they are also chastised for not embracing modernity and liberal individualism.

The racialisation of Indigenous peoples has in fact had a profound impact on contemporary racism in the US. In the nineteenth century, 'manifest destiny', which rested on a bedrock of white supremacy, animated territorial expansion. The land seized from Indigenous people was understood to be 'unsettled' and 'empty' (because it was not individually owned but part of the commons) and therefore available for 'free white persons'. Putting aside their own history of enclosures, white Anglo settlers came to see themselves as a breed apart from, and superior to, the 'savage' because of their ability to cultivate the land and extract value. Long before the concept was coined in the mid nineteenth century, the British and the Anglo-American colonists had developed their own idea of 'manifest destiny', derived in part from their sense of divinely bestowed racial and cultural superiority. They also believed in the right of conquest of backward peoples in the name of civilisation, an attitude they had first developed closer to home, particularly against the Irish, who were subjected to many of the same practices later applied to Native Americans. (Interestingly, it is the neoconservative Robert Kagan who makes this argument most forcefully, see Kagan, 2006.)

We might say then that the project of settler colonialism was central to the historical process of racialisation, which then served to inform later projects of racial formation. Indeed, Patrick Wolfe traces what he calls the 'elementary structures of race' in several settler-colonial contexts (e.g. North America, Australia, Palestine and Brazil) to demonstrate similar processes of racialisation in various contexts (Wolfe, 2016).

However, even while the past influences the present and practices of racialisation have been transplanted from one location to others, the specific context for the production of racialised subjects often necessitates new vocabularies and practices, not least because struggles against racism limit the unreconstructed use of previous ideologies. In addition, moments of racialisation are often a response to real world events and interests which demand particular responses. Put another way, while racist ideologies develop in particular contexts, they can and often do build upon the repository of past modes of racialisation. In this sense, anti-Muslim racism in the twenty-first century is informed by the past, for example, through the trope of Muslim as Native American or the image of Muslim piracy in the Barbary coast. However, it is also tied, perhaps more immediately, to the racialisation of other contemporaneous groups, such as Japanese Americans in the context of World War II. Similarly, Nixon's drug war and its particular racialisation of African Americans can also be said to have a bearing on the racialisation of Arabs, just as Carter's racialisation of Iranians informed the language of the 'Muslim threat' of the 1980s.

The evolution in the racialisation of Arabs and Muslims is also tied to expanding US political interests in the Middle East. Melani McAlister traces the ways in which popular culture reflects and shapes US perceptions of the Middle East, examining the shift from the racialised Arab to the racialised Muslim (McAlister, 2005). The resistance to US policies in the region by such secular nationalists as Mossadeg and Nasser in the 1950s had a significant impact on the development and deployment of anti-Arab and anti-Iranian stereotypes (Little, 2002). The connection between the growing strategic importance of Israel following the 1967 war (Said emphasised the importance of the US relationship to Israel in the growth of US Orientalism) and the US response to Munich, mentioned above, is another example. Following the overthrow of the Shah of Iran in 1979 and the election of Ronald Reagan in 1980, anti-Arab and anti-Muslim racism intensified significantly in the US.

These developments cannot be divorced from the broader process of racialisation taking place within the US. Anti-Arab racism also impacted all those who 'looked Arab/Muslim', including brown-skinned Latino/as. Not coincidentally, at the same time as Arab and Muslim men were being turned into violent terrorists, African American men were being cast as violent predators in the context of the War on Drugs and the rise of mass incarceration (see Alexander, 2012; Reeves and Campbell, 1994). The 1980s saw the intensification of the War on Drugs alongside the introduction of various counter-terrorism measures; ideologically the threat of black and brown male violence was the bedrock of these policies.

The criminalisation of black men, of course, has a much longer history. It has its roots in the post-Civil War imposition of 'slavery by another name', a process that ensnared former slaves and their descendants in a new form of involuntary servitude by criminalising them (Blackmon, 2009). It also built on post-Civil War notions of the 'black brute' who supposedly posed a threat to white women. Fredrick Douglass argued that when all the other methods of demonising black people had failed, the myth of the black rapist was developed to justify lynchings and white terror during the era of reconstruction (see Davis, 1983: 183–6). Vigilante groups like the Ku Klux Klan justified their brutality by claiming to keep white women safe from the black rapist as visualised, for instance, in D.W. Griffith's *Birth of a Nation*. Such constructions of white women in need of protection from predatory black men were reminiscent of the 'captivity scenarios' of the seventeenth century, in which Native American men were accused of kidnapping white women, a charge that then justified genocide (Slotkin, 1973; see Zinn, 2003 for an alternative take on these narratives – one that restores agency to white women who not infrequently sought refuge from their patriarchal communities among Native American societies). This history of 'black men as brutes' continues to feed the logic of mass incarceration today, which has imprisoned more African Americans than were enslaved in the ante-bellum south (Smiley and Fakunle, 2016).

With Arabs and Muslims, Orientalism provided a handy explanation for their violence: the Arab/Muslim terrorist is violent because he is driven by rage rather than rationality. Bernard Lewis, in a now famous article titled 'The roots of Muslim rage', argued that it was not politics that motived Muslims, but an existential rage that is fundamentally cultural and characterises the 'clash of civilisations'. Through this, Lewis, and later Huntington, would give Orientalism a new lease on life. Like past Orientalists, this duo forwarded the argument that Muslims lacked rationality and reason and therefore lay outside modernity. The Muslim man is driven by Islam to take fanatical actions which have no real or political basis. In the 1980s, Ayatollah Khomeini personified all things irrational and it was suggested that Muslim 'culture' made him behave in certain ways. If Iranian students took Americans hostage it was not because they had legitimate political reasons to do so – such as US support for the coup that overthrew the democratically elected Mohamad Mossadeg or CIA training of the Shah's secret police that savagely repressed and tortured dissenters. Rather, it was 'Islam' that drove these actions (Said, 1997). Just as African American 'culture' was said to have stunted their economic development through a 'culture of poverty', the culture of Islam was seen to distort the mindset of Muslims.

The 'clash of civilisations' recycled older Orientalist arguments about modernity. For Orientalists, as well as other liberal imperialists, modernity was the hallmark of the West. Since other regions of the world had failed to break from their traditional pasts, it was the 'white man's burden' to facilitate this process on a global scale. This was the dominant ideology in the nineteenth century in various imperial nations (see, for instance, Lasurdo, 2011). The remaking of Europe in the nineteenth century was premised on its superiority in the world system due to its ability to go through a Renaissance and discard its old pre-modern ways of the 'dark ages'. Further, since modernity, the scientific revolution and the Enlightenment brought a belief that humans were rational beings, capable of making their own history, Europeans were seen as unique in their ability to cast off their traditional culture. Further, modernity was presented as a product of nascent capitalism and it was therefore necessary for the West to bring both capitalism and 'civilisation' to the rest of the world in the industrial capitalist era.

In the racial hierarchy that developed, non-capitalist countries were depicted as traditional and backward. Max Weber famously argued that because certain mechanisms for social change were absent in the Middle East (such as free labour or rational law), an internal social virus prevented the development of capitalism. This internalist, essentialist, teleological/stageist view of history influenced many thinkers both within the Orientalist tradition as well as within the US school of modernisation theory (e.g. Lerner, 1953; Rostow, 1960).

Several scholars have debunked this argument in a variety of ways. Recent work on the intellectual advancements made by Muslims during their 800-year rule in the Iberian peninsula suggests that the Renaissance would not have occurred had it not been for their advancements in science, astronomy, architecture and rationalist thought (see, for instance, Menocal, 2003; Saliba, 2011), Bryan Turner in *Marxism and the End of Orientalism* (2014) takes on the economic dimensions of this argument, stressing the global and interdependent nature of capitalist development. More recently, Alexander Anievas and Kerem Nişancıoğlu offer a sweeping account of the origin of capitalism as a global process in which non-European societies played a decisive role in *How the West Came to Rule* (2015). Similarly, Sven Beckert in *Empire of Cotton* (2014) and Robin Blackburn in *The American Crucible* (2013) point to the global system of production and trade that enabled the growth of capitalism in Europe. Thus, even to pose the question of why 'Islam' didn't experience a Renaissance is absurd when historical developments are placed within their global economic and geopolitical contexts. (The origin of capitalism is of course a hotly debated topic whose contours are beyond the scope of this chapter.)

Nevertheless, it has now become an entrenched dogma in the West that Muslims are outside modernity and must be brought, forcibly or otherwise, out of their traditional ways. Presumably, even while they live in the midst of gleaming shopping malls and towering sky scrapers as seen in Dubai, Abu Dhabi or Bahrain, their clothing choices mark them as having never left the 'dark ages'. One telling scene in the film *Sex in the City 2*, set in Abu Dhabi, and the only moment when the four women from New York feel any affinity with Muslim women, is when the latter throw off their burqas to reveal the latest fashions underneath. Modernity is reduced quite literally to clothing within the neoliberal logic of liberation through consumption (Kumar, 2016). Even when they live in the West, and hold jobs, attend university, buy groceries, visit hospitals and lead their day-to-day lives in ways similar to white Christian/secular citizens, their clothing choices, particularly those of women, are presented as a danger to modernity. The burkini ban that swept France in 2016 is an example of the ubiquitous nature of this thinking. Women's bodies become markers of modernity, in a move that objectifies both the burkini-clad Muslim woman and the bikini-clad French woman.

Also, just as the US developed notions of the Native American and later African American as threats to white middle-class femininity and virtue, various European powers justified colonial brutality as the key means by which to control the excessive/deviant sexuality of the colonised male because of the threat he posed to upper-class white women. In Europe today, the idea of 'Muslim rape' and gangs of Muslim men terrorising white women has become a key trope of the counterjihad movement (Horsti, 2016). This is part of an argument about what the Islamisation of Europe would look like, or what the threat of 'Eurabia' represents. This argument was then given a hearing in the US by the likes of Pamela Geller of Stop Islamization of America and various other far right-wing ideologues.

Similarly, the US far right learned from Europe to shame feminists for their alleged failure to 'speak out' about the oppression of Muslim women. But US liberals too have started to give voice to this argument, albeit in more nuanced and sophisticated ways (e.g. Rogers, 2015). The far right has also taken a page from the liberal establishment. Whereas Jerry Falwell blamed gays for the attacks of 9/11, when the Orlando shooting occurred in 2016 the far right took a page both from official liberalism as well as Israel's pink washing strategy to cast themselves as friends of the gay community.

It is important to emphasise that ideas gain strength and the capacity to travel to the degree that they coincide with political and material interests, a point that tends to be underemphasised in the literature on global cultural flows. In the 'movement from above', ideas travel in multiple directions because they suit the interests of various constituencies within the global neoliberal system. For instance, German Chancellor Angela Merkel, who had previously taken a liberal approach towards Muslim immigrants and refugees, did an about-face by advocating a ban on the Muslim veil after the Christian Democrats lost electoral support to the far right. While the number of women who wear the veil in Germany is miniscule, Merkel nonetheless targeted them as a convenient political scapegoat, an act of crass political expediency not unlike Switzerland's decision to ban minarets in a country that has a total of only four. What is at stake is not only the political future of the Christian Democrats domestically but also Germany's political and economic hegemony within the EU. If Ulrich Beck is right that German hegemony within Europe is based on both its dominant economy and rejection of its Nazi past, the rise of far right-wing parties poses not only a serious political threat but an economic one as well (Jeffries, 2013).

In sum, an intermestic approach to Islamophobia is one that both roots ideologies and practices within their specific national contexts but is also attentive to the transnational context. This transnational context, the global War on Terror, is a system whose contours need to be fleshed out in order to gain a fuller understanding of the phenomenon of Islamophobia. Most fundamentally, anti-Muslim racism can only be understood if placed in the context of empire – that is, a system for the management and development of global capitalism under the control of powerful nation-states which both compete with and cooperate with one another. By 'empire', I do not mean the Hardt and Negri use of the term, but rather empire in ways that political economists have understood it. *Islamophobia* was focused more on the political aspects of empire, but as Chibber (2004) correctly argues, the economic aspects of empire in the age of the War on Terror need to be studied in greater depth. In the next section, I raise some questions for future research that such a focus implies.

Future directions

The state is a crucial site for the study of Islamophobia. Miller, Massoumi, Mills and Aked argue that the state is one 'pillar' of Islamophobia, and Kundnani also emphasises the significant role of the state. But the state, as these scholars are well aware, is not a monolith or unitary actor. It consists of various institutions and actors that come into conflict with one another over various approaches to the world, even if they share a common focus on the reproduction of capitalism. There is a vast body of scholarship on the capitalist state and debates about the relationship between structure and agency, as well as the state and imperialism. If we accept, for instance, Leo Panitch and Sam Gindin's theory of a US-led informal global empire that has at its core the 'internationalisation of the capitalist state' (Panitch and Gindin, 2012), what does that mean for the study of Islamophobia? When and how do subordinate states within the informal empire exert their 'relative autonomy' and how do they come together to reproduce racism? How does conflict between elites within a nation, as well as conflicts between nation-states, impact the 'movement from above' and shape the contours of Islamophobia? Here we need to pay particular attention to the ways in which neoliberalism creates the conditions for new forms of racialisation. For instance, in *The End of Tolerance*, Kundnani argues that the impact of neoliberalism on migrant labour, particularly job and spatial displacements, would be instrumental to the emergence of new discourses on race.

A second, and connected area, is the development of the carceral state and the interconnected ways in which racialised groups are policed around the world. What are the new configurations of the national security state and the carceral state in the era of neoliberal imperialism? If we look at the current surveillance system, it is one marked by an unprecedented merger of military and commercial networks. What this indicates is the deepening and strengthening of the relationship between capital and the state in the neoliberal era, contrary to the mythology of the death of the nation-state, and a further entrenchment of the 'military-industrial complex'. Scholars of the carceral state similarly note the ways in which the state and the private sector come together to create a vast apparatus for punishment and control (e.g. Hallett, 2006; Selman and Leighton, 2010). (Recent historical work on the carceral state can be found in a special issue of the *Journal of American History*. For an overview of the various contributions, see Hernández et al., 2015.)

In an important new book, Jordan Camp argues that in the context of the global economic crisis of the early 1970s, as well as the social crises wrought by race and class conflicts, the neoliberal carceral state emerged to manage these crises (Camp, 2016). As older racial narratives wore thin, a new common sense developed that blamed racialised Others for social problems and offered the carceral state as a solution. Camp's focus on the 'outgrowth of the long counterinsurgency against the Black freedom, labor, and socialist alliance' is one important part of the story (Camp, 2016: 5). This work can be productively advanced by examining the contemporaneous ways in which Arab/Muslims, Latinos and African Americans are racialised in the neoliberal era by the US carceral state. Kundnani and I initiated the first steps of such analysis (Kundnani and Kumar, 2015). Drawing on W.E.B. Du Bois's notion of the 'psychological wage', we argued that 'security' has become one of the primary means through which racism is ideologically reproduced in the 'post-racial', neoliberal era. The neoliberal state we suggest has in part been legitimised through racialised notions of security that offer a new 'psychological wage' as compensation for the decline of the social wage and its reallocation to 'homeland security'.

We might also internationalise this analysis by studying the ways in which technologies for social control travel the globe and how racialised Others are managed within the system of global neoliberalism. How does neoliberalism inform contemporary modalities of racist ideologies and practices on a global scale? Finally, how does the dialectic of dominance and resistance from below get played out within this context? In short, we need to develop an intermestic account of the growth of Islamophobia. The task for us is to unpack the global infrastructure of empire in the twenty-first century while being attentive to national dynamics and concrete economic and political circumstances.

Bibliography

Abdel-Malek, A. (2000), 'Orientalism in crisis', in A.L. Macfie (ed.), *Orientalism: A Reader*. New York: New York University Press, pp. 47–56.

Ahmed, A. (1994), *In Theory: Classes, Nations, Literatures*. Delhi: Oxford University Press.

Al-Azm, S.J. (2000), 'Orientalism in reverse', in A.L. Macfie (ed.), *Orientalism: A Reader*. New York: New York University Press, pp. 217–38.

Alexander, M. (2012), *The New Jim Crow*. New York: The New Press.

Anievas, A. and Nişancıoğlu, K. (2015), *How the West Came to Rule: The Geopolitical Origins of Capitalism*. London: Pluto Press.

Beckert, S. (2014), *Empire of Cotton: A Global History*. New York: Alfred A. Knopf.

Bender, T.A. (2016), *Nation Among Nations: America's Place in World History*. New York: Hill and Wang.

Blackmon, D.A. (2009), *Slavery by Another Name: The Re-enslavement of Black Americans from the Civil War to World War II*. New York: Anchor Books.

Blackburn, R. (2013), *The American Crucible: Slavery, Emancipation and Human Rights*. London: Verso.

Brulin, R. (2011), 'Defining "terrorism": the 1972 General Assembly debates on "international terrorism" and their coverage by the *New York Times*', in B. Baybars-Hawks and L Baruh (eds), *If It Was Not for Terrorism: Crisis, Compromise, and Elite Discourse in the Age of War on Terror*. Cambridge: Cambridge Scholars Publishing, pp. 12–30.

Camp, J.T. (2016), *Incarcerating the Crisis: Freedom Struggles and the Rise of the Neoliberal State*. Oakland, CA: University of California Press.

Chibber, V. (2004), 'The return of imperialism to social science', *Archives Européennes de Sociologie/European Journal of Sociology*, 45 (3), 427–41.

Dabashi, H. (2009), *Post-Orientalism: Knowledge and Power in Times of Terror*. New Brunswick, NJ: Transaction Publishers.

Dabashi, H. (2011), *Brown Skin, White Masks*. Chicago, IL: University of Chicago Press.

Dabashi, H. (2015), *Can Non-Europeans Think?* Chicago, IL: University of Chicago Press.

Davis, A. (1983), *Women, Race, and Class*. New York: Vintage Books.

Delphy, C. (2015), *Separate and Dominate: Feminism and Racism after the War on Terror*. New York: Verso.

Fields, K.E. and Fields, B.J. (2012), *Racecraft: The Soul of Inequality in American Life*. New York: Verso.

Foner, E. (2005), *Give Me Liberty: An American History: Vol. 1*. New York: W.W. Norton.

Hallett, M. (2006), *Private Prisons in America: A Critical Race Perspective*. Urbana Champaign, IL: University of Illinois Press.

Hernández, K.L., Muhammad, K.G. and Heather, A.T. (2015), 'Introduction: constructing the carceral state', *Journal of American History*, 102 (1), 18–24.

Horsti, K. (2016), 'Digital Islamophobia: the Swedish woman as a figure of pure and dangerous whiteness', *New Media and Society*, 25 April, 1–18.

Jeffries, S. (2013), 'Is Germany too powerful for Europe', *Guardian*, 31 March. www.theguardian.com/world/2013/mar/31/is-germany-too-powerful-for-europe. Accessed 15 August 2016.

Kagan, R. (2006), *Dangerous Nation*. New York: Alfred Knoff.

Kumar, D. (2007), *Outside the Box: Corporate Media, Globalization and the UPS Strike*. Urbana Champaign, IL: University of Illinois Press.

—— (2010), 'Framing Islam: the resurgence of Orientalism during the Bush II era', *Journal of Communication Inquiry*, 34 (3), 254–77.

—— (2014), 'Mediating racism: the new McCarthyites and the matrix of Islamophobia', *Middle East Journal of Culture and Communication*, 7, 9–26.

—— (2016), 'Imperial feminism', *International Socialist Review*, 102, 56–70.

Kundnani, A. (2007), *The End of Tolerance: Racism in 21st Century Britain*, Ann Arbor, MI: Pluto Press.

—— (2016), 'Islamophobia: lay-ideology of US-led empire'. www.kundnani.org/wp-content/uploads/Kundnani-Islamophobia-as-lay-ideology-of-US-empire.pdf. Accessed 2 September 2016.

Kundnani, A. and Kumar, D. (2015), 'Race, surveillance, empire', *International SocialistReview*,96.http://isreview.org/issue/96/race-surveillance-and-empire. Accessed 10 September 2016.

Lasurdo, D. (2011), *Liberalism: A Counter-History*, New York: Verso.

Lentin, A. and Titley, G. (2011), *The Crisis of Multiculturalism: Racism in the Neoliberal Age*. New York: Zed Books.

Lerner, D. (1953), *The Passing of Traditional Society: Modernizing the Middle East*. New York: Free Press.

Little, D. (2002), *American Orientalism: The United States and the Middle East since 1945*. Chapel Hill, NC: University of North Carolina Press.

Loveman, B. (2010), *No Higher Law: American Foreign Policy and the Western Hemisphere since 1776*, Chapel Hill, NC: University of North Carolina Press.

Macfie, A.L. (2000), 'Introduction – Orientalism in crisis', in A.L. Macfie (ed.), *Orientalism: A Reader*. New York: New York University Press, pp. 2–23.

Matar, M. (2000), *Turks, Moors, and Englishmen in the Age of Discovery*. New York: Columbia University Press.

McAlister, M. (2005), *Epic Encounters: Culture, Media, and U.S. Interests in the Middle East since 1945*, Berkeley, CA: University of California Press.

McCoy, A. (2009), *Policing America's Empire: The United States, the Philippines and the Rise of the Surveillance State*, Madison, WI: University of Wisconsin Press.

Menocal, M.R. (2003), *The Ornament of the World: How Muslims, Jews and Christians Created a Culture of Tolerance in Medieval Spain*. New York: Back Bay Books.

Miller, D., Massoumi, N., Mills, T. and Aked, H. (2015), 'Five pillars of Islamophobia', OpenDemocracy. www.opendemocracy.net/opensecurity/david-miller-tom-mills-hilary-aked-narzanin-massoumi/five-pillars-of-islamophobia. Accessed 6 September 2016.

Mills, C.W. (1997), *The Racial Contract*. Ithaca, NY and London: Cornell University Press.

Omi, M. and Winant, H. (1994), *Racial Formation in the United States*. New York: Routledge.

Panitch, L. and Gindin, S. (2012), *The Making of Global Capitalism: The Political Economy of American Empire*. New York: Verso.

Price, D.H. (2016), *Cold War Anthropology: The CIA, the Pentagon, and the Growth of Dual Use Anthropology*. Durham, NC: Duke University Press.

Rana, J. (2007), 'The story of Islamophobia', Souls, 9:2, 148–61.

Reeves, J.L. and Campbell, R. (1994), *Cracked Coverage: Television News, the Anti-Cocaine Crusade, and the Reagan Legacy*. Durham, NC: Duke University Press.

Rogers, H. (2015), 'Holding our tongues: why aren't more non-Muslim feminists decrying violence against women in Muslim majority countries?', Tablet. www.tabletmag.com/jewish-news-and-politics/189292/holding-our-tongues. Accessed 5 September 2016.

Rostow, W.W. (1960), *The Stages of Economic Growth: A Non-Communist Manifesto*. Cambridge: Cambridge University Press.

Said, E. (1997), *Covering Islam*. New York: Vintage.

Salaita, S. (2006), *Anti-Arab Racism in the USA: Where it Comes From and What it Means Today*. Ann Arbor, MI: Pluto Press.

Saliba, G. (2011), *Islamic Science and the Making of the European Renaissance*. Boston, MA: MIT Press.

Selman, D. and Leighton, P. (2010), *Punishment for Sale: Private Prisons, Big Business, and the Incarceration Binge*, Lanham, MD: Rowman & Littlefield.

Slotkin, R. (1973), *Regeneration Through Violence: The Mythology of the American Frontier, 1600–1860*. Middletown, CT: Wesleyan University Press.

Smiley, C.J. and Fakunle, D. (2016), 'From "brute" to "thug:" the demonization and criminalization of unarmed Black male victims in America', *Journal of Human Behavior in the Social Environment*, 26 (3–4), 350–66.

Stampnitzky, L. (2014), *Disciplining Terror: How Experts Invented 'Terrorism'*. Cambridge: Cambridge University Press.

Steinberg, S. (2016), 'Decolonizing sociology', Stanford University Press Blog. http://stanfordpress.typepad.com/blog/2016/08/decolonizing-sociology.html. Accessed 11 September 2016.

Steinmetz, G. (2013), *Sociology and Empire: The Imperial Entanglements of a Discipline*. Durham, NC: Duke University Press.

Turner, B.S. (2014), *Marxism and the End of Orientalism*. Abingdon: Routledge.

Vitalis, R. (2015), *White World Order, Black Power Politics: The Birth of American International Relations*. Ithaca, NY: Cornell University Press.

Wolfe (2016), *Traces of History: Elementary Structures of Race*. New York: Verso.

Yilmaz, F. (2016), *How Workers Became Muslims: Immigration, Culture and Hegemonic Transformation in Europe*, Ann Arbor, MI: University of Michigan Press.

Zinn, H. (2003), *A People's History of the United States*. New York: HarperCollins.

4

The UK Counter-terrorism Matrix: Structural Racism and the Case of Mahdi Hashi

Asim Qureshi

Introduction

The organisation CAGE (formerly CagePrisoners) was launched in October 2003 in order to provide a platform for communities to learn about the plight of those detained at the US detention camps on Guantanamo Bay, Cuba. Within the first year of launching the website, many individuals began contacting us complaining directly of family members who were unlawfully detained by the US military and security agencies, well beyond the camps at Guantanamo Bay. CAGE expanded its role from republishing information pieces to conducting investigations and writing reports that highlighted the extent of abuses, particularly by Western countries, in the global 'War on Terror'. While the organisation's initial concerns focused on abuses stemming from US/UK military action abroad, this in turn led us to scrutinise counter-terrorism policy and legislation at home – and in particular the relationship between the two. Through the extensive interviews we conducted from hundreds of detainees, their families and experts, we have been able to signpost the dangers of structural racism within Western counter-terrorism policy.

The UK government's counter-terrorism strategy CONTEST has four key areas: Pursue, Prevent, Protect, Prepare (Home Office, 2011). Key to the development of the UK government's legal policy are the first two areas, Pursue and Prevent, where communities intersect with counter-terrorism. Pursue concentrates on those who are alleged to be planning terrorist attacks while Prevent concentrates on the 'pre-crime' space, effectively seeking to stop individuals becoming terrorists in the future. The entire counter-terrorism strategy is supposed to work together, in an interdepartmental way.

In July 2016, I was invited to Chatham House to discuss the UK's counter-extremism policy that included, NGOs, lawyers and government officials. One of the features of this meeting related to the way in which the officials would distinguish their work from other parts of counter-terrorism policy. One of the consistent refrains we heard from officials was that the government's counter-extremism policy had nothing to do with the government's Prevent strategy, and, in fact these pro-Prevent officials (who cannot be identified due to rules of the discussion) were against some of the counter-extremism policy directions being taken. For me, there was something missing from this thinking, that these officials did not see how their particular area or work within Prevent intersected with the government's counter-extremism strategies, but further wider terrorism legislation and policy.

It is precisely in the intersection between the different aspects of the CONTEST strategy that we see a picture emerge of a structural form of racism that undermines communities. Structural racism here is understood as the way in which racism manifests from intra-institution to inter-institution (Powell, 2007: 796). This is well captured by the editors of this collection in their introduction:

> We regard the state, and more specifically the sprawling official 'counter-terrorism' apparatus, to be absolutely central to production of contemporary Islamophobia – the backbone of anti-Muslim racism.

Islamophobia as a form of racism manifests itself within the nexus of counter-terrorism. By treating the counter-terrorism apparatus in the UK as an interconnected matrix, I will argue that Prevent and Pursue, are two sides of the same coin despite claims to the contrary. With Pursue, the police are interested in disrupting potential acts of terrorism that are in the process of being engaged. Prevent claims that it is attempting to operate in a 'pre-criminal' space, removing individuals from a path that might lead to future violence. This picture is not as binary as it is presented, and there is a great deal of overlap between the two.

When an individual is suspected of being some kind of threat to the UK, the security agencies along with the Home Office on occasion will make determinations as to the way that individual should be treated. Since before the 'War on Terror' began, the UK government has been enacting legislation and policies that limit the freedom of individuals, often without having to present any evidence before a court. There are questions though about the starting point of investigations, and to what extent they are based on profiling or actual investigations.

The empirical data in Chapter 1 shows how counter-terrorism measures are disproportionately targeting Muslim communities. Such data is important in demonstrating the racist nature of counter terrorism policy, however, this data is not made readily available especially with respect to religious breakdown. For example, the systematic profiling of young black males by police is well documented with reports indicating that in 2015, black men were 17 times more likely to be stopped and searched than any other group (Morris, 2015). However, the police do not record data by religion, but only by ethnicity, thus making it more difficult to identify whether Muslims are being systematically discriminated against.

The latest figures from stops at UK ports under Schedule 7 of the Terrorism Act 2000 show that 78 per cent of those detained under the power came from ethnic minorities (CAGE, 2016a). This is at a time when the ethnic minority population of the UK constitutes 14 per cent of the entire population. Although the general numbers of stops have decreased, prolonged detentions (up to 6 hours) have increased by 75 per cent (CAGE, 2016a). With schedule 7 stops, it is difficult to ascertain the extent to which these stops are based on religious or racial profiling, but projects such as Schedule 7 Stories (www.schedule7stories.com) provide anecdotal examples of how Muslims are largely targeted by the powers.

A June 2016 briefing paper for the UK House of Commons by Benjamin Politowski highlights the ethnic break-up within counter-terrorism operations. Since 9/11, the numbers indicate that 39 per cent Asian, 29 per cent White, 12 per cent Black and 19 per cent Other were arrested under terrorism legislation (Politowski, 2016). What commentators, such as the Independent Reviewer of Terrorism Legislation David Anderson, often fail to recognise in relation to such statistics is the percentages are often based on ethnic categories, not on religion. By focusing on ethnic make-up much of the actual discrimination against Muslims is lost (Anderson, 2016: 44). Muslims are roughly 5 per cent of the UK population, so high percentages among that demographic in terms of ethnicity and religion presents a disproportionate targeting – exacerbated by the fact that Muslims can also appear in the 'White' category. The second reason why such statistics are skewed is due to those from the far right not being arrested under terrorism legislation. An example of this would be the case of Robert Cottage, the former British National Party candidate who was jailed for stockpiling explosives – although caught with both the desire and ability to cause serious harm, was not treated as a potential terrorist (Campbell, 2007). As recognised by Politowski, the aim of arresting appears to be a fishing exercise:

> The relatively low ratio of arrests to charges suggests that alongside the aim of investigating and prosecuting terrorists, key objectives of terrorism related arrests include opportunities for intelligence gathering as part of the Pursue strategy and deterrence and disruption under Protect. (Politowski, 2016)

The religious make-up of profiling stops and arrests are perhaps best reflected in the statistics around citizenship removal cases. Since 2002, there have been 53 citizenship revocations by the UK Home Secretary, at least 27 on the grounds of national security. The current UK Prime Minister and former Home Secretary Theresa May having been responsible for 37 of those revocations. While the entire policy is shrouded in secrecy, particularly due to the protection the courts give to the government through secrecy invocations based on national security, we know from the ethnic origins of those who have had their British citizenships removed that they hail from Muslim countries (Ross and Galey, 2013).

The UK counter-terrorism matrix

The attacks of 9/11 were not the beginning of the 'War on Terror' era of terrorism policies in the UK. One year prior to those attacks in the US, the UK government passed the Terrorism Act (TA) 2000, defining for the first time what an act of terrorism constituted and how it would be defined. The Act replaced the previous Prevention of Terrorism (temporary provisions) Act 1974. Significantly, the legislation permitted certain powers that would make existing profiling practices into institutional forms of structural racism and violence. Until 2010, Section 44 of the TA 2000 was used in order to stop and search individuals within a specific area without the need for any form of reasonable suspicion. Later Section 47A would be used in order to carry out the same policy of stop and search, with the exception that some form of reasonable suspicion would be required.

As mentioned above, Schedule 7 of the Terrorism Act 2000, gives the police unprecedented powers to detain and question individuals with little recourse to normal processes of rights. For example, under the legislation it is an offence to refuse to answer questions, leading to a great deal of consternation about how such self-incriminating information might be used. Projects like Schedule 7 Stories clarify that particularly where individuals have been detained, the focus is much more on political and religious views rather than questions on any specific lines of inquiry or investigation. For many people, this will be the first moment they enter into the matrix of counter-terrorism – having been forced to hand over not only their electronic devices, but also the information that is contained inside their hearts and minds.

There is a notion that such information has no specific impact on the individual, and that communities should be willing to share such information as no prosecutions will emerge from it. However, the legal system has been constructed in order to neutralise any potential threat, even if it is in what is termed the pre-criminal space – one in which an individual could be placed on a number of terrorism/extremism databases kept by the government (Webb, 2015). Such assessments are almost impossible to challenge due to the layers of secrecy that surround them (Lewis et al., 2009), but can impact on an individual's ability to exercise their rights to freedom of expression, to gain lawful employment or work with vulnerable groups.

After the 7 July 2005 bombings, successive UK administrations pushed to move terrorism out of the framework of the criminal justice system and into the civil law system. Through this, they had the opportunity to present secret evidence in what are euphemistically called 'closed material proceedings' (CMPs) where the accused and their legal team are unable to hear or see the evidence being presented against them, being forced to rely on a system of special advocates who represent the defendant/appellant on their behalf against the state. The system is so controversial that even the special advocates involved in the system have publicly criticised it:

CMPs represent a departure from the foundational principle of natural justice that all parties are entitled to see and challenge all the evidence relied upon before the court and to combat that evidence by calling evidence of their own. They also undermine the principle that public justice should be dispensed in public. (European Parliament, 2014)

While there was an attempt by the UK government to re-establish interment in the UK through the Anti-Terrorism, Crime and Security Act 2001, this was struck down by the House of Lords in 2005 in the historic case of A and Others (House of Lords, 2004). Partly as a response to indefinite detention without charge being ruled unlawful, the government introduced a line of legislation that permitted CMPs to be used under civil law sanctions: Prevention of Terrorism Act 2005; Terrorism Prevention and Investigation Measures Act 2011; Counter Terrorism Act 2008; Justice and Security Act 2013; Counter-Terrorism and Security Act 2015 (European Parliament, 2014).

Deportation orders had already been in place for a long period, but what connected all of these measures was the notion that secret evidence could be used in them since they technically existed outside the criminal justice system – they were civil law sanctions. As the matrix in Figure 4.1 highlights, this could include: deportation orders, financial sanctions, extradition orders, passport revocation, citizenship deprivation, barred re-entry into the UK (even for UK citizens for two years), and potentially referrals to health and social services through Prevent – all through various pieces of legislation that has been passed piecemeal since 2001.

Based on the way such counter-terrorism policies have operated, there are a wide variety of options available to the UK security apparatus to sanction any individual on whom there is even the slightest suspicion. This is demonstrated best through the case of Mahdi Hashi, a British man (with citizenship removed), whose trajectory took him as a 16 year old being questioned by the security agencies in Egypt to years later pleading guilty to terrorism charges in the US. At each stage of his story, there are important questions about the way in which he was surveilled and treated.

By presenting the matrix of the counter-terrorism apparatus, my hope is that we begin to see and understand counter-terrorism policy as a form of structural violence, where the entire system works interdependently to reinforce threats, intimidation and coercion.

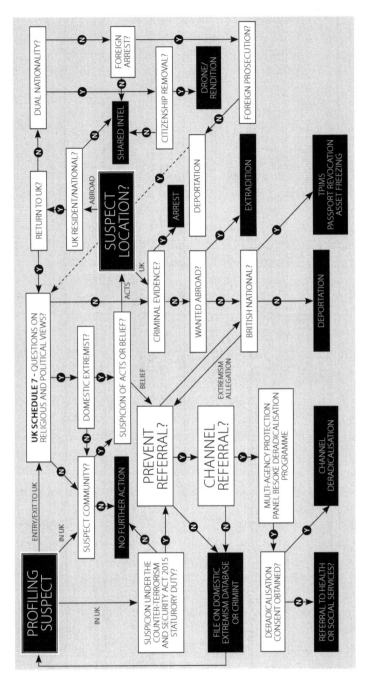

Figure 4.1   An overview of the UK counter-terrorism matrix

The model presented takes an individual through the range of counter-terrorism processes that currently take place in the UK and abroad, providing potentialities that derive from a suspect's location. If the suspect is detained abroad, depending on his citizenship status, there are a number of ways in which the British authorities engage with foreign governments. This is in order to extract intelligence, provide intelligence for foreign prosecution or even remove as a threat through citizenship deprivation, leading to rendition or assassination by drone strike.

If the individual is in the UK, the matrix we present suggests sanctions based on whether an individual is under police suspicion, profiled at a UK port or referred to Prevent. The matrix provides a view, however, that wherever the point of suspicion begins, the construction of counter-terrorism policy always provides an alternative form of sanction as a way of subverting the criminal justice process. Thus, in many scenarios we witness the burden of proof is reversed in order to remove threats.

Where foreign nationals have not committed any crimes, they can be deported (or subjected to other sanctions) under secret evidence based on arbitrary orders. Where UK nationals have not committed any crimes, they can have their citizenship removed (and other sanctions) over an arbitrary allegation of extremism. All of this works to provide the UK government with wide powers to be able to remove perceived threats, even where those threats pose no imminent or long-term danger to the security of the UK.

Cases such as that of Mahdi Hashi exemplify the difficulties that surround the counter-terrorism matrix, that once one is profiled within the system it becomes difficult to escape it. Proving innocence can be futile as there is no way to disprove a false positive, but further, that such a construction can ultimately become a self-fulfilling prophecy. It is precisely in this nexus that UK counter-terrorism can be seen as a form of structural racism.

The cases presented below are based on extensive interviews conducted by CAGE staff with the individuals themselves, as well as family members, lawyers and publicly sourced accounts and court documentation. The information spans different periods of each individual's experience, reflecting the varying degrees of access possible for primary source material.

Background of Mahdi Hashi

Mahdi Hashi was born in Mogadishu, Somalia, on 18 September 1989. Within two years of his birth, the civil war in Somalia in 1991 began, resulting in his family's life being under threat due to the general state of the conflict. In 1995, Mahdi's family chose to relocate to the UK as asylum seekers in order to escape the difficulties of their own country. By early 2004, the family received news that Mahdi's British citizenship had been granted.

In 2005, he completed his GCSEs and rather than continuing his education in the UK, chose to leave with his family in Egypt in order to study the Arabic language. It is this decision that starts a process of scrutiny into Mahdi Hashi's life by the security agencies, a path that will lead to his eventual rendition to the US.

Arbitrary detention by Egyptian security

In July 2006, the Egyptian National Security police came to the students' dwelling where Mahdi was living around 4 pm requesting all the foreign students to show their passports. Four months after this incident, the same security agents returned, however, on this occasion with the Egyptian army who came carrying heavy weapons including shotguns, machine guns and pistols.

On the completion of the raid, the security agents decided to detain 16-year-old Mahdi, claiming that his visa had expired and so would need to be interrogated. After spending the day in the hands of the security agency and being questioned by them, he was released, immediately after which he renewed his visa. A short while later, he was again requested to return to the police station in order to answer further questions. Mahdi arrived at the station a little after midnight, and was bundled into the back of a car after two hours of questions. There was no official knowledge of Mahdi's detention until the British Embassy contacted the Egyptian National Security regarding Mahdi's dual nationality; five days later they received confirmation of his detention.

Mahdi was detained for a total of eleven days in Egyptian custody, in a cell that was roughly 3 x 3 m. It was not until the British Embassy spoke to him that Mahdi had any inkling of why he was being detained. Speaking to me about his detention, he explained:

how I felt at the time, that they are trying to make me admit something, to make me say it first. I was speaking to the embassy they were trying to ask me why I was here, 'The Egyptian authorities are telling us something else.' And when they actually realised that I was completely confused about the situation, bearing in mind I was only 16, they go to me, 'Well, the Egyptian authorities are saying that you have links to Al-Qaida and other terror networks, specifically the Chechen mujahedeen and also the mujahedeen in Caucasus.' I didn't know what 'Caucasus' was. They said that you've actually trained as well, you done training with them, extremist training. (Qureshi, 2010)

After the eleven days of detention, the Egyptians claimed that his visa had expired and deported him back to the UK, banning him from returning to Egypt.

On Mahdi's arrival back in the UK, his family were waiting for him at the airport, having been provided the full flight details. All the passengers on the flight from Egypt made their way through customs, except Mahdi. After the family made an enquiry into his location, they were told that he had not boarded the flight, and were shown a passenger list which did not contain his name.

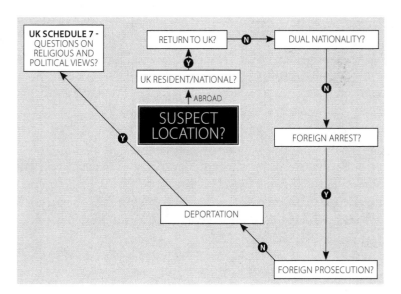

Figure 4.2   Arrest abroad to deportation to the UK

Worried and confused, the family made their way back home, when they received a call from a neighbour informing them that Mahdi had called from Heathrow airport and was waiting for them to pick him up. It turned out that the family had been lied to by airport staff, as he had been on the flight and should have been on the passenger list – Mahdi had been in the airport – except he was being interrogated for three hours by security agents who took his fingerprints and DNA (Figure 4.2).

Kentish Town youth workers

After almost a year from his detention in Egypt, Mahdi decided to continue his Arabic studies, this time choosing Syria. He remained there for about a year having no problems during that period. It was on his return that he was again subjected to harassment by the UK security agencies. According to Mahdi:

> When I came back, I came back at Heathrow airport. I was stopped by two police officers. They were asking questions like, 'Why did you go there? Did you want to go to Iraq?' and 'What do you think about …?' They asked me scholarly questions about religion and jihad and suicide bombing, for example, they would ask me about the Palestinians. Then afterwards they took my DNA and my fingerprints and they told me that we are putting this on a Terrorism Database, they had me under the Terrorism Act 2000, Sch 7. (Qureshi, 2010)

On Mahdi's return from Syria in 2008, he got involved with a local group known as the Kentish Town Community Organisation (KTCO). Their aim was to assist young people who were having difficulties in their personal lives. The group of friends who all assisted in the project went on to become victims of harassment by the UK security agencies after the Ethiopian invasion of Somalia in 2007.

As with the other men from the Kentish Town youth group, Abshir Mohammed had studied the Arabic language in Egypt at the Al Fajr centre in Cairo. In July 2008 he went to Egypt again, having returned to the UK, in order to attend his brother's wedding. On his arrival in the country he was detained for 16 hours and interrogated about his previous movements in Egypt and why he had returned. It was on his return to the UK that he was stopped at immigration by UK security officials from MI5 who used the stop as an opportunity to question him:

> I was just about to speak when he said that he wanted to finish. At that moment I felt very threatened and thought they were going to try and put me away for life despite not having done anything wrong. He said that basically they knew I had committed or suspected that I had committed terrorist activities abroad. I was stunned and said excuse me. I gathered myself together and said to him, listen, I went to Fajr Centre in Egypt in order to study Arabic, renowned all over, even non-Muslims study there. He said look, if I want your CV I can get it, I want to know who you are as a person and what your aims were in wanting to go, and you know your links? I explained that I work for a youth organisation that in fact had encouraged me to go and study this course. He said that was fair enough but that really we would need to meet on another day. He then said that we would need to meet again in order to sort out these issues, otherwise I would find it very difficult to go to America or Yemen. I said that I didn't even want to go to those places, fine I have some family in Yemen but I had no real desire to go at all. (Qureshi, 2009a)

Another member of the KTCO group, Mohammed Nur, was not stopped at a port by UK security officials, he was visited at his home. In August 2008, he was at home leaving for work when there was a knock on his door with police and MI5 officers pretending to be post office workers in order to gain entry into his home. They accused him of being an extremist and then attempted to induce compliance by threatening him:

> The MI5 agent then came back into the conversation and said, 'Mohammed, for your own benefit, it is best that you cooperate with us. You travel regularly, if you want to travel more, then I suggest you cooperate as we have very good connections all around the world. Any country that you go to, we can give you problems. If you don't want those problems, then I suggest you cooperate with us.' I then said that there was no way I was going to cooperate when I did not even know what I did. I said that if they explained to me what I had done wrong then I would be more than willing to help, however they said that they

could not discuss that. They then said that if we were to meet in three days time, they would be able to tell me why they were interested in me. (Qureshi, 2009c)

Over that entire year there were extensive discussions between large groups of friends who were all feeling subjected to the scrutiny of the security agencies. Whether the intelligence officials had direct knowledge of individual involvement in activity abroad or not, a scattergun approach was taken towards the community, resulting in a great deal of mistrust and alienation. The KTCO men would eventually publicly reveal their plight, as they became desperate to end the abuses that were being carried out against them; however, this would not take place for at least another year (Figure 4.3).

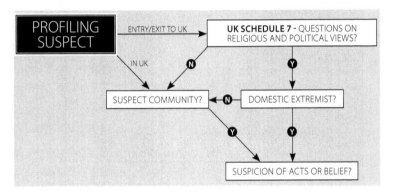

Figure 4.3   Profiling leads to suspicion of acts or beliefs

Harassment in the UK and abroad

In keeping with the tactics that were used by the security agencies against Mahdi Hashi and the Kentish Town Community Organisation workers between 2008 and 2009, the case of Ahmed Diini provided yet further evidence of abusive way in which the agencies interacted with individuals and communities. Unsurprisingly, his presence on the security agency's radar was once again due to the wider stratosphere of friends and associates connected to the North West London community.

Ahmed Diini's situation has very much revolved around the abuses that have taken place against him by the security agencies. Diini was not only stopped at ports during his time in the UK, but also approached directly at the Birmingham school where he was employed. According to Diini,

> I personally got morally and mentally affected since I am being victimised. Even now I have to live with the fact that I won't be able to travel somewhere without being stopped for a minimum of two hours and being seen as a criminal, since the people around me in the queue don't get stopped but I am the only one that gets picked on. (CAGE, 2013a)

As with Diini, as a naturalised British citizen, Mahdi Hashi was facing problems based on his desire to visit his country of birth, and keep connected to the family he had there. It was also in 2009 that Mahdi's family received the unfortunate news that his grandmother in Somalia was very unwell. At the time it was felt that the best person in their family who could leave to care for her was Mahdi.

Having booked his flight through Gatwick airport for Somalia with a stopover in Djibouti, Mahdi left for the airport. As he made his way through security, he was stopped by two members of MI5 who questioned him for a few hours. As a result, he missed his flight, although MI5 reimbursed him by having another booking made for him seven days later.

When he returned to catch his flight, he was again detained. Speaking to me about his treatment at the hands of the detaining officer, he said,

> He goes, 'Because of your extremist friends we suspect you're an extremist yourself. We hope that we're wrong, you know we hope so, but we have reason to believe that you're extreme. We hope that we're wrong.' After that he threatened me, 'We warn you not to get on that flight for your own safety.' I'm like, 'What you trying to say to me, what's happened?' I'm thinking like he's going to arrest me in Djibouti, and torture me, might wanna take me to Morocco like Binyam Mohamed, that story. So I'm like, 'Are you telling me not to get on that flight?' He said, 'I'm not telling you not to get on that flight but it would be better for your own safety if you didn't. But it's your choice mate.'
>
> I got to Djibouti when the police grabbed me. When I spoke to some of them properly on the level, he said, 'We don't know why you're here

but we've been told to keep you here. It's coming from the government and it's coming from your government. (Qureshi, 2009b)

Mahdi was held in Djibouti for 16 hours before he was eventually deported back to the UK. On his return, his plight had not ended as MI5 waited for him. After waiting with him to collect his luggage, he was taken to a private room. There he was accused of being a terrorism suspect. They opened a book which had the pictures of a number of Muslim men, and asked him to identify all those that he knew, some being from the community centre. They explained that they wanted his help, and that in doing so, his status as a terrorism suspect would be lifted. They claimed that this was the only way for him to prove his innocence (Figure 4.4).

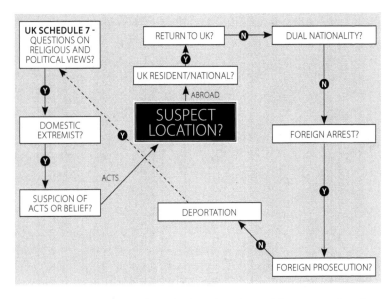

Figure 4.4   Suspicion at home leads to detention and deportation abroad

The arbitrary detention, statelessness and rendition of Mahdi Hashi

Once out of the country, the UK Home Secretary is given a much wider range of powers in order to be able to take a decision on the fate of an individual. Recently the Counter-Terrorism and Security Act 2015 has permitted the government to exclude British citizens from returning to

THE UK COUNTER-TERRORISM MATRIX

the UK, a move that previously had been reserved for foreign nationals such as Ahmed Diini.

While Diini was on a trip to Germany to get married, the Home Office issued an exclusion order. Sent in February 2011, the letter read:

[T]he Home Secretary personally directed that you should be excluded from the United Kingdom on the grounds that your presence in the country would not be conducive to the public good. (CAGE, 2014b)

Theresa May simply asserted that the man had been 'identified as a person involved in Islamist activity', without providing further evidence – seemingly a vindictive move following his public complaint. He was then forced to remain in Germany. In April 2011, he decided to settle in Egypt with his wife.

Shortly after his arrival in Egypt, his phone rang, 'Good morning Ahmed Diini, you are speaking with the British (security) service(s).' The unidentified agent explained that the UK had warned its partners in the region against him.

You are aware that you are not allowed to enter the UK. But if you consider cooperating with us, we might rethink the matter and allow you to come back. We are aware you have family here. (CAGE, 2014b)

Ahmed did not engage with the threats. Rather, he assumed that they were empty threats and so instead chose to concentrate on his studies. A miscalculation on his part, as he would go on to face many more difficulties.

Once Mahdi Hashi decided to relocate his life to Somaliland, he planned to set roots down. In 2010, he met his future wife in Somalia and by 2011 they were married. The following year in February, they had a son together.

In early 2012, Mahdi's family in the UK were sent a letter by the Home Office, explaining that they must inform him that his citizenship had been revoked on the grounds of alleged extremism, and that he would not be permitted to return to the UK.

By the middle of summer 2012, his family were informed that he had been detained in Djibouti. The family had no official confirmation of this, however. They were contacted by a man who claimed that he had been previously detained with Mahdi in a Djibouti prison. The man claimed that Mahdi was being interrogated by US authorities. The last piece of information the man gave was that he was being mistreated and consistently requesting assistance from the British Embassy, unaware that he had already had his citizenship revoked.

The Foreign Office only told the family that as they had revoked his citizenship, they were unwilling to take any responsibility for his plight. What seems to be clear though is that the British revoked Mahdi's citizenship while he was in custody in Djibouti, leading to questions of whether this was an attempt to wipe their hands clean of their own citizen, and to allow the US to do what they liked to him. This tactic has been witnessed elsewhere, with the citizenships of Belal el-Berjawi and Mohammed Sakkar having been revoked, only for both men to be soon killed by US drone strikes.

The British Nationality Act 1981 provides the circumstances in which an individual can be deprived of British nationality. The grounds of such deprivation have recently been broadened to include where the Secretary of State 'is satisfied that deprivation is conducive to the public good' (British Nationality Act, 2006). However, the Secretary of State may not make an order on those grounds if it would make a person stateless.

In the circumstance where Mahdi Hashi's entitlement to Somali nationality was at the very least under great doubt, the UK government were obliged to verify the fact that he had another nationality before depriving him of British citizenship. Practically speaking, this was almost impossible to do with the Somali authorities, and so in all likelihood did not engage in a proper exercise of due diligence.

Mahdi's mother-in-law attempted to find him by travelling to Djibouti and searching for him, but none of her family or connections were able to find the location of his detention. Later, when it emerged that he was being detained at the US military base Camp Lemonier in Djibouti, he would describe the torturous conditions he and fellow detainees were held in,

[The man was] stripped to his underwear and hung upside down ... They beat the soles of his feet, poured cold water on him and said they would electrocute him. There was screaming all around me and it was pretty horrific. (Verkaik, 2013)

Despite a campaign by his family, friends and CAGE to have Mahdi brought before a court, he was instead placed on a rendition flight to the US without any due process or an extradition proceeding. In January 2013, Hashi was brought before a New York court charged with providing material support to terrorism for the Islamic group al-Shabab operating in Somalia.

What is not known is that he was detained by non-state militia for many months during the period he was missing from Somaliland. During that time, he was suspected of being a British spy among other things. It is part of the tragedy of this case that wherever Mahdi Hashi went in the world, he would be treated as a pariah, from the age of sixteen.

In May 2015, Mahdi Hashi was convicted of the charges against him. The FBI claimed that between December 2008 until August 2012, he was involved in terrorism activities with al-Shabab, an accusation which is difficult to prove. In response to his conviction, the chairman of the Kentish Town Community Centre, Sharhabeel Lone, said of Mahdi's conviction:

Let down by his own country and at the mercy of a foreign power's skewed judicial system – three years of solitary confinement have extracted a confession from Mahdi that he was a member of a terrorist organisation in Somalia for four years. But that can't be true because, for nearly two of those years, he was helping young people out of gang crime and drugs as a junior youth leader with our organisation. (Verkaik, 2015)

Mahdi's statelessness was only one such example of the consequences of the UK forcibly removing the protections of citizenship. Another case is that of Belal el-Berjawi, who after having allegedly joined al-Shabaab in Somalia found himself stateless, having left the UK due to his claims of unwarranted harassment by the security agencies. He contacted me at CAGE requesting a lawyer to assist in an attempt to regain his citizenship status. Like so many others, el-Berjawi's story began with being detained and harassed abroad. The security agencies were monitoring him and his close acquaintants for potential travel to Somalia to join al-Shabaab. Those stops led to Schedule 7 interrogations followed by on the ground surveillance in the UK. Ultimately, el-Berjawi was able to leave the

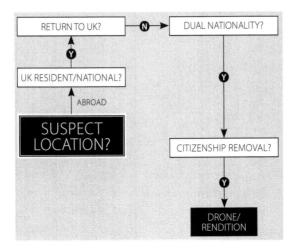

Figure 4.5   Citizenship removal while abroad can lead
to killing by drone or rendition

country and there is evidence that he joined the militant group despite
the efforts of the UK security agencies.

On Saturday, 27 January 2012, el-Berjawi was killed by a US
unmanned aerial vehicle on the outskirts of Mogadishu (Cobain,
2012). Belal el-Berjawi's death illustrates how a matrix of suspicion,
harassment, unaccountable measures and disenfranchisement can
lead to extra-judicial assassination by the US (Figure 4.5). The British
government was to evade all responsibility of el-Berjawi's killing by
claiming that they had already removed his citizenship, so no longer had
any obligations towards him. Yet, it was the very act of removing his
citizenship that made the UK government complicit in this extra-judicial
killing. This process has become endemic within UK policy, where the
authorities seek to limit their footprint on any activity that might be
considered outside the rule of law.

Back to the beginning: the torture of Ahmed Diini

One of the central difficulties in the counter-terrorism matrix is that it is
very difficult to claim your rights in any circumstances except a formal
arrest and charge. Processes of arbitrary sanction, secret evidence and

international cooperation make it almost impossible to ever know why an individual is considered a threat.

On 19 August 2013, just ten days before the family planned to return to Germany for the birth of their child, a team of armed men broke into their apartment in Cairo. Diini was forced to the ground. He was then taken away in front of his wife and son. Upon his arrival, he witnessed the guards discussing his fate, 'This guy will definitely talk if we electrocute him!' Shortly after, he was taken by a man into a dark room and tied to a piece of metal. During his detention, he was subjected to routine forms of abuse in Egypt. He was repeatedly hooded, beaten, forced into stress positions for hours, kept in a 'dog cage' and racially abused. Eighty days into his detention, Ahmed Diini explained to CAGE from his Egyptian cell,

> After a couple of days, I came to the realisation that this matter had full connection to the British MI5. The reason being that the Egyptian secret services which were interrogating me at the police station mentioned things which only the British security services could know of. (CAGE, 2013a)

In a letter, he wrote, 'They are clearly trying to drive me mentally crazy, day in and day out from the torture that I see and hear in this place' (CAGE, 2013b). It was only on 17 February 2013 that a British officer physically visited him in his Egyptian prison, 'I am now 100 per cent sure the British security services are part of this trouble because I met one of their … agents (who) in short tried to induce me to work with them in exchange for my freedom', Diini wrote in a letter made available to CAGE (CAGE, 2014a).

On 23 March 2014, after seven months of detention without charge, Diini was suddenly released without explanation and ordered to leave the country on the very same day. His family immediately booked him the first flight to the Netherlands, which happened to stop over in Turkey. To his surprise, the Turkish authorities arrested him on 24 March 2014, while he was in transit. He was informed that Interpol had issued a notice for his arrest. He was wanted by the US on terrorism-related allegations.

He had shortly before been sitting in his Turkish cell, waiting to know if he would be sent to the US.

It is quite clear that the United States were aware of his detention in Egypt. They must have known the terrible conditions Ahmed was being held under there. Yet, as far as we can tell, they did nothing to prevent his ill treatment, even though they could have made use of their influence. Moreover, according to his Dutch lawyer, Andre Seebregts, the US has an extradition treaty with Egypt. (CAGE, 2014a)

The international complicity between the Egyptian government, UK security agencies and the US in issuing the arrest warrant highlights how individuals who come under the radar of suspicion can be continually harassed where they go. Ahmed Diini has never been charged with a single offence and since his designation as an 'extremist' by the UK has been suffering a continual form of arbitrary punishment. Diini eventually fled his captivity in Turkey; his current whereabouts are still unknown.

Conclusion

This chapter has provided a snapshot of the way that counter-terrorism policy works interdependently, so that no part of the system is ever separate from the other. This contradicts the claim that there are 'soft' as opposed to 'hard' parts of the law as the entire system works in tandem as a weapon of coercion. Thus, we see that those who do not comply are threatened, and then sanctioned with parts of the apparatus as forms of intimidation and punishment (CAGE, 2016b). The problem with such a system is that the law fails to have any equilibrium between the rights of the individual and the power of the state.

There is a cycle of criminalisation within the system. Stops at airports under Schedule 7 powers of the Terrorism Act 2000 permit police and security officials to question individuals about their activities and beliefs. As it is a criminal offence not to answer questions in such circumstances, the ability to not incriminate oneself is removed. A profile is created, which can then be used further down the line, either as part of criminal proceedings or as part of the UK government's Prevent strategy in order to allegedly prevent future harm.

The provisions of counter-terrorism measures in the 'law' provide a legal framework for intervention by the state, but in my view, this amounts to forms of structural violence and racism against communities. It is important to note that in cases such as the 2006 transatlantic bomb plot, and Operation Crevice, the police and the CPS did not need to rely on terrorism legislation and structures to disrupt and prosecute those individuals. They were convicted based on a criminal justice system that was well established, and that also gave the defendants their full rights of representation. The majority of terrorism cases we now see do not involve plots being carried out against the state or public. In fact, terrorism statistics often constitute breaches of Schedule 7 powers for refusing to answer questions or hand over passwords to electronic devices, as well as reading publications considered to be 'terrorist' in nature and quality.

In order to understand how communities can resist against the structural racism of the state, we first must understand how it is the entire system that undermines due process and the rule of law, rather than simply looking at specific cases or isolated examples of abuse. The macro and micro aggressions against individuals and communities should thus never be treated or spoken of as specific matters, but must always be drawn back to the root of the issue, that the UK government's entire modality of counter-terrorism is predicated on the notion that genuine rights must be eviscerated in order for the law to be an effective tool of manipulation and coercion.

Bibliography

Anderson, D. (2016), *The Terrorism Acts in 2015*. London: Independent Reviewer of Terrorism Legislation.

British Nationality Act (2006), Section 40 (2) substituted by Immigration, Asylum and Nationality Act 2006. London: HM Government.

CAGE (2013a), Interview with Ahmed Diini, CAGE, London.

—— (2013b), Letter, from: Ahmed Diini, to: CAGE, London.

—— (2014a), Interview with Ahmed Diini, CAGE, London.

—— (2014b), Profile: Ahmed Diini, CAGE, London.

—— (2016a), 'What you should know about the terror arrest stats', CAGE, London.

—— (2016b), 'I refused to work with MI5 and now I can't see my daughter', CAGE, London.

Campbell, D. (2007), 'Ex-BNP candidate jailed for stockpiling explosives', *Guardian*, 31 July.

Cobain, I. (2012), 'British "al-Qaida member" killed in US drone attack in Somalia', *Guardian*, 22 January.

European Parliament (2014), *National Security and Secret Evidence in Legislation and Before the Courts: Exploring the Challenges*. Directorate General for Policies, Policy Department C: Citizens' Rights and Constitutional Affairs.

Home Office (2011), *Counter-terrorism strategy (CONTEST)*. London: HM Government.

House of Lords (2004), Judgment of A and Others v Secretary of State for the Home Department.

Lewis, P., Evans, R. and Taylor, M. (2009), 'Police in £9m scheme to log "domestic extremists"', *Guardian*, 25 October.

Morris, N. (2015), 'Black people still far more likely to be stopped and searched by police than other ethnic groups', *Independent*, 6 August.

Politowski, B. (2016), *Terrorism in Great Britain: The Statistics*. London: House of Commons Library.

Powell, J.A. (2007), 'Structural racism: building upon the insights of John Calmore', *North Carolina Law Review*, 86, 791–81.

Qureshi, A. (2009a), Interview with Abshir Mohammed, CAGE, London.

—— (2009b), Interview with Mahdi Hashi, CAGE, London.

—— (2009c), Interview with Mohammed Nur, CAGE, London.

—— (2010), 'The Horn of Africa inquisition', CAGE, London.

Ross, A.K. and Galey, P. (2013), 'Rise in citizenship-stripping as government cracks down on UK fighters in Syria', The Bureau of Investigative Journalism. www.thebureauinvestigates.com/stories/2013-12-23/rise-in-citizenship-stripping-as-government-cracks-down-on-uk-fighters-in-syria. Accessed 26 March 2017.

Verkaik, R. (2013), 'Latest on Mahdi Hashi's ordeal: kidnapped, tortured and rendered', *Mail on Sunday*.

—— (2015), 'Mahdi Hashi: guilty of supporting al-Shabaab – but was his plea coerced?', *Independent*, 15 May.

Webb, O. (2015), 'Am I on a domestic extremism database?', London Review of Books Blog.

5

The 'War on Terror' and the Attack on Muslim Civil Society

Shenaz Bunglawala

The onset of the War on Terror has reshaped the contours of state-Muslim civil society relations with the mobilisation of British Muslim actors across several domains contesting the legislative, political, social, cultural and discursive tenets of policies aimed at a 'disciplinary mode of regulation' (O'Toole et al., 2016: 162). While studies have revealed the extent to which top-down approaches have been frustrated by the variable geometry displayed by local implementation, the steady centralisation of policy and the expansion of its reach, the hollowing out of spaces for 'contested practice' (O'Toole et al., 2016) and the shift from prevention to 'pre-emption' has further strained the boundaries between the state and Muslim civil society. If 'disciplinary' modes failed in an earlier iteration of counter-terrorism policy, the current preoccupation with non-violent extremism leaves Muslim civil society actors confronting a dual challenge: the interpenetration of civil society by the state and the threat to political dissent.

This chapter examines these developments using the experiences of two British Muslim organisations, MEND, CAGE, and select British Muslim charities. It draws on the work of Nilsen and Cox on 'social movements from above' and the defensive/offensive strategies they deploy to 'expand or maintain the position of dominant groups' (Nilsen and Cox, 2013: 71). It explores the social, cultural, administrative and political resources employed by the state to espouse and entrench its conception of Muslim identity politics, with a particular focus on security policy. Analysing the interaction between 'social movements from above' and 'social movements from below', I hope to show that while the British state has actively and aggressively sought to preset conditions on the contours and direction of Muslim identity politics, Nilsen and Cox's theory of social movements delineates the opportunities available to Muslim actors to resist efforts to suppress their voices and stymie their opposition to policies that strengthen structural racism.

British Muslim civil society

Interest in British Muslim participation in politics and civil society has largely focused on self-organisation among civil society actors and developments in procedural and substantive electoral participation; from early concerns about the presence of a 'Muslim vote' to public policy agenda-setting by Muslim advocacy groups (see McLoughlin, 2005; O'Toole et al., 2013). Research has explored political engagement by British Muslim organisations on issues ranging from anti-war campaigning to lobbying for religious equality legislation, and the relations between national British Muslim organisations and the state, vis-à-vis 'pressures from below' arising from Muslim identity politics (see Peace, 2015). Less attention has been paid to two new developments which are shifting the modalities of Muslim political engagement and reframing Muslim identity politics: the shift to tackle 'non-violent extremism' and the growing encroachment in the sphere of Muslim civil society from aggressive state policies targeting British Muslim civil society organisations.

Consideration in the academic literature on the topic of British Muslim participation has principally examined several key factors; the state of Muslim self-organisation at the national level and its representational mandate; the emergence of an identity politics that challenges the premise of the secular state; and the role of power and patronage in relations between Muslims and the British state focusing on the modalities of self-description, participation and influence at a national level.

The role of the state in respect of the latter consideration is often portrayed as the loci for Muslim projections of citizenship rights and equality with the greater emphasis on government, not the state per se. The relationship is rarely portrayed in terms which examine the state's relationship with Muslim groups as a non-neutral actor traversing the boundaries of state and civil society to reflexively position and consolidate its power over Muslim groups through direct patronage of some and the aggressive undermining of others. While earlier research has uncovered the degree of structural racism on policy issues; whether differential access to policy-making networks for Muslims (for example, favouring race over religion in assessment of policy questions; the 2016 Race Audit commissioned by Theresa May, which documents equality as outcomes in relation to race but not religion, is a germane example), or the framing of issues in terms which actively circumscribe the agency of Muslims as a collective group, the fundamental rebalancing of relationships *within* British Muslim civil society and *between* British Muslim civil society actors and the state under the more recent iteration of the counter-terrorism strategy have been less well examined.

The War on Terror and the dominance of security policy in interactions between British Muslims and the state has demonstrably shifted the basis of power relations and the modes of participation from earlier models which privileged notions of the state as a neutral actor among competing interests in civil society. In more recent times, the state has become an active player, beyond the power to grant patronage to Muslim groups evident in earlier periods, in reshaping the conditions for Muslim participation in politics and civic life through the deliberate exercise of powers of exclusion over Muslim actors in civil society. If earlier counter-terrorism strategies were marked by a focus on violent extremism and the conferring by the state of 'legitimacy' on Muslim civil society actors through (dis)engagement, the current drive to tackle 'non-violent extremism' and the expansion of the state's repertoire of disciplinary measures has left Muslim civil society actors not merely struggling to assert 'contested practice' but to engage in contestation at all.

'Social movements from below'

British Muslim identity politics has been characterised as suffering from claims of 'exceptionalism' arising from strains of 'misrecognition' which treats the condition of collective Muslim agency as divisive, sectarian and indisposed to common projects on the basis of a singular (and insular) preoccupation with a faith identity. The virtue of recognising Muslim identity politics has been criticised for overplaying the premium that British Muslims place on their faith identity when engaging in the public sphere (see Mirza et al., 2007) and for consigning British Muslims to frustrated subjectivities by privileging faith identity constructs over more secular constructs preferred by other Muslims.

Moreover, self-description in the framing of Muslim identities in the public sphere has been suffused with recourse to a reductive nomenclature which often masks the complexity of Muslim identity politics under a simple binary construction of 'Islamist' and 'non-Islamist'. The former, in part, is used synonymously with Muslim identity politics in order to propagate a view of Muslim political agency as 'reactive, grievance-based, or "pariah politics"' (Dobbernack et al., 2014: 5).

In their analysis of the British Muslim actors and the 2010 British general election, Dobbernack, Meer and Modood, evaluate the strategies used by Muslim groups to 'oppos[e] ... the refusal to acknowledge their desired self-description' (Dobbernack et al., 2014: 2) and criticise the presumption of Muslim identity politics as 'reactive', noting that 'Excluded groups seek respect for themselves as they are or aspire to be, not simply a solidarity on the basis of a recognition of themselves as victims; they resist being defined by their *mode of oppression* and seek space and dignity for their *mode of being*' (Modood, 2005: 159, emphases in the original).

It is the search for space and dignity for their 'mode of being' that determines the articulation of Muslim identity politics as 'Muslim' insofar as the prevailing landscape of political identities and political groupings makes it possible to respect and accommodate this self-description by subaltern groups. As Dobbernack et al. argue, the reflexivity and mobilisations evident among Muslim actors in the 2010 general election suggest Muslim identity politics avers the claims-making mobilisations of other constitutive groups in politics where various 'modes of being' conflict and contest the myriad 'modes of oppression' which promulgate their exclusion.

We can fairly characterise Muslim identity politics and the actors who advance it in the face of 'misrecognition' as acting in the manner of social movements from below, 'to either *challenge the constraints that a dominant structure of needs and capacities imposes upon the development of new needs and capacities*, or to defend aspects of an existing, negotiated structure which accommodate their specific needs and capacities' (Nilsen and Cox, 2013: 73, emphasis added).

The depiction of Muslim civil society actors as evincing the features of social movements from below rests upon several interrelated developments: (a) the shift away from elite-level interactions between Muslim civil society actors and the state to encompass a wider variety of Muslim actors advancing claims-making conceptions of citizenship (Isin and Turner, 2003) – a generational shift is also evident in the composition of these new groups with the reshaping of Muslim identity politics among a younger generation of Muslim civil society actors; (b) the broadening of counter-terrorism policy to encapsulate non-violent extremism and in so doing giving rise to modes of resistance against dominant constructions of 'non-violent' extremist beliefs; (c) the mode or organisation shifting from membership constituted by groups (to communally representative bodies) to membership constituted by individuals (to movements for mass mobilisation).

The interplay between the assertiveness of claims-making citizenship in (a) and the patterns of resistance in (b) are mutually reinforcing with conceptions of citizenship among younger British Muslim actors in civil society, as articulated through the prism of Muslim identity politics, informing and influencing the strength of their pushback against attempts to engineer new modes of exclusion.

A decade of (dis)engagement

Interventions by the British state in Muslim civil society is not without precedent. Earlier iterations of the government's counter-extremism strategy, Prevent, included state-funded 'capacity-building' programmes and 'leadership development' as part of an overall strategy to build communities resilient to messages propagated by violent extremists. Nor was there any reluctance to identify the strategy as requiring community involvement and engagement, with the emphasis being on cooperative methods managed by the state and voluntarily entered into by British Muslim organisations (*Guardian*, 2008).

But co-operation turned to implicit coercion under the dual pressures of the refusal by government to countenance critical engagement from the Muslim Council of Britain and exhortations from neocon think tanks for 'choosing our friends wisely' (Maher and Frampton, 2009).

The speech given by then Communities Secretary, Ruth Kelly, in October 2006 was a turning point in the relations between British Muslim civil society actors and the state with Kelly iterating the shift from cooperation to tacit coercion, stating 'our strategy of funding and engagement must shift significantly towards those organisations that are taking a proactive leadership role in tackling extremism and defending our shared values' (Kelly, 2006).

In a foreword written to the report, *Choosing our Friends Wisely*, in which Policy Exchange set out criteria for (dis)engaging Muslim civil society groups on the basis of their stoking 'grievances' and alleging 'state-sanctioned "Islamophobia"', Kelly referred to a limited description of the state's role in shaping Muslim civil society, mentioning that 'dealings government has with both individuals and groups can act to "legitimise" or "delegitimise" those individuals or groups' (Maher and Frampton, 2009).

The positioning of the state in relation to Muslim civil society as the act of conferring 'legitimacy', or not, described a period in state-Muslim civil society relations when the presence of unpalatable actors was handled through exclusion and the denial of 'dealings' with government. The conferring of 'legitimacy' was connected to the act of engagement whose denial epitomised the state's active role in 'delegitimatisation'.

The corollary of delegitimising some and legitimising others was further evident in the discursive shift in the labelling of actors as 'Islamists' and 'non-Islamists', respectively, and in the early calls for uniformity across 'government and the public sector' on the 'new criteria for engagement', recognising the capacity for the broad arm of the state to demur from rules set at the national level when tasked with policy implementation in local contexts (Maher and Frampton, 2009: 7).

While the act of 'delegitimising' through disavowal of dealings with government displaced the primacy of organisations like the Muslim Council of Britain in their standing among others in the sphere, government involvement in restructuring British Muslim civil society was limited to these exclusionary practices, which closed off avenues to government consultation from those groups that fell out of favour, replacing them with more pliant groupings that benefited from access and influence at senior government levels. Though implicit in its criticism of Muslim leadership that was deemed to be 'part of the problem', yesteryear's policy of exclusion differs from the wider-scale deployment of offensive and defensive strategies that inform present day attempts to undermine claims-making politics among British Muslim civil society actors.

The discernible shift of the last decade led to what has been termed a 'democratic constellation' (Hussain, 2013) of British Muslim civil society actors emerging as a consequence of government efforts to fund pliant British Muslim organisations and 'consult' with a broader range of Muslim voices.

The intended consequence has been praised for broadening the range of actors populating British Muslim civil society as well as for dissipating 'gatekeeper' models of community engagement by dislodging established interlocutors and widening the field to include newer, albeit smaller, players. But the 'helping hand' of the state has ventured beyond merely facilitating the democratisation of Muslim civil society and the early intervention to consciously restructure the balance of power between the state and Muslim civil society has spread further and deeper as the counter-terrorism strategy has developed to encompass 'non-violent extremism'.

Furthermore, and paradoxically, the celebration of the emergent 'democratic constellation' has been short-lived as the state's intervention in Muslim civil society reneges on engaging with a constellation of groups and instead pursues a policy of cementing the voices of the few.

Non-violent extremism and the 'pre-criminal space'

The Coalition government which came to power in 2010 continued its predecessor's recalibration of funding to groups with the revised Prevent strategy in 2011, noting the refusal to fund groups which 'oppose our values' and casting a vast net over the categorisation of British Muslim civil society organisations as 'extremist' by inferring a causal link between 'non-violent extremism' and 'terrorist ideology' (Home Office, 2011).

The most significant shift came in the form of the widening of the parameters of exclusion to encompass groups deemed to exacerbate the 'vulnerability to radicalisation' on the basis of espousing 'non-violent extremism'.

The 2011 Prevent strategy iterated the need to 'stop people moving from extremist groups or from extremism into terrorist-related activity' and to do so on the basis of challenging 'terrorist ideology [which] makes use of ideas espoused by extremist organisations' (Home Office, 2011: 7).

The strategy identifies a causal link between 'extremist organisations' and the move to terrorist activity, claiming 'Terrorist groups of all kinds very often draw upon ideologies which have been developed, disseminated and popularised by extremist organisations that appear to be non-violent' (Home Office, 2011: 19).

A key objective of the strategy to challenge terrorism is, therefore, 'to challenge apologists for terrorism' (Home Office, 2011: 8).

The strategy goes on to describe tenets of 'non-violent extremism' as claims that 'the West is perpetually at war with Islam'; that 'there can be no legitimate interaction between Muslims and non-Muslims in this country or elsewhere'; and that 'Muslims living here cannot legitimately and or effectively participate in our democratic society' (Home Office, 2011: 20).

The strategy further notes the wiliness of 'Islamist extremists' who 'purport to identify problems to which terrorist organisations then claim to have a solution' (Home Office, 2011: 20).

The move from violent extremism to non-violent extremism and the targeting of the 'conveyor belt to radicalisation' (Cameron, 2013) is described by Phil Edwards as moving beyond the consideration of violent extremism to focus on 'ideological alignment with terrorism' (Edwards, 2015: 57).

In an accompanying report, Lord Carlile of Berriew, who conducted the Prevent review, argued that 'dissipation of [a] sense of victimhood' is a 'proper and important part' of counter-terrorism policy and gave as an example that of Muslims 'feeding assertions of victimhood' at an event in East London organised to discuss the rise of Islamophobia in the UK and Europe (Carlile, 2011: 4).

This tendency to conflate claims-making citizenship and Muslim identity politics with 'victimhood' grievances which might pave the way for more nefarious manipulation by terrorist groups is one demonstrable way in which British Muslim civil society actors have found self-agency and articulations of their 'mode of being' and mobilisation against 'modes of oppression' enter what is described as the 'pre-criminal space'.

The expansion of the counter-terrorism strategy to encompass non-violent extremism and the introduction of the Prevent duty, which enforces compliance across a range of specified authorities with the requirement to have 'due regard to the need to prevent people from being drawn into terrorism', has had two far-reaching consequences for British Muslim civil society actors (Home Office, 2015).

Firstly, it reduces legitimate activity to address structural racism to culpably feeding 'victimhood' which can be exploited by terrorist groups. In so doing, it reduces the capacity of Muslim civil society actors to adopt claims-making articulations, as 'strategies of ... "preventing" "terror" ... [come to] include mundane requests for Muslim provisions' (Nabi, 2011: 120).

Secondly, by widening the reach of counter-terrorism to encompass 'pre-crime', the strategy has moved from prevention to pre-emption where 'measures based on what is described as 'circumstantial evidence' come perilously close to criminalising risky types (rather than acts) and thoughts (rather than deeds)' (McCulloch and Pickering, 2010: 21).

It is, as Edwards puts it, about 'policing the limits of the thinkable and speakable' (Edwards, 2015: 57).

The double whammy for British Muslim civil society actors is traversing a terrain in which speaking out against encroachments to civil liberties is perceived as 'feeding assertions of victimhood' and where espousing Muslim identity politics can be construed as 'purport[ing] to identify problems to which terrorist organisations then claim to have a solution'.

By problematising the activities of Muslim civil society actors in this way, the counter-terrorism strategy presents a stark choice between acquiesce and alienation, and where alienation is seen as tacit evidence of an 'ideological alignment with terrorism'.

The difficulties faced by Muslim civil society organisations are compounded by the active involvement of the state in deterring those actors it regards as 'facilitators and cult leaders' (Cameron, 2015) for 'extremism', such that alienation does not mirror the status quo ante, where Muslim civil society actors were ignored or supplanted with more compliant types. Under the current guise, alienation provokes an aggressive undermining of those Muslim civil society actors who refuse to conform to the 'our way or the high way' mantra.

In his speech setting out the Conservative government's counter-extremism strategy in 2015, David Cameron reinforced the earlier shift in engagement strategy and, going further, committed to government support for 'reforming and moderate Muslim voices'. He spoke of government backing in the form of 'practical help', 'campaigns' protection' and 'political representation' (Cameron, 2015).

Cameron identified the challenge ahead for the government in its displacement of 'extremists' with 'reformists' and 'moderates' as reversing the 'overpowering' voice of the former over the latter, dismissing the notion of 'stand[ing] neutral in this battle of ideas' (Cameron, 2015).

Cameron evinced the active role of government in 'back[ing] those who share our values', while the scope of the new Prevent duty emboldens deployment of the state to similar ends (Cameron, 2015).

While it is unclear what 'political representation' consists of in this regard, beyond the reassertion of earlier models of 'disengagement' and the conferring of 'legitimacy' on some Muslim groups over others, the notion of government providing backing in the form of 'political representation' and 'protection' evokes the privileged access to 'the political power that is pre-eminently ascribed to the state' and the manner of offensive/defensive strategies employed by 'social movements from above' to 'expand or maintain the position of dominant groups'.

British Muslim civil society and 'social movements from above'

Cox and Nilsen define social movements from above as 'a collective project by dominant groups, consisting of skilled activities centred on a rationality that seeks to maintain or modify a dominant structure of entrenched needs and capacities'.

Evaluating the means used by dominant groups to entrench their position using privileged access to various resources, Cox and Nilsen describe an array of 'defensive' and 'offensive' strategies that are employed.

Among the defensive strategies are the options of accommodation or repression whereas offensive strategies range from violent coercion to the suspension of civil rights.

The manner in which 'defensive' and 'offensive' strategies have been used against two British Muslim civil society organisations, CAGE and MEND, is explored below, while a further section examines how British Muslim charities have fared under the new Prevent strategy amid consideration of whether 'the rules on charities are too lax [that] they can allow extremists to prosper' (Cameron, 2013).

The selection of these two civil society organisations rests on several points of coherence in the nature of attacks launched against them, often simultaneously, and on common platforms shared in regards to the

Prevent strategy as curtailing Muslim identity politics and restraining capacities to address structural racism.

A point of reference between the two organisations is concurrence with the view that British Muslims are faced with 'an aggressive anti-Muslim narrative that is based on assumptions [which] subverts the political expression/identity of [Muslim] individuals by turning them into potential threats' (Qureshi, 2015: 181).

It should further be noted that CAGE and MEND occupy a common status concerning offensive/defensive strategies, with both organisa-tions identified as the main protagonists against 'social movements from above'. The classification of the two organisations as constituting, among others, 'extremist opposition to Prevent' is illustrative of this (Sutton, 2016: 12).

The two organisations emerged from vastly different circumstances, the birth of CAGE was closely connected to the immediate aftermath of the War on Terror and communities, domestic and international, affected by it, while the emergence of MEND is due to two intervening factors: the challenges faced by British Muslims under the twin onslaught of high volumes of negative media output and the misrepresentation of Islam and Muslims fuelling hostile public attitudes and low levels of (formal) political participation among British Muslims; and the effort to move away from a Muslim civil society organisation as a body for communal representation to a model for advancing public accountability through active citizenship and collective advocacy.

Both CAGE and MEND demur from models of communal repre-sentation, whether in the form of mosques or umbrella-type Muslim organisations, preferring to establish credentials of legitimacy on direct engagement with British Muslims and through mass mobilisation on issue-based politics.

Both groups also share an avowed Muslim political agency and an unabashed Muslim identity politics while maintaining a fierce independence from external interference in internal affairs through direct funding from British Muslim communities. Their independence from the state and autonomy, in the face of pressures exerted by social movements from above, has to some extent shaped the type of strategies and the vigour with which they have been deployed to unsettle their status. As with the purpose underlying the use of these strategies, the endgame is to ensure the prevailing power of social movements from above, though an intended by-product is to weaken these Muslim civil society organisations relative to those favoured by the state.

Defensive strategies

Cox and Nilsen describe accommodation as a defensive strategy consisting of concessions or co-optation which can 'often involve playing on existing differences within movements from below'.

Co-optation is a tried and tested policy glibly portrayed as 'divide and rule', with its use against Muslim civil society actors character-ised as deeming 'secular Muslims' as good and 'non-violent devout Muslims' as bad (Oborne, 2016). Co-optation has been broadly used since the onset of the War on Terror with government relations towards Muslim communities in the late 2000s largely shaped by the deliberate exploitation of 'existing differences' and the resulting concessions in the form of new forums for engaging 'good' Muslims. The 'concessions' are, necessarily, in favour of social movements from above as evident in criticisms levelled by one of the women who stepped down from a women's advisory group, citing principled objections to the cosmetic nature of the group's supposed functions (*Guardian*, 2010).

The Community Engagement Forum, established as recently as October 2015 (Prime Minister's Office, 2015), is the latest incarnation of a familiar pattern of co-optation that seeks to elevate some groups over others by granting the concession of an audience with senior politicians. Now, as before, the logic of participation is governed by misplaced notions that privileged access is an opportunity to influence government policy 'from within'.

What has changed more profoundly from earlier modes of co-optation is the deliberate interpenetration of Muslim civil society by the state using existing organisations as a conduit for marshalling state-sanctioned com-munications into civil society masquerading as the autonomous outputs of civil society actors.

The disclosure of secret documents reveals how a number of British Muslim civil society organisations were wilfully managed to 'become tools of government' (Hayes and Qureshi, 2016: 7).

The report by CAGE uncovered evidence of how 'the government is attempting to engineer the contours of debate around the legitimacy of Muslim life in the UK by promoting certain organisations and views, and that the veil of secrecy [under the Official Secrets Act] is there to allow organisations to present themselves as independent and based within the grassroots of their communities' (Hayes and Qureshi, 2016: 13).

The report identified a number of campaigns 'fronted' by civil society organisations but which were created and state-managed by a government department, the Research, Information and Communications Unit (RICU), which has rolled out 'counter-narrative campaigns' and provided 'communications advice' (Intelligence and Security Committee, 2010), using the services of a media and communications company, Breakthrough Media.

The centrality of media and communication strategists in the implementation of this defensive strategy is particularly revealing. Co-optation serves to subdivide Muslim civil society actors between those who maintain autonomy through independence from the state and those whose co-optation compromises the authenticity of their 'civic' articulations. In the case of the latter, co-optation functions as more than just 'concessions' in the form of privileged access. It also takes the form of reflexively consolidating the power of the state by allowing its position, vis-à-vis social movements from below, to be articulated from *within* the non-state sector. Communication strategies play a vital role in this by disseminating on-point messaging and diffusing central narratives via channels opened up by the state and those open to its co-opted civil society partners.

The dual challenge faced by social movements from below is thus to take on those civil society actors who 'speak for' the state as well as the state itself. Social movements from above utilise access to resources to engage in direct struggles with social movements from below as well as indirect struggles, through the proxy battles waged by select groups whose co-optation adds a different material advantage: a resource that gives all the appearance of being a 'non-state' intervention.

There are several cases that exemplify the proxy wars fought, seemingly, from within civil society, which to a less astute observer may appear as little more than 'turf wars' between Muslim civil society organisations and the jostling for pole position amid competitive struggles for communal resources; funding, prestige or the expansion of a membership base.

As mentioned above, the role of strategic communications is key as civil society actors co-opted by the state parrot its misgivings in order to undermine the activities of British Muslim civil society actors, like

MEND and CAGE. Secondly, the use of media as a means to attack British Muslim civil society organisations allows for the easy dispersal of central narratives as well as the added infliction of intimidation or fear.

Ironically, sections of the British print media have fought tenaciously against what it considers state interference in the workings of a free press, in respect of calls for more robust media self-regulation through the implementation of the Leveson report recommendations, but have displayed more noticeably subdued reaction to disclosures contained in the aforementioned CAGE report about campaigns directed by the state which have, for example, 'featured' in the largest selling national daily in the UK.

Both MEND and CAGE have found themselves the targets of hostile campaigns in the media for engaging in 'extremist' speech on campus or for facilitating the presence of 'extremist' preachers on campus. The sustained campaign by these two organisations against the Prevent strategy and specifically the Prevent statutory duty, with its institution-alisation of Islamophobia through deliberate and sanctioned religious profiling in respect of Islamic beliefs and practice, has attracted a spate of critical media coverage.

As the Prevent statutory duty marked six months since its imposition on universities from July 2015, the *Daily Mail*'s 'investigations unit' targeted MEND and CAGE in articles soliciting responses from both organisations about events they had either organised or spoken at on various UK campuses. The events were said to have been 'filmed by an undercover *Daily Mail* reporter'.

Emails bearing a multitude of questions and offering the right to reply to allegations which were to feature in the news reports referred to various statements made by individuals affiliated to the respective organ-isations or to other members of the panel at the listed events. The emails also explicitly mentioned the Prevent statutory duty and questioned the organisations about whether their participation or organisation of events put the higher education institutions in 'breach [of] the legal duty for universities to facilitate the challenging of extremist beliefs' (email com-munication to MEND, 11 December 2015).

In the case of MEND, many of the events which were the subject of the *Mail*'s article involved activities organised by the organisation during Islamophobia Awareness Month (IAM). Each year, MEND organises numerous activities to raise awareness about Islamophobia in the UK and to highlight significant trends in its manifestation. In 2015, a matter of principal interest was the new Prevent statutory duty.

The orchestrated attacks were described by CAGE as evidence of a 'Home Office pushback'. CAGE, which was handed a list of 85 questions and granted a mere 24 hours to respond, labelled the scheme 'a thinly veiled effort, quite possibly influenced by the Home Office and lauded by right wing organisations, to discredit a growing opposition movement' (CAGE, 2016).

There are two important factors about the episode that I want to expose.

Firstly, in at least one case involving a volunteer with MEND, a veiled Muslim female, the *Daily Mail* sent two individuals to her home address with documents making various allegations about her involvement with MEND and her participation in events during Islamophobia Awareness Month on behalf of the organisation. The woman described the experience as 'very intimidating' and noted that the publication did not contact her via phone or email before dispatching individuals to confront her at her home with a list of questions. The experience, she said, caused her 'a lot of stress' and prompted her appeal that the organisation does more to 'protect their members' (email communication to MEND, 4 January 2015).

Secondly, the uncritical adoption by the newspaper of the prevailing characterisation of MEND and CAGE as 'extremists' and its reliance, in articles published in the recent past, on material published by the Henry Jackson Society, denotes the use of a different instrument in defensive strategies employed by social movements from above: repression.

Cox and Nilsen explain the use of repression as a defensive strategy as 'involv[ing] violent coercion or the suspension of civil rights', (Nilsen and Cox, 2013: 71). I make a point of noting that suspension used in this context does not relate to the withdrawal of civil rights but to their denial using strategies to frustrate the active exercise of freedom of expression and freedom of association.

The newspaper's attack on MEND and CAGE by itself does not constitute what can be regarded as the suspension of civil rights though it clearly represents an attempt to provoke hesitation among civil society actors when engaging in public events for fear of the possibility of inviting unsolicited media attention and intrusive harassment.

But the newspaper's attack on MEND and CAGE is not to be seen in isolation from other acts to actively suppress their activities, nor should the use of published articles as a means of 'scaring off' civil society organisations be treated as discrete events with a short life cycle.

As MEND and CAGE have learned, the maxim that an author 'publish and be damned' has shifted the cost from author to subject with the result that these organisations suffer material impact in their exercise of freedom of expression and freedom of association.

Articles published in the national dailies which stop short of actual defamation but are nonetheless skilled pieces of character assassination can be regurgitated *ad nauseum* as social movements from above exploit them as demonstrable evidence of the subject's harbouring 'extremist' credentials. Having on record, in the form of published newspaper articles, accusations of extremism can, and do, serve as necessary and sufficient conditions for the closure of avenues, to MEND and CAGE, when booking public venues to hold meetings of a campaigning or political nature. Examples abound of planned events being sabotaged when venues are openly publicised by those seeking to deter meetings from taking place.

The convenient use of the media serves yet another purpose which is furthered by the uncritical posture adopted by newspapers when presented with privileged information; raising concerns without the added burden of substantiating their reliability or credibility. In an article commenting on how the 'hard left are sabotaging anti-extremism plans', *Times* columnist Rachel Sylvester relayed criticism about Prevent 'singl[ing] out Muslims' by shadow Home Secretary, Andy Burnham, at a MEND fringe event at Labour's annual party conference in 2016, noting that MEND was an organisation 'about which the Home Office's extremism analysis unit has "significant concerns"' (*The Times*, 2016).

What these concerns might be and whether they are warranted is of much less interest than recording, in print, that concerns have been aired. The act places the burden of proof on the subject without compelling the accuser to substantiate the basis of claims made. It also, under the Orwellian operations of the Extremism Analysis Unit, forces the subject into an asymmetric struggle in which the state can land killer punches but the subject is confined to shadow boxing, neither comprehending the allegations made nor being offered the opportunity to contest them openly and directly.

This, however, is resorting to a milder form of curtailment when compared to more drastic measures where pressure is applied on public venues by individuals, sometimes belonging to co-opted groups, to cancel bookings and thereby coercing venues to adopt risk-averse strategies with the intended effect of incapacitating the ability of social movements from below to organise and mobilise in civil society.

The new Prevent duty has the pernicious effect, as universities which have been 'named and shamed' for allegedly hosting so-called 'extremist preachers' have found, of requiring the specified authorities to whom the duty applies to engage in pre-emptive strikes against what 'may' be said rather than act against that which is uttered on their premises. Edwards's distilling the Prevent strategy as tantamount to 'policing the limits of the thinkable and the speakable' is apposite here. The danger lies in these limits being tightly bound and narrowly defined.

Actions pursued for the purposes of suspending the civil rights of British Muslim civil society organisations represent the repressive dimension of defensive strategies. Take, for example, the strategy recently adopted by one of the organisations to unlist venues from publicity material about events to prevent interference with future planned meetings. The suppression of civil rights rests not merely on what freedoms a subject can no longer exercise but also, more malevolently, on what he or she thinks they can no longer freely do.

As argued by Cox and Nilsen, defensive strategies are not necessarily applied as binary options with methods more likely to involve '*some* accommodation and *some* repression' (Nilsen and Cox, 2013: 72, emphasis in the original). The examples I have related above fit this matrix and expose how defensive strategies are flexibly used to aggressively constrain the capacity of British Muslim civil society actors to challenge dominant positions.

Offensive strategies

Cox and Nilsen further elaborate methods employed by social movements from above to entrench dominant position as the use of offensive strategies, which they describe as involving 'attacks on the truce lines left by movement struggles of the past, undermining and reversing the victories and concessions won by movements from below' (Nilsen and Cox, 2013: 72).

I want to focus on the aspect of 'attacks on the truce lines' in this section. The context against which I set forth my examples is the legal framework governing the constitution of Muslim civil society organisations as legal entities and the legal rights and obligations that flow therefrom. I include British Muslim charities as other actors in Muslim civil society that have been worst affected by offensive strategies used to 'restore the power of already-dominant groups'.

The process for registering a company as a charitable organisation or a not-for-profit company is straightforward enough, involving the filing of an application with the Charities Commission or documentation with Companies House and registering bank accounts for the purpose of conducting transactions for and on behalf of the organisation. While the procedure may seem simple enough on paper, the practice, for some British Muslim civil society organisations, has been far from simple and fraught with disquiet over discriminatory application of the rules.

I offer by way of example a problem which has afflicted both MEND and CAGE as well as several British Muslim charities, the closing of bank accounts; CAGE had its bank accounts with Barclays and the Co-operative Bank terminated in May 2014. A number of British Muslim charities have later suffered a similar fate. In July 2014, HSBC notified a number of British Muslim charitable organisations that it would be closing their accounts (Third Sector, 2014). The aid charity Ummah Welfare Trust, the Finsbury Park Mosque and the Cordoba Foundation were informed that HSBC would withdraw banking facilities and close their accounts. The Muslim Association of Britain, which opened an account with HSBC in 2014, had it closed by the bank three days later. In January 2016, HSBC closed the bank account of the UK's largest British Muslim charity, Islamic Relief (Sunday Times, 2016).

The strain of withdrawing banking facilities from organisations that are reliant on community funding models and grant funding cannot be overstated. Nor can the banks' decision to revoke arrangements under the guise of a 'risk-averse' calculus dispel the perception that what was being revoked were legal entitlements to service provision, or 'concessions' won in earlier struggles.

The withdrawal of banking facilities was attended by attempts at reputational harm under which at least one major Muslim charity was forced to investigate an accusation of transgression at its own cost (BBC News, 2014). In another case, involving Finsbury Park mosque, a profile report produced by the multinational media company, Thomson Reuters, falsely ascribing to the mosque continued 'links to terrorism' led to HSBC withdrawing its banking services. The mosque later won a libel claim against Thomson Reuters who admitted producing a profile report about the mosque which 'made the false allegation that there were grounds to suspect that the claimant had continued connections to terrorism' (BBC News, 2017).

The matter came to light following a BBC investigation by political journalist Peter Oborne, who has extensively researched the plight of British Muslim charities and the 'continuing war' (*Daily Telegraph*, 2014) they face from media assaults on their reputation and 'overzealous' attention from the charity regulator, the Charities Commission (Civil Society, 2015).

Paradoxically, and perhaps a benign unintended consequence quite unforeseen by social movements from above, is the strengthening of community funding that has ensued after the revoking of banking facilities. If revocation signalled an attack on the truce lines from above, the advantage to British Muslim civil society actors has been the strong assertion of solidarity from below.

A related though distinct type of attack in the case of MEND came from other quarters. In one odd development and quite unexpected, the organisation received a letter from Companies House, more than two years after its registration, informing that 'unless cause is shown to the contrary, at the expiration of 2 months [from date shown] the name of MEND UK Limited will be struck off the register and the company will be dissolved'.

It is not known why the letter was sent or what 'cause' needed to be demonstrated to avert de-registration. A separate incident involved billing for corporation tax, even though the company is registered as limited by guarantee and not-for-profit.

As with the withdrawal of banking services, letters reneging on normal practice have left some British Muslim civil society organisations wondering at the shifting goalposts that have come to characterise their more perilous situation though none have been shown to have violated rules or regulations. The question that persists is why their situation should be fraught with undefined risk. The challenge has been to overcome obstacles and hurdles placed in their way and continue, as far as possible, to fulfil their objectives.

Conclusion

Advocacy by British Muslim civil society organisations in pursuit of equality and non-discrimination preceded the War on Terror as Muslim actors sought to advance claims-making citizenship and highlight the growing prevalence of discrimination based on grounds of religion; Islamophobia.

The War on Terror both heightened fears of the spread of Islamophobic hatred and created spaces for Muslim civil society actors to be more visible. But with visibility came threats to autonomy and the burden of displaced responsibility. Using Cox and Nilsen's theory of offensive and defensive strategies used by social movements from above in interactions with social movements from below to entrench the position of dominant groups, I have tried to show how British Muslim civil society organisations have struggled to maintain and progress claim-making projects.

In an earlier phase of the War on Terror, British Muslim civil society actors found themselves confronted with the demand to do more to tackle the threat from violent extremism while being effectively silenced through exclusion from political dialogue. Defensive strategies used in this phase were fairly rudimentary with established organisations that challenged dominant positions undermined through the cultivation of more pliant bodies that neatly fit into the restricted models of engagement foreseen by social movements from above but articulated as the benign production of a 'democratic constellation'.

As Muslim civil society has matured amid generational shifts in models of organisation and claims-making articulations have taken on a more pronounced form, defensive and offensive strategies at the disposal of social movements from above have taken on greater power. This has been coupled with the expansion of the War on Terror to encompass violent and 'non-violent' extremism necessitating a wider range of defensive and offensive strategies.

Non-violent extremism and the incursion into a 'pre-criminal space' has rebalanced the boundary between the state and Muslim civil society as the realm for operating defensive and offensive strategies has further broadened to include the space previously designated the 'non-state' sector.

Examples of defensive strategies that have been discussed here comprise attempts by social movements from above to co-opt and embolden some

Muslim civil society organisations over others. Defensive strategies have also taken the form of aggressive undermining of Muslim civil society actors who threaten the entrenched position of dominant groups and that of their co-opted partners.

Offensive strategies discussed here entail efforts to 'pull the rug' from under Muslim civil society in a demonstration of the power of social movements from above. The efforts, in many ways, perfectly illustrate the relevance of claims-making articulations by Muslim civil society actors with their demands for equal treatment and non-discrimination.

The defensive and offensive strategies that have been used to suppress the voices of Muslim civil society actors and stymie their opposition to policies that strengthen structural racism have rendered a number of benign consequences that offer a ray of optimism. They remind us that though there remain challenges for Muslim civil society organisations to overcome, the challenges are not symptomatic of 'a finished and monolithic ideological formation' but constitute transient settlements in the ongoing 'political process of struggle' in which they play a vital and formative part.

Bibliography

Websites were last accessed 12 February 2017.

BBC News (2014), 'Audit "clears Islamic Relief" of terror funding claim', 12 December.

—— (2017), 'Finsbury Park Mosque wins libel payout from Reuters', 1 February.

CAGE (2016), CAGE statement, 'Upcoming Daily Mail investigation evidence of Home Office push back', 5 January. https://cage.ngo/press-release/upcoming-daily-mail-investigation-evidence-home-office-push-back/.

Cameron, D. (2013), *Statement to the House of Commons*. HC Deb 3 June, cc 1245, 1235.

—— (2015), 'Extremism' speech, 20 July.

Carlile, A. (2011), *Report to the Home Secretary of Independent Oversight of Prevent Review and Strategy*. London: The Stationery Office.

Civil Society (2015), 'Bubb: "overzealous" regulatory approach to Muslim charities harming fight against terror'. www.civilsociety.co.uk/news/bubb---overzealous--regulatory-approach-to-muslim-charities-harming-fight-against-terror.html.

Daily Telegraph (2014), 'The continuing war against Islamic charities', 2 December.

Dobbernack, J., Meer, N. and Modood, T. (2014), 'Misrecognition and political agency. The case of Muslim organisations in a general election',

British Journal of Politics and International Relations, 17 (2), May, doi: 10.1111/1467-856X.12033.

Edwards, P. (2015), 'How (not) to create ex-terrorists: Prevent as ideological warfare', in C. Baker-Beall, C. Heath-Kelly and L. Jarvis (eds), *Counter-Radicalisation: Critical Perspectives*. London: Routledge, pp. 54–70.

Guardian (2008), 'Whitehall draws up new rules on language of terror', 4 February.

——(2010), 'Muslim women are not political pawns', 9 April.

Hayes, B. and Qureshi, A. (2016), *'We are Completely Independent'. The Home Office, Breakthrough Media and the PREVENT Counter Narrative Industry*. London: CAGE.

Home Office (2011), *Prevent Strategy*, Cm 8092. London: The Stationery Office.

——(2015), *HM Government: Revised Prevent Duty Guidance for England and Wales*, 12 March (updated 16 July 2015). London: HMSO.

Hussain, D. (2013), 'Winning the battles but losing the war?', Public Spirit. www.publicspirit.org.uk/winning-the-battles-but-losing-the-war/.

Intelligence and Security Committee (2010). *Intelligence and Security Committee Annual Report 2008–2009*, Cm 7807. London: The Stationery Office.

Isin, E.F and Turner, B.S. (eds) (2003), *Handbook of Citizenship Studies*. London: Sage.

Kelly, R. (2006), 'Britain: our values, our responsibilities', Speech, 11 October.

Maher, S. and Frampton, M. (2009), *Choosing Our Friends Wisely: Criteria for Engagement with Muslim Groups*. London: Policy Exchange.

McCulloch, J. and Pickering, S. (2010), 'Counter-terrorism: the law and policing of pre-emption', in N. McGarrity, A. Lynch and G. Williams (eds), *Counter-terrorism and Beyond: The Culture of Law and Justice after 9/11*. Abingdon: Routledge, pp. 13–29.

McLoughlin, S. (2005), 'The state, "new" Muslim leaderships and Islam as a "resource" for public engagement in Britain', in J. Cesari and S. McLoughlin (eds), *European Muslims and the Secular State*. Aldershot: Ashgate, pp. 55–69.

Mirza, M., Senthilkumaran, A. and Ja'far, Z. (2007), *Living Apart Together: British Muslims and the Paradox of Multiculturalism*. London: Policy Exchange.

Modood, T. (2005), *Multicultural Politics: Racism, Ethnicity and Muslims in Britain*. Edinburgh: Edinburgh University Press.

Nabi, S. (2011), 'How is Islamophobia institutionalised? Racialised governmentality and the case of Muslim students in British universities', University of Manchester, PhD thesis.

Nilsen, A.G. and Cox, N. (2013), 'What would a Marxist theory of social movements look like?', in C. Barker, L. Cox, J. Krinsky and A.G. Nilsen (eds), *Marxism and Social Movements*. Leiden: Brill, pp. 63–81.

O'Toole, T., DeHanas, D., Modood, T., Meer, N. and Jones, S. (2013), *Taking Part. Muslim Participation in Contemporary Governance*. Bristol: Centre for the Study of Ethnicity and Citizenship.

O'Toole, T., Meer, N., DeHanas, D., Jones, S. and Modood, T. (2016), 'Governing through Prevent: regulation and contested practice in state-Muslim engagement', *Sociology*, 50 (1), 160–17.

Oborne, P. (2016), 'A soft apartheid towards Muslims is emerging in Britain', Owen Jones meets Peter Oborne. www.youtube.com/watch?v=PXkKbFQRH cs&app=desktop.

Peace, T. (ed.) (2015), *Muslims and Political Participation in Britain*. London: Routledge.

Prime Minister's Office (2015), Prime Minister: 'I want to build a national coalition to challenge and speak out against extremism', 13 October.

Qureshi, A. (2015), 'PREVENT: creating "radicals" to strengthen anti-Muslim narratives', *Critical Studies on Terrorism*, 8 (1), 181–91.

Sunday Times (2016), 'Terror fear makes HSBC cut ties to Muslim charity', 3 January.

Sutton, R. (2016), 'Myths and misunderstandings: understanding opposition to the Prevent strategy', Policy Paper No. 7, Henry Jackson Society.

The Times (2016), 'Hard left are sabotaging anti-extremism plans', 11 October.

Third Sector (2014), 'Cage lodges complaint with financial ombudsman over closure of bank accounts', 7 October.

PART 3

Social Movements From Above

6

Mainstreaming Anti-Muslim Prejudice: The Rise of the Islamophobia Industry in American Electoral Politics

Nathan C. Lean

Since the late 2000s, academics, activists and others who work on the issue of anti-Muslim prejudice, or Islamophobia, have increasingly turned their attention to its mechanics. Specifically, a new body of literature has emerged that examines the degree to which individuals and organisations with varying levels of influence and reach partner with one another to advance, often for great sums, anti-Muslim messages. In the media, in the blogosphere, in political circles and in grassroots networks, their goal is often the same: awaken concerns about the alleged threat posed by the religion of Islam and its followers, and advocate for policies that aim to thwart that threat. In my writing on this subject, I have referred to this phenomenon as the 'Islamophobia industry', or what I see as a well-greased and tightly woven cadre of people and groups that share funding and institutional structures (Lean, 2012). The relatively newfound focus on this network comes not as a result of academic postulation that typifies some approaches in the ivory tower, nor is it a conspiratorial charge that sees ghosts in every shadow. Rather, it is based on recognition over the years that the bulk of anti-Muslim content on the Internet, in the political arena, and in spaces 'on the ground' tends to come from the same cast of characters, and those characters have become more vocal, and more prominent, since the end of the twenty-first century's opening decade.

It has become rather conventional to dismiss many of the individuals and groups that comprise the Islamophobia industry as lunatics, fringe actors or aggravators who occupy merely peripheral spaces. This is especially so when it comes to the coterie of armchair 'scholars' and bloggers that have turned the World Wide Web into a breeding ground for Islamophobic information and imagery. Their presence within the dark corners of obscure websites, online forums and comment sections has rendered them somewhat comparable to pests or other nuisances; they are sufficiently irritating, but at the end of the day their ultimate effect is minimal. (For characterisations of American blogger Pamela Geller as a 'fringe' figure, see Feffer, 2012; Kaczynski and Massie, 2015; Sales, 2016.) The purpose of this chapter is to argue for a different inter-pretation of the Islamophobia industry – one that understands its central figures and organisations not as bizarre or cryptic but rather as highly influential and increasingly central to the worldviews of leading political figures, especially in the US. This shift to the mainstream is not one that happened overnight, it is rather recent. Nowhere else is this sharpened into fuller relief than within the arena of the 2016 presidential election cycle. During this time, as I will show below, the Islamophobia industry became a powerful force in driving anti-Muslim messaging that resonated with leading candidates for high office. This was undoubtedly due, in part, to a general rise of populist-like sentiment that was birthed in preceding European elections and trickled into the American electorate, giving rise to a swath of politicos that might have otherwise been seen as out of touch, if not too eccentric for serious consideration altogether. With the election of Donald Trump, however, those messages transcended the hyper-partisan and bombastic climate of the campaign and landed squarely in the White House. Thus, figures in the Islamophobia industry that had long been lobbying for influence and labouring to move their messaging beyond the borders of the computer screen or marginally influential circles found that they had the ear of the most powerful leader of the so-called free world. This chapter will analyse two specific people and platforms that speak to the increasing centrality of Islamophobia and its purveyors within the American government: Frank Gaffney and his Washington, DC think tank, the Center for Security Policy (CSP); and Senior Advisor to the President, Steve Bannon, and his former media enterprise, Breitbart. While other figures certainly exist, my focus on these two will highlight the role of politics in the person of Gaffney and the role of the media in the person of Bannon. Similarly, Gaffney's history in Washington, DC, and his long involvement in conservative political circles, shows the ease with which a figure like him, who touts wild conspiracy theories about Muslims, can slip into the presidential sphere of influence in ways that are not so outwardly obvious. Bannon, on the other hand, demonstrates the way in which a relatively unknown figure who hides behind the writings published on a conservative website can be jerked out of obscurity overnight and offered one of the most prized and significant posts in the White House.[1] In what follows, I will briefly trace the background and the emergence of the Islamophobia industry in the US, with emphasis on the individuals and groups that can now claim greater influence in the political world. I will chart their evolution and rise over the course of the 2016 presidential election, and show how their proposals ended up as talking points that major candidates deployed. Finally, I will problematise the influence of Frank Gaffney and Steve Bannon in the Trump White House, giving special attention to the role of Trump campaign manager and advisor Kellyanne Conway in facilitating those relationships. I will also underscore the potential proximity of anti-Muslim voices like Pamela Geller and Robert Spencer, which Bannon's appointment makes possible.

An industry on the fringes?

A curious thing happened after the attacks of 9/11. At a time when many would suspect that negative public sentiment towards Muslims would be especially high, polling data that was released at the time showed just the opposite. Two months after the attacks, 59 per cent of Americans reported having a generally positive image of Islam. Pew Research reported in a study released in December 2011 that favourable views of Muslim Americans had risen by 12 per cent in eight months, and that despite not being familiar with the religion of Islam – and believing that it played some role in the terrorist attacks – this oft-targeted religious minority was actually becoming more accepted in the mainstream.[2] These warming views, however, did not last. The years following 9/11 saw increased animosity towards American Muslims, with hate crimes and other attacks on the rise. Ten years after the tragedy, in 2011, a survey of polls verified in statistics what many felt to be true: Muslims were loathed by a substantial swath of the population. In fact, views of favourability had virtually flipped with more than half of all Americans reporting that Muslims made them feel uncomfortable and the same percentage suggesting that American values and Islamic values were incompatible (Pubic Religion Research Institute, 2011). Ironically enough, these anxieties came at a time when the number of attacks carried out by Muslims was strikingly small. A study conducted by the Triangle Center on Terrorism and Homeland Security in 2011 found that since 9/11, only eleven Muslims had successfully executed attacks in the country. In a span of more than nine years, they killed 33 people. By comparison, the country witnessed 150,000 murders in the same amount of time (Kurzman, 2012).

While other factors undoubtedly contributed to these views – and contribute today to negative sentiment directed at the Muslim community – I have argued that these antipathies are a result, in part, of the Islamophobia industry's efforts since the early 2000s to sustain an expressly negative discourse about Muslims in the media, on the Internet and in policy circles. For more than a decade, this group of bloggers, politicians, pundits, religious leaders and activists has laboured to convince their compatriots that Muslims are engaged in a zero-sum quest to uproot the Constitution and take over the US with violence. They write best-selling books, appear frequently on television and radio, and demand eye-popping fees for their speaking engagements. In a climate of fluctuating political and economic realities, their messages have attracted a steady band of anxious followers.

It is possible to cleave this network into two discernible parts: a ferocious squad of propagandists that flood the Internet with skewed information and outright falsehoods; and a more measured group of policy-oriented warriors who inject prejudiced views of Muslims and Islam into legislative and governmental arenas. Though not always obvious, the relationship between the two camps is one of mutual benefit. Without the bloggers who rile their large online bases towards action, state and national policy proposals may not have the apparent grassroots support they need. Similarly, without the government-minded activists and lobbyists, warnings of 'creeping Sharia' or narratives about the supposedly impending threat of the Muslim Brotherhood would likely swell on social media, only to fizzle out and die before they materialised in action. Over the past few years, bloggers like Pamela Geller and Robert Spencer have occupied the former category. On average, their websites feature between 300 and 400 new blog posts on Islam and Muslims each month, and those posts are spun out through their social media accounts and reposted on dozens of other websites and blogs, including BareNakedIslam, Front Page, the Middle

East Forum and Blazing Cat Fur, among others.[3] This has the effect of crowding the Internet with information such that search strings related to a news event involving Muslims or Islam are likely to generate those stories among their results. A paradigmatic example of this is a Google search string for the word 'jihad'.[4] Such an inquiry routinely generates Robert Spencer's Jihad Watch website within the first five results, often just after the Wikipedia entry. For newcomers to the web in search of information on this Islamic principle, Spencer's thorough (and abjectly imbalanced) articles are low-hanging fruit. Thus, while it may appear that Spencer himself is a lesser-known figure with no obvious political influence, his website is supported financially by the David Horowitz Freedom Center, a California-based outfit whose namesake founder has led anti-Muslim initiatives throughout the US, including 'Islamofascism Awareness Week' on college campuses (The Freedom Center itself has received funding from philanthropists Nina Rosenwald and Elizabeth Varet, as well as the Bradley and Scaife Foundations.) With this financial support, Jihad Watch enjoys prime Internet real estate and has the ability to mobilise online foot soldiers into on-the-ground activists. In recent years, this has taken several different forms. In 2010, it was Geller and Spencer's organisation, the American Freedom Defense Initiative (AFDI), that organised the raucous protests against Park 51, a proposed Islamic community center in New York City. The duo have also been behind numerous public signage and placards which juxtapose gory and sensationalised imagery of Muslims with cherry-picked verses from the Quran. These have appeared on public buses in various American cities, as well as in Metro stops and on billboards. Most recently, AFDI organised a 'Draw Muhammad' cartoon contest in Texas in 2015 – an event so controversial that it prompted two would-be assassins to ambush the gathering. The event, carried out in the name of advancing free speech, highlighted the nexus between online Islamophobia and grassroots activism, and showed the degree to which seemingly fringe actors may grab the national spotlight and gain mass attention for their ideological programme. Notably, Georgetown University's Bridge Initiative showed in a 2015 article that Geller and Spencer's group increased their funding drastically between 2012 and 2013; tax records indicated that their assets increased by more than 15,000 per cent, with Geller drawing an annual salary well over $200,000 (for an estimated ten hours of work each week) while Spencer, whose salary was augmented by the Horowitz Freedom Center, received nearly $215,000 (Bridge Initiative, 2015).

If the anti-Muslim blogosphere is led by Geller and Spencer, the world of anti-Muslim policy is led by Frank Gaffney, a former Reagan administration official who has established recognisable influence within the far right and neoconservative circles of the Republican Party. Unlike Spencer and Geller, Gaffney is not bombastic in his approach nor is he a particularly able mobiliser of the general public when it comes to organising around issues related to opposing Muslims or Islam. Gaffney's CSP is represented by Geller and Spencer's attorney, David Yerushalmi, and for several years the two have partnered on various policy documents, wonky memos, presentations and other legal material that shrouds pernicious views of Islam beneath lofty jurisprudential jargon. In this way, their influence is less felt among ordinary factions of the general public that may search for digestible information about the world's second-largest religion, but rather by key lawmakers and others who stand ready to cement such ideological views in national laws. Gaffney's approach is one that rocks on two hobbyhorses: the alleged threat posed by Sharia law and that posed by the Muslim Brotherhood. Despite deploying wild conspiracy theories (that Hillary Clinton's chief of staff was a secret member of the Muslim Brotherhood; that Barack Obama was a closeted Muslim; that the new Missile Defense Shield logo indicated a submission to Islam; that Supreme Court Justice Elana Kagan prefers Sharia to the US Constitution), it is necessary to focus on the less sensational work that Gaffney has done over the years that has attracted far less public attention. When it comes to Sharia, or Islam law, Gaffney has aligned himself with neoconservative politicians, lobbyists and others to advance the idea that Muslims in key positions of influence (especially in state and local governments) hope to upend the American Constitution. To this end (and with a 2012 operating budget of more than $3 million), he has argued for increased surveillance of American mosques, advised Senator Ted Cruz on possible congressional measures that would supposedly curtail the perceived threat, and with Yerushalmi, crafted blueprint legislation that would effectively ban Islamic law in American courts – a bill that more than a dozen states have adopted into law. Virtually all of Gaffney's evidence for his claims rests on one single document from 1991 that supposedly outlines a Muslim Brotherhood strategy for exerting its influence, and spreading Sharia, in the US. A closer inspection, however, reveals that the 'Explanatory Memorandum' is not a smoking gun. Rather, it was little more than one whimsical fantasy of a man who was once affiliated with the Brotherhood, but who had no capability of carrying out such a grand scheme – a reality which is further evidenced by the document's lack of impact in the 25 years since it originated (Bridge Initiative, 2016). Still, for Gaffney, the perception of a threat was so palatable that it spawned a ten-part video series about the Muslim Brotherhood's alleged takeover, and numerous national conferences where such a thing was discussed with key figures of the Republican Party, many of whom were written off as fringe figures within that group but who, in the wake of Donald Trump's election and the rise of populism within American and European electorates, have been thrust to the fore as leading contenders for key government posts and cabinet positions. Now, into the first term of Trump's presidency, figures like Gaffney have been pulled into the mix and are set to become more influential than perhaps they ever were before. Additionally, while it may seem easy to write off Spencer and Geller as inconsequential nodes of the anti-Muslim network (Trump even once blamed Geller for 'taunting' Muslims), the inclusion of Breitbart's Steve Bannon as White House Senior Advisor is reason to believe that their ideas will enliven the imaginations of those who dwell in Pennsylvania Avenue (the street that connects the White House and the US Capitol) and craft American policy.

Anti-Muslim influence in the 2016 presidential campaign

The 2016 American presidential election was unusual in many regards. Yet, it may be argued that chief among the peculiarities was a deep-seated populism that, like a sleeping giant, needed only to be nudged in order to awaken. With Europe having recently experienced the paroxysm of populist electoral uprisings, the US stood well primed to experience the same as frustrations with the Obama era were channeled into angry messages that resonated with working-class voters and rested on narratives of race, immigration, national security threats and 'taking the country back'. Perhaps unsurprisingly, this resulted in a campaign season of intense anti-Muslim rhetoric and draconian policy proposals that identified the religion of Islam as the primary culprit for terrorism around the globe. Certainly, other election years had experienced similar rhetoric though the reality of an outgoing African American president, who had endured two terms of scepticism about his birthplace and alleged connections to the Islamic faith, brought about an opportunity for discourses that were pillared on similar themes. It is through this lens that we get a glimpse of how the not-so-fringe cast of the Islamophobia industry were able to deliver anti-Muslim conspiracy theories to more mainstream audiences. Two specific moments stand out in that regard.

Republican presidential candidate Ben Carson set off a firestorm of controversy in September 2015 when, in an interview with *Meet the Press*, he suggested that a Muslim could not – and should not – be the president of the US because of their alleged adherence to Sharia and their alleged tendency to engage in *taqiyya*, an Islamic principle that has historically allowed Muslims in danger to deny their religious beliefs in order to save their lives. (For Carson, this was evidence that Muslims are permitted to lie and cannot be trusted.) Just months later, during a campaign stop in Charleston, South Carolina, Carson told Breitbart that the Council on American-Islamic Relations is a terrorist organisation with clear connections to the Muslim Brotherhood, which hoped to engage in 'civilisational jihad' in the US. The proof for his claim was the aforementioned 1991 'Explanatory Memorandum' (Swoyer, 2016). These two moments revealed the influence of Frank Gaffney, and the ease with which seemingly bizarre conspiracy theories could be adopted and spread by a once-leading presidential contender. Though it is unknown if Gaffney was advising Carson in an official way (he was advising Senator Ted Cruz, who proposed a bill to declare the Muslim Brotherhood a terrorist organisation), he was quick to defend Carson and took to various national media outlets to buttress the claim that Sharia was antithetical to the US Constitution. Narratives about *taqiyya* had long been a part of Gaffney's playbook, and were central to his understanding of Islamic law and its supposedly nefarious influence in Congress and other Washington halls of power (Gaffney, 2012).

Gaffney's presence within the 2016 campaign became clearer in December 2015, when then-candidate Donald Trump announced his controversial 'Muslim ban', a policy proposal that would effectively suspend immigration to the US from certain Muslim-majority countries for an undetermined period. During the press conference in which he announced this proposal, he cited a study conducted by CSP which alleged that 51 per cent of American Muslims wanted to be governed by

Islamic law, and that 25 per cent of them claimed that violence against Americans 'is justified as part of the global jihad' (Trump, 2015). The poll, it was later revealed, was fraught with methodological problems and was swiftly debunked (Lean and Denari, 2016). But beyond that, an investigation of the poll and the polling company behind it showed a relationship that further underscored the proximity of Gaffney to the Trump campaign, and now the Trump administration. While CSP was at the vanguard of promoting the poll's findings, it was an organisation called The Polling Company which conducted the poll as a paid consultant for Gaffney's group. At the helm of The Polling Company was Kellyanne Conway, the woman who would later become Trump's campaign manager and secure a role as Counselor to the President. In a June 2015 interview on Gaffney's radio show, Conway referenced the poll, and reinforced the idea that a substantial percentage of American Muslims were violent:

> I think this is important because the answer from lots of folks always is, 'Look, don't cast a wide net and call all Muslims non-peaceful and violent and adhering to jihad and Shariah and bloodthirsty.' Fine. However, look at the data. The Muslims living in the US themselves – 27 percent of them, anyway – say that this is what the purpose of jihad is, to either punish nonbelievers (16 percent) or, the other 11 percent, to undermine non-Muslim states. (Center for Security Policy, 2015)

Conway's relationship with Gaffney dates back years. As Mother Jones reported, her company had conducted surveys for CSP as far back as 1998. She has appeared multiple times on Gaffney's podcasts and is featured in various places on his website (Levy, 2016). Conway is also tied to the Federation for American Immigration Reform (FAIR), a once-fringe group that has advised Trump on matters of immigration, and which, as a result of its connections to white supremacists, has been labeled a hate group by the Southern Poverty Law Center (Levy, 2016). FAIR credits Conway as having bolstered Trump's hardline position on immigration, which included his so-called 'Muslim ban'. With Conway's connections to Gaffney and other extreme anti-immigrant groups, it is not difficult to imagine how these ideas would play out in terms of policies. Also of critical concern is the presence of Steve Bannon, Trump's Senior Advisor, and a man whose online platform, Breitbart, has given rise to the ideas of not only Frank Gaffney, but the less measured and more maleficent voices of the anti-Muslim blogosphere.

An anti-Muslim White House?

When Donald Trump appointed Steve Bannon, the former Breitbart editor, to the post of Senior Advisor, many Washington pundits suggested that signaled a sharp turn to the right on the part of the incoming president. Indeed, Bannon is a controversial figure, and as some have noted, that is due in no small part to an array of blatantly prejudiced statements that he has made in the past about Jews. Even the *Times of Israel*, a newspaper that has traditionally enjoyed warm relations with American conservatives, criticised the pick. But apart from the conversation surrounding Bannon's tendency to deploy anti-Semitic language, his former website was also a space for virulent anti-Muslim writers. Apart from the columns authored by staff writers that were a mix of screed and conspiracy, Breitbart featured the writings of outsider contributors too. The anti-Muslim hate group leader and American blogger Robert Spencer published seven posts on the site between April 2014 and December 2016. Shockingly, Geller's partner, blogger Pamela Geller, published a whopping 271 pieces between October 2009 and December 2016. And Frank Gaffney also published on the site, with more than a dozen pieces penned for Bannon's enterprise between 2014 and 2016.[5] As recently as 9 November 2016 (the day after the US presidential election), Gaffney appeared on Breitbart radio to declare that Trump must designate the Muslim Brotherhood as a terrorist organisation (Hayward, 2016). It is impossible to know for certain what the nature of Trump's White House will be when it comes to issues related to Muslims and Islam, and political forecasts have limited value. Yet, judging from the group of people to whom he is most closely connected, there is reason for grave concern. What is clear in the case of Bannon is that the cast of the Islamophobia industry that once relied on his website for a platform now have the ability to do more with their messages than saber rattle. In effect, bloggers like Geller and Spencer, and neoconservative policy wonks like Gaffney are reaping the produce of a field that they have long sewn; their narratives over the years have ushered into being a populist uprising comprised of predominantly white, working-class Americans that hold fast to the idea that immigrants and racial minorities are a threat not just to their jobs but also to national security. Having helped swell that portion of the American electorate and having roused them when it came to the issue of Islam, they elected a man who would, in turn, give them space through people like Bannon and Conway to continue to exert their maleficent influence.

Part of what is so concerning about the future of anti-Muslim prejudice in the US, and the White House dynamics that will likely embolden it, is the broader members of Trump's cabinet and team of advisors that have advanced stereotypes and abjectly bigoted remarks about Muslims and Islam over the course of their careers. This is especially the case in the example of General Mike Flynn, Trump's National Security Advisor (Flynn has said, among other things, that 'Islam is a cancer') (Khan, 2016). On the whole, the bombastic statements are worrisome and suggest that when it comes to issues of national defence and military engagements, ideological underpinning of a virulently anti-Muslim nature may well factor into policy decisions. Yet, I would argue that despite the danger that such bold-faced prejudice poses, the greater threat to the American Muslim community, and indeed to Muslim communities all around the world that are affected by American policies, lies in the advisory roles occupied by Bannon and Conway. It is no secret that Senior Advisors and Counselors to the American President are among the most trusted and respected figures within the White House and the American government writ large. Often, their influence is even greater than that of decorated generals or other cabinet officials whose tasks do not entail a daily presence in the Oval Office. They are constants in a world of change, and to that end, it is their advice that often reaches the president first; they are also the people who usually have the president's ear before final decisions are made. Thus, Bannon and Conway, with their shared commitment to ramping up domestic surveillance of Muslim communities, curtailing immigration from Muslim-majority countries, and otherwise dismantling Islamic institutions within the US that they perceive as threatening, present extraordinary challenges for those who value civil rights and equality, and those who loathe prejudice. The fact that both of these individuals have worked closely with – and that their incomes have depended upon – people like Spencer, Geller and Gaffney, whose ideas about Muslims and Islam are not only con-spiratorial, but dangerous, further underscores the possibility that the Trump White House will adopt a mantle of Islamophobia. Unfortunately, with the 2016 elections having generated Republican control of both bodies of Congress, it is likely that whatever policy proposals that emerge within the corridors of the West Wing will find support on Capitol Hill. Of course, the fact that Gaffney has long lobbied various members of Congress on these ideas already, and hosted various neo-conservative factions at policy gatherings in Washington over the past several decades, is all the more reason to believe that the anti-Muslim network, or the Islamophobia industry, will thrive in the years to come.

Notes

1. It should be noted here that while I characterise Bannon's former website, Breitbart, as 'conservative', it may be more accurately described as a platform for white nationalists, neo-Nazi sympathisers, anti-Muslim and anti-immigrant bloggers, as well as people who have espoused anti-Semitic views (including Bannon himself).
2. Though it is impossible to know exactly what accounted for these views, many, including Pew, point to President George W. Bush's rhetoric in the immediate days following 9/11, which characterised Islam as a religion of peace and lambasted attempts to paint the terrorist attacks as a war between the US and Muslims.
3. This number is based on a tabulation of yearly blog posts on these sites between 2014 and 2015, and averaging them to arrive at a monthly figure. Additionally, using social media tracking technology, it is possible to see how specific URLs are spread across the Internet and reposted on various websites.
4. For the purposes of this chapter, I conducted ten Google searches (clearing the browser cache each time) over a ten-day period between 1 December 2016 and 11 December 2016. In each daily query, Jihad Watch was within the first five results.
5. Calculations are based on a tabulation of authored pieces featured on the author page of each respective writer on the Breitbart website.

Bibliography

Bridge Initiative (2015), 'Group behind Muhammad cartoons increased assets by 15,000% in 2013', 6 May. http://bridge.georgetown.edu/group-behind-muhammad-cartoons-increased-assets-by-15000-in-2013/. Accessed 4 December 2016.

—— (2016), 'Civilization Jihad: debunking the conspiracy theory', 16 February, http://bridge.georgetown.edu/civilization-jihad-debunking-the-conspiracy-theory/. Aaccessed 4 December 2016.

Center for Security Policy (2015), 'The ominous trade agreement' Center for Security Policy, 25 June. www.centerforsecuritypolicy.org/2015/06/25/the-ominous-trade-agreement/. Accessed 15 December 2016.

Feffer, J. (2012), *Crusade 2.0: The West's Resurgent War on Islam*. San Fransisco, CA: City Lights.

Gaffney, Jr, F. (2012), 'The truth or taqiyya?', Center for Security Policy, 2 April. www.centerforsecuritypolicy.org/2012/04/02/the-truth-or-taqiyya-2/. Accessed 13 December 2016.

Hayward, J. (2016), 'Frank Gaffney: Trump foreign policy must start with designating Muslim Brotherhood a terrorist organization', Breitbart, 9 November. www.breitbart.com/radio/2016/11/09/frank-gaffney-trump-foreign-policy-start-designating-muslim-brotherhood-terrorist-organization/. Accessed 17 December 2016.

Kaczynski, A. and Massie, C. (2015), 'White nationalist and anti-Muslim fringe embrace Trump proposal', Buzzfeed, 8 December. www.buzzfeed.com/andrewkaczynski/white-nationalist-and-anti-muslim-fringe-embrace-trump-propo?utm_term=.dg5D6zN1zv#.ym2A3jN2jp. Aaccessed 4 December 2016.

Khan, M. (2016), 'Donald Trump National Security Advisor Mike Flynn has called Islam "a cancer"', 18 November. http://abcnews.go.com/Politics/donald-trump-national-security-adviser-mike-flynn-called/story?id=43575658. Accessed 18 December 2016.

Kurzman, C. (2012), 'Muslim-American terrorism in the decade since 9/11', Triangle Center on Terrorism and Homeland Security, 8 February. http://kurzman.unc.edu/files/2011/06/Kurzman_Muslim-American_Terrorism_in_the_Decade_Since_9_11.pdf. Accessed 28 March 2017.

Lean, N. (2012), *The Islamophobia Industry: How the Right Manufactures Fear of Muslims*. London: Pluto Press.

Lean, N. and Denari, J. (2016), 'Here's why you shouldn't trust the latest poll on Muslim Americans', *Huffington Post*, 7 July. www.huffingtonpost.com/nathan-lean/heres-why-you-shouldnt-trust-the-latest-poll-on-american-muslims_b_7688204.html. Accessed 14 December 2016.

Levy, P. (2016), 'Long before Trump, Kellyanne Conway worked for Anti-Muslim and anti-immigrant extremists', 9 December. www.motherjones.com/politics/2016/12/kellyanne-conway-immigration-islam-bannon-trump. Accessed 17 December 2016.

Public Religion Research Institute (2011), '"What it means to be an American" attitudes in an increasingly diverse America ten years after 9/11', 6 September. http://www.prri.org/wp-content/uploads/2011/09/PRRI-Brookings-What-it-Means-to-be-American-Report.pdf. Accessed 28 March 2017.

Sales, B. (2016), 'Stephen Bannon: 5 things Jews need to know', *Times of Israel*, 14 November. www.timesofisrael.com/stephen-bannon-5-things-jews-need-to-know/. Accessed 17 December 2016.

Swoyer, A. (2016), 'Dr. Ben Carson: CAIR wants "civilizational jihad" to "destroy us from within", 6 January. www.breitbart.com/big-government/2016/01/16/dr-ben-carson-cair-clear-ties-to/. Accessed 13 December 2016.

Trump, D.J. (2015), 'Donald J. Trump Statement on preventing Muslim immigration', Donaldtrump.com, 7 December. www.donaldjtrump.com/press-releases/donald-j.-trump-statement-on-preventing-muslim-immigration. Accessed 14 December 2016.

7

Terror Incognito: Black Flags, Plastic Swords and Other Weapons of Mass Disruption in Australia

Scott Poynting and Linda Briskman

Introduction

Anti-Muslim racism in Australia actually pre-dates the federation of British colonies into a nation-state at the beginning of 1901; it grew up with the 'white Australia policy' from the late nineteenth century, and has long outlived it, changing with the times. A New South Wales Contingent was despatched in 1885 to assist the ill-fated Sudan campaign, with a Sydney notable and imperial military veteran Sir Edward Strickland earlier that year urging public subscriptions for this military assistance in confronting 'England's and all Christendom's old enemies, the Saracens' (cited in Hutchinson and Myers, 1885). This Islamophobia was thus a child of British colonialism and racist supremacism at the far reaches of Empire, and yet has proven very adaptable to the contemporary 'Empire of Capital' (Meiksins Wood, 2003) under US hegemony. The 'white Australia policy' as well as being instituted to bar immigration from China, indentured labourers from the Pacific Islands and other non-white labour immigration was contemporanouesly deployed against 'Afghans' who came in the late nineteenth century as cameleers, from the North West Provinces (today's Pakistan) and Afghanistan (Deen, 2011; Kabir, 2004). They were few, but the public outcry was out of proportion with their numbers or their influence. Their Islam was represented as bound up with their non-whiteness and other undesirable attributes. Also under the white Australia policy, Syrian immigrants (from today's Lebanon) strove from the same time to emphasise to state officials their

Christianity, where they could, and tenuous connections with Europe as elements of 'whiteness'.

This potted history is offered to make the following points. Firstly, anti-Muslim racism has always (since the Australian state has existed) been part of white hegemony sustained by the state, stemming from and imbricated in Empire and subsequent legacies of colonialism. Secondly, it has been rooted in various degrees of common sense within the national popular, at times welling up in panics and racist campaigns. (That is not to say that it is caused by Islamophobic moral panic, nor manifested solely in it.) Thirdly, it has been related to national security, and has notably been whipped up manipulatively in wartime: examples being the Mahdi in Sudan, 'the Turk' in World War I, within the contemporary post-World War II US-led empire during the Gulf War of 1990–91 (in purported rescue of Arab and Muslim Kuwait!) and during the post-2001 wars on Afghanistan, Iraq and against a generalised and globalised Muslim 'terror'.

It is the Islamophobia of today's Australia that is the subject of this chapter. Regretfully, this could fill several books. So we present in this chapter a series of recent case-study snapshots of state and media Islamophobia in Australia, which we believe build up a bigger picture of the current situation faced by Muslims in the 'War on Terror' downunder. For the most part, the multifarious and complex connections between contemporary Islamophobia and the Australian state, its coercive apparatus (military, police, courts) and the consent-constructive apparatus of hegemony (notably the media), the common sense of folk wisdom found in civil society and informing its movements, and counter-hegemonic movementswill need to be merely gestured at here. Following Morgan and Poynting (2012), we assert that Islamophobia is now as thoroughly globalised as the world's media, and is sustained with stock images, circulated transnationally. If we are right, then readers from other continents will readily recognise similar tropes and indeed the same ideology. *De te fabula narratur.*

A few prefatory words about Islamophobic moral panic are called for. The notion of moral panic, famously expounded by Stan Cohen (2002), accounted for the social construction of folk devils and their deployment in processes of social control. We contend that foremost among the folk demons of the contemporary 'West' is the Muslim Other. As Morgan and Poynting (2012: 5–6) explain:

Moral panics usually involve a supposed identification of a society's ills – fixating on and aggregating a range of symptoms – and prescriptions to remedy these by both accredited experts and ordinary people. What makes the diagnoses 'ring true' is that they resonate with ordinary people's experiences; those suffering from particular anxieties about, say, the direction or extent of social change, can identify elements of their worries as a generalized and shared sense of a social ailment. 'Explanations' offered by the 'experts' take up their inchoate concerns, render them more articulate, plausible, and sometimes even scientific-sounding, and deliver them back to the anxious audiences in a feedback loop which works to the extent that it reverberates with popular anxieties. 'Folk Devils' serve as simplified, easily grasped apparent causes of the problem (often obscuring real structural causes).

The cases of local or national moral panic in Australia about the 'Muslim Other' outlined in this chapter each project real anxieties onto this imagined cause, integrating local concern and outrage about a particular issue concerning Muslims, with the globally circulating construction of a Muslim folk devil and reinforced by the clash of civilisations ideology (Huntington, 1993; Lewis, 1990). This ideology posits that Islam and Western 'ideals' are incompatible, spurred on by what Lean (2012) refers to as the Islamophobia industry that manufactures fear and, we would argue, loathing.

An example might help here. The front page of Rupert Murdoch's high-circulation Sydney tabloid *Daily Telegraph* on 14 October 2016 was headlined, 'MOTHER OF ALL MONSTERS'. This was superimposed on a large colour photograph of a figure in a dark burqa, looking for all the world like Darth Vader. There was a bright, yellow-backed banner with 'SYDNEY TERROR' at the top. The introductory heading prefigured the story: 'ISIS teen warns mum of plot. She does NOTHING'.

All the elements of Islamophobic moral panic were there: monsters, impending danger, familiar and demonising symbols associated with moral threats (the burqa), exaggeration (the 16-year-old son of the 'monster' had made vain boasts about an imagined but undetailed terrorist assassination in which he was to star), projection of anxieties onto the Other, and strident demands that 'something be done'.

But something has already been done. Counter-terrorism police have already arrested the child and charged him with carrying out an act done in preparation for a terrorist act (allegedly buying a military-style knife) and membership of a terrorist organisation (which, under Australian anti-terrorism laws, can be him and his mates – see Dagistanli and Poynting, 2017). The police have given the story to the tabloid media. But the media have long demanded action of the police and the state more generally against this particular example of a folk devil. The boy had been targeted by the media (and the police) since his appearance, at twelve years old, in a demonstration carrying a 'radical' banner: 'Terror teen at the Hyde Park protests' (Banks, 2016: 3). He has since been panicked about for leading prayer groups at lunch time at his state high school and thus attempting to 'radicalise' his fellow students. Here we see demonstrated the triangular relationship between the media (with their identification of evils and demands for action), the police (with their use of the media to prosecute their case, to promote their worldview, to garner support and to secure further resources both material and legislative) and politicians vying for popular support through 'toughness' on terrorism and their scapegoating through 'plain speaking'. Accredited experts and moral entrepreneurs play their part in the cycle of amplifying deviance, largely via the media, in offering diagnoses, dire prognoses should nothing be done, and inevitably over-simplified solutions calling for strong state action. Burqas, protests, prayer groups and radicalisa-tion of young Muslims are all packaged up as elements of the problem. Heightened surveillance, draconian laws, criminalisation of protest and suspension of civil liberties are all part of the remedy (Hocking, 2004; Williams, 2011), and it is demonstratively observant and/or politically active (either can be designated as 'radical') Muslims who must be subjected to the cure (Dagistanli and Poynting, 2017; Sentas, 2014).

Sources

Given the contemporary nature of these events, our sources are largely from media reports and the like. If we are looking to sample Islamophobic common sense, then these are as good a place as any to find it. We do find some exemplary ideological elements in Hansard (the record of parliamentary proceedings in Australia), since the political populism of fear-mongering and 'the enemy within' is very much a part of the phenomenon. Some observations from recent court documents are also adduced here. Our case studies traverse individual events and systemic policies, practices and ideologies, as opportunistic convergence of all these factors serves to entrench Islamophobia in the Australian landscape.

Black flags

Abdul Numan Haider, an 18-year-old Australian from suburban Melbourne, had come to the attention of police. He had been reported displaying a black and white Islamic flag and arguing loudly in a shopping centre. He had railed online against the Australian spy organisation, the Australian Security Intelligence Organisation (ASIO), which had caused his Australian passport to be cancelled on suspicion of support for terrorism in Syria and an imputed desire to travel there. His family home had been raided by counter-terrorism police (with no arrest) under the same suspicions, and he had been harassed by intensive surveillance and police visits. His family had become concerned about his state of agitation, and had encouraged him to see a counsellor (Lillebuen, 2014). They did not want him to go out on the evening of 23 September 2014, when he met, as arranged, with two counter-terrorism police intent on 'warning' him about his confronting behaviour. He attacked both of them with a small knife, and one shot him dead. The counsellor would have been a far less lethal option, but might not have been necessary had it not been for the police hounding of this disturbed young man. (He had called them 'dogs' on Facebook, while posing provocatively with an 'Islamic State in Iraq and the Levant' (ISIL) banner – hardly the actions of a member of a terrorist cell involved in a clandestine plot.) As Islamic Council of Victoria secretary Ghaith Krayem pointed out, waving a flag and posting disparaging comments about Australian security agencies 'did not make a person a terrorist' (Houston et al., 2014).

Police admitted that Haider was 'acting on his own' (Noble et al., 2014), but under the circumstances the discovery of a terrorist plot would have been handy to them. Police sources briefed *The Age* that they feared Haider planned to decapitate the officers on orders from the Islamic State, drape their bodies in the ISIL flag and post pictures of them on the web (Silvester, 2014). There was never a scintilla of evidence for this wild speculation, though police had found a black flag and a larger knife in Numan Haider's bag. Lack of evidence did not prevent the media, security services, police and politicians from referring to the stabbing attack as an act of terrorism. The dead youth could not defend himself against the accusation.

Plastic swords

The wider circumstances, in pressing need of a terrorist plot, were the raids by Australian police and security agents – some 800 officers in all – on the homes of Australian Muslims in the state capital cities of Brisbane and Sydney, which took place five days before Haider was shot in the head. These were the biggest counter-terrorism raids in Australia's history: far larger than those highly mediated swoops in 2001 after 9/11, after the Bali bombing in 2002 (Poynting et al., 2004: 168–77), and after the London 7/7 bombings in 2005. In the similarly publicised and orchestrated anti-terror raids of 2014, there was but one terrorism charge proffered: against Omarjan Azari, who remained in jail a year later, yet to face trial, under maximum security conditions roundly criticised by a supreme court judge for the prisoner's inability to access lawyers effectively to prepare his defence (Hall, 2015). The original charge has been dropped: that of conspiracy to commit a terrorist act. He is now charged with 'doing acts in preparation to commit a terrorist act' under legislation that leaves great scope for prosecutions to construct a scenario with little and circumstantial evidence, since the future act allegedly prepared for need not be specific nor achieveable by the persons charged (Dagistanli and Poynting, 2017). The accusation is that someone connected with Azari was being prepared to cut the throat of a random stranger in a public place and – the same story – drape the body in the black ISIL flag and post a video of it on the Internet. One other man was charged in the raids for possessing an unlicensed firearm and ammunition; he pleaded guilty and was fined $500 and placed on a good behaviour bond: hardly terrorist material. Dozens of others subjected to the raids however – police and government would not say how many – were detained without charge in secrecy under anti-terrorism laws, pending investigation, and – failing charges – placed under control orders (see Williams, 2011 for a useful catalogue of this array of legislation).

Azari's lawyer later complained in court that the-then Prime Minister Tony Abbott had improperly interfered with his case by releasing misinformation about it (Hoerr, 2015). Abbott had publicly commented that all that was needed to commit a terrorist attack was 'a knife, and iPhone, and a victim' (Bourke, 2014). Abdul Numan Haider's knife attack on the two police officers, of course, was widely portrayed as fulfilment of this prophesy.

One man detained – and not charged – during the 18 September raids was Mustafa Dirani, a 21-year-old painter. During the raid on his parents' home in a Sydney suburb, a plastic 'sword of Ali' decoration was removed from the wall and confiscated by police. The media were told, amid hysteria about beheadings, that a sword had been found. Not only is this sword decoration commonplace in Shiite households, it is also unlikely to belong to a supporter of the Islamic State, given their implacable enmity with Shia Muslims – an obvious conclusion left undrawn in the fevered media reportage at the time.

Institutionalising hate speech

The next episode of anti-Muslim hysteria in Australia arose under the pretext of free speech, fortuitously made possible by events in faraway France in January 2015. We will show how in Australia, as elsewhere in the West, the 'Je suis Charlie' outpourings became a convenient vehicle for Islamophobic hatred.

Following the slaying of staff at the *Charlie Hebdo* office in Paris in January 2015, champions of 'free speech' made their voices freely heard, ranging from reasoned debates by civil libertarians on the 'absoluteness' of free speech to the opportunism of right-wing groups of different degrees of dangerousness. The assault on those associated with the iconic satirical magazine unleashed debates on freedom of the media and of artistic expression, with the diminishing of the voices of critics who opposed its production of material deliberately and gratuitously hurtful to Muslims. Madeleine Byrne, an Australian now resident in Paris, is perceptive. 'Some would argue,' she says, 'that *Charlie Hebdo* carries on a long tradition of anti-authoritarian jesting ..., but there was also something unpleasant about its obsessional targeting of Islam' (Byrne, 2015).

Backing free speech post-*Charlie* was less an Australian obsession and rather a minor rhetorical interest that insidiously manifested itself in some unpleasant vilification. In March 2014, the Attorney-General

George Brandis had defended his amendment to dilute the Racial Discrimination Act 1975, insisting in parliament that Australians had 'a right to be bigots' (Australian Senate Hansard, 24 March 2014 at 14:16). In October 2015, the notion of free speech at any price became strikingly apparent when Geert Wilders, the anti-immigration, anti-Muslim member of the Dutch parliament was granted a visa to visit Australia (see, for example, House of Representatives Hansard, 14 October 2015 at 13:29). The purpose of his visit was to launch the Australian Liberty Alliance (ALA), a political party premised on similar values to that of his own Party for Freedom. The somewhat middle-class ALA presents itself as slick, intelligent and thoughtful and would take umbrage at suggestions that it is racist and dangerous: yet its formation has served to institutionalise Islamophobia in the Australian political process. Its popularity was tested at the federal election of 2016 when, despite standing a significant number of candidates, it did not win one parliamentary seat. Nonetheless, it has been a haven for extremist groups from which the ALA professes to distance itself. These provocative anti-Muslim rally-holding organisations, such as Reclaim Australia, declaim (in a manner similar to the English Defence League, or PEGIDA in Germany) that 'we are losing our democratic freedom to speak openly and honestly, we're losing our voice and our NATIONAL character' (Reclaim Australia, 2015).

For all the professed openness and freedom, attending the Perth talk by Wilders in 2015 was nigh impossible as it was held exclusively for an inner circle in a secret location, somewhat ironically for a political party trying to garner electoral support. But attendance at a 2013 visit to Melbourne was revealing. Once the shrewd Wilders realised he had a sympathetic audience, his anti-Muslim fervour reached fever pitch. Particularly disturbing was his proclamation on the superiority of Western culture (Briskman, 2015). His inflammatory language about mosques and halal food ought have rung alarm bells, but rather than failing the visa 'character test' for his propensity to incite racial hatred, he was permitted to return for the 2015 ALA political party launch to further propagate and institutionalise anti-Muslim rhetoric.

The elevation to sacred proportions of the right to free speech has little regard for its impact on the unleashing of verbal and physical terror on Muslims by the repressive arm of the state, creating a climate whereby small knives and plastic swords can strike so much fear into the nation that there is benign acceptance of the strong and even deathly arm of the law.

The aptly named 'terror' swoops of 2014 were accompanied, as in 2001 and 2005, by a wave of hate crime vigilantism by right-thinking citizens, emboldened by the example of their state. In Australia, it was not only the unrestrained rhetoric of former Prime Minister Tony Abbott that caused further harm, but a relentlessly unhinged media. This included the broadsheet national newspaper of the Murdoch stable, *The Australian*, that, unlike the tabloids, prides itself on an educated readership. During 2015, it rolled out a season of polemics that it described as an 'unflinching series of articles analysing Muslim Australia' (The Australian, 2015), with 'unflinching' translating into opinion pieces virulently hostile to Islam and Muslims. Alongside this media frenzy, in order to sow fear of terrorism and to display animosity towards Muslims that could reap electoral advantage, ministers of government deployed their portfolios divisively in populist appeals. The first matter that Treasurer Joe Hockey mentioned in his 2015 budget speech was terrorism (Hockey, 2015). Foreign Minister Julie Bishop linked people-smuggling to terrorism (Wroe, 2015) and Kevin Andrews used his Defence portfolio to announce training of Iraqi troops to counter the terror threat that he claimed was 'reaching out to Australians'. Education Minister Christopher Pyne announced that education officials would work to stop schoolchildren from being 'radicalised' and Liberal Senator Cory Bernardi initiated an inquiry into halal certification, wildly alleging that under its guise funds were being directed to support terrorism (Latham and Briskman, 2015; see also Hussein, 2015a).

Prime Minister Abbott was particularly colourful in his selection of words, which until he was deposed in an inner-party coup in September 2015, regularly littered his populist inflammatory statements delivered while surrounding himself with a growing forest of Australian flags. 'Death Cult' (them) and 'Team Australia' (us) were among his favourites – the former 346 times in the seven months to May 2015 (House of Representatives Hansard, Tuesday, 16 June 2015: 23; Olding, 2015). If this was not enough, the public was confronted with statements such as 'they're coming after us' and a new 'dark age that is beyond us' (Tlozek, 2015). Abbott had the audacity to ask Muslims to declare Islam to be a religion of peace, and to 'mean it' (Seccombe, 2015). This simply implied that when Australian Muslims had continually espoused peace (since 2001 and before), they were not genuine. (Shakira Hussein's 2015b, 'The myth of the lying Muslim' is an instructive piece of ideology analysis on this theme within current Islamophobia.)

Asylum seekers as Muslim terrorists

Prior to the federal election of November 2001, then Defence Minister Peter Reith, in four separate interviews, drew a link between asylum seekers and terrorism (Henderson, 2002). Coming as it did just after the events of 9/11, this official response set the scene for rhetoric that continues to the present, with some fluctuation according to global events and local circumstances. Although he did not refer specifically to Muslims, there would have been no doubt in the minds of a nervous Australian public that the terms 'Muslim' and 'asylum seeker' were synonymous – and meant 'terrorist'. 9/11 allowed successive Australian governments to introduce increasingly harsh measures to deter and contain asylum seeker boat arrivals. It legitimised the government's military response to the 'Tampa affair' a few weeks earlier when a Norwegian cargo vessel had rescued 438 mainly Afghan asylum seekers from their foundering fishing boat, but was unlawfully interdicted and boarded by Special Air Service forces to prevent them from claiming asylum on Australian soil. The 'Pacific solution' of 'offshore' asylum seeker detention, beginning in debt-struck and beholden Nauru, was devised by the Australian government at that time (Poynting, 2002).

Reith's cynical utterances were possibly the most overt political linking of asylum seeking with terrorism, but since that time the joined-up expression, 'Middle Eastern Muslim asylum seeker' uncritically entered the Australian lexicon (Briskman and Mason, 2015). Ghassan Hage (2003: 67) speaks of how 9/11 'sealed the position of the Muslim as the unquestionable other in Australia'. A consequence has been to reduce refugees, whatever their background, religious affiliation or religiosity to a singular category (Poynting and Noble, 2004).

Harmful discourses emerged that preceded, and opened the door for, strident official reactions noted elsewhere in this chapter. Media campaigns commonly represent Middle Eastern immigrants and asylum seekers as 'abusing the hospitality of the host' (Levey and Moses, 2009); the politics of fear undermines social inclusion and moral panic triggers anxieties (Abu-Raya and White, 2010); and the question of 'values' frames fear with the view that if migrants are left to their own devices they will 'inflict' their backward cultures on the majority (Aly, 2011). In the intervening years, from 2001 until Paris in 2015 and Brussels in 2016, political discourse that marginalises Muslims has been insidious, media analysis increasingly rabid and community reaction progressively ignorant, fear-driven and hateful.

Islamophobia and resentment of asylum seekers are global in nature (Morgan and Poynting, 2012). Hyperbole increased during 2015 and 2016 when desperate people fled Syria in mounting numbers for the safety of the West. No matter that 3.2 million Syrian refugees had earlier fled into neighbouring countries and North Africa (UNHCR, 2014), or that Turkey currently has the highest numbers of refugees per capita of population of any nation, it was Western borders – and Western values – that were consistently portrayed as threatened. As barriers were erected, borders closed, detention centres put in place, turnbacks increased, tear gas used and policing intensified in a number of European countries, Australia could claim to have led the way. As with *Charlie Hebdo*, perceived 'threat' resonated in distant Australia, which under pressure from home and abroad agreed to take 12,000 Syrians with preference given to 'persecuted minorities': code for non-Muslim (Henderson and Borello, 2015), since Prime Minister Abbott had previously referred to the 'Christian minorities ... being persecuted in Syria' (Henderson and Uhlmann, 2015). The fact that one of the Paris attackers apparently carried a Syrian passport (later shown to be false[1]), and had travelled the refugee route, exacerbated rejection of the idea of Muslim Syrians, resulting in admonishment of Australia by the United Nations High Commissioner for Refugees (UNHCR) for its discriminatory approach (McNeill, 2015).

All the boxes

In the endless cycle of global Islamophobic moral panicking, each event builds on another, recirculating the ideological elements. One of the most telling instances in the Australian context is the case of Man Haron Monis, which conveniently for Islamophobes ticked all the boxes for the categories of Middle Eastern, refugee, Muslim and 'terrorist', as well as bearded 'hate preacher'.

On 15–16 December 2014, a lone gunman, former Iranian refugee and recent convert to Sunnism, Man Haron Monis, held hostage ten customers and eight employees of the Lindt chocolate cafe in Sydney. In what became widely referred to as an act of 'lone wolf terrorism', two hostages died: one at the hands of Monis, and one in police crossfire. Monis was shot dead by police. What is remarkable about this event is not that it happened (other mentally disturbed people, mainly non-Muslims, have notoriously committed serious and murderous acts in Australia[2]), but that the terrorist label was invoked, as in other incidents referred to earlier in this chapter. Prior to the siege, Monis, who had a firearm licence, faced serious charges in Australia including that of being an accessory to his wife's murder in April 2013 (for which his then girlfriend, Amirah Droudis, was convicted of murder in 2016) (Macmillan, 2016) and, in October 2014, to sexually abusing a large number of women in the guise of being a 'spiritual healer' (Ralston, 2014).

According to Iranian officials, Monis was a criminal who had fled Iran after the theft of a considerable amount of money from a travel business. Barely reported in Australia is that Iran had previously warned Australia about Monis's 'psychological conditions' (Schliebs and Taylor, 2014). His violent mood swings from that time, as recounted to an Australian journalist by a university contemporary of Monis, have been retold to the ongoing inquest. Certainly, he had been involuntarily admitted to hospital in Australia for psychiatric treatment, and had been diagnosed as schizophrenic and prescribed anti-psychotic drugs.

Three days before the Lindt cafe siege, Monis had lost a High Court appeal against the lawfulness of charges made in 2013 of 'using a postal or similar service to menace, harass or cause offence' arising from offensive letters that he had sent to families of Australian soldiers killed in Afghanistan (Monis & Droudis v The Queen [2014]). His former lawyer on that case, Manny Conditsis, offered the opinion that Monis was 'unhinged at some point prior to taking hostages', venturing: 'I'm convinced he walked into that cafe knowing he would not come out alive, whether at his own hand or the hand of police' (Feneley, 2014). That seems logical. A Daesh (ISIL) operative he was not, despite his declaration and his calling for their black flag to be brought to him at the cafe. Normally more than ready to claim 'credit' for a terrorist operation, Daesh made no attempt to own this atrocity. As the counsel assisting the inquest into the Lindt cafe deaths told the inquest, 'Mr Monis' claimed nexus with IS did not – it seems – exist' (Gormley and Callan, 2015: 43).

This did not stop Tony Abbott from citing the incident as a case in point regarding the need to temper civil liberties for the protection of the community. The gunman was a 'monster' who 'should not have been in our community'.

> The system has let us down because plainly this guy shouldn't have been in the country, he shouldn't have been out on bail, he shouldn't have had a gun and he shouldn't have been radicalised to the extent that he claimed to be conducting an Islamist death cult attack here in Australia. (Crane, 2015)

He was right about the gun. When Martin Bryant went on his murderous shooting rampage, then Prime Minister John Howard merely made the point about the gun. In Haron Monis's case, Tony Abbott had to bring refugees and death cults into it.

Counter-terrorism opportunism

By seizing upon the notion of terrorism, even though Australia's distance geographically, culturally and politically are protective factors, the Australian government has introduced a raft of measures (as mentioned above) promoted as protecting Australians from the Muslim terror 'threat'. The first of these, the post-9/11 anti-terror laws, are discussed below in the case of Zaky Mallah. More recent policies include limiting the granting of citizenship in some circumstances, incrementally adding to counter-terrorism laws and revoking passports of dual nationals believed to be involved with terrorist groups abroad – or even suspected of intending to join military conflict abroad (as in Syria), including those supported by Australia and its allies. One particular example of note was the targeting of Hajj pilgrims in 2015. On 25 August, the Department of Immigration and Border Protection issued special instructions to those making the pilgrimage, advising them to arrive early at the airport and warning that Australian Border Force officers 'may examine you and/or the items you are carrying'. Apparently oblivious to the irony, the Border Force issued a statement emphasising that individuals would never be stopped based 'simply on race, religion, ethnicity or travel destination' (Department of Immigration and Border Protection, 2015). In addition, immigration authorities publicly brag about how they have stopped more than 76,000 people for questioning since August 2014 (Xinhua, 2015). In what we can only speculate to be an attempt at fulfilling key performance indicators, one of the authors was interrogated in July 2015 before travelling to Iran for academic reasons. The Border Force personnel seemed to have little knowledge of the geopolitics of the Middle East and the author was perhaps fortunate to be a woman of a certain age and not of the dreaded 'Middle Eastern appearance'.

The Australian media displays of Islamophobic opportunism reinforce counter-terrorism measures. Following the mayhem in Paris in November 2015, banners appeared in the front-page headlines, adorned with the French flag and a procession of lead-ins to articles, which not only condemned the terrorist attacks but also rebuked Muslims and migrants. The broadsheet *The Australian* reproduced a *Wall Street Journal* article by notorious anti-Muslim crusader, Ayaan Hirsi Ali, in which she gave three pieces of unsolicited but unsurprising advice to European countries: to learn from the way Israel has responded to 'Islamic terrorism'; promote the superiority of 'liberal ideas'; and confine immigration to those who adopt 'European values' (Hirsi Ali, 2015).

In another example of media reaction over values and the national culture, schoolchildren who left a school assembly during the singing of the Australian national anthem were the butt of sensationalist reporting. Their exit was to comply with restrictions on singing during the Shia holy month of Muharrem. The principal of Cranbourne Carlisle Primary School in Melbourne incurred the ire of the tabloids for pandering to the Muslim Other and breaching the iron law of national bonding. Kevin Donnelly (2015), Tony Abbott's right-wing right-hand man with the national school curriculum, weighed in: 'Advance Australia Fair, is an essential part of Australian identity and should be compulsory.'

In another example of media 'leadership', the spiritual leader of Australian Muslims, the Grand Mufti, was criticised by commentators and politicians for his attempts to join the many voices which delve into the motives behind the lethal attacks in Paris. Explanations that he posited seemed eminently sensible: racism, Islamophobia, curtailing of freedoms through securitisation and foreign policies and military intervention. He condemned acts of terrorism (Owens, 2015) and clearly rebuked those who had murdered in Paris, but his words arguably fell into Abbott's category of not being genuine.

Government and media opportunism also converge with attacks, reported and unreported, on 'visible Muslims', notably women wearing the hijab and other religiously prescribed covering, in Australia and other countries. As noted by Zempi and Chakraborti in the UK (2015: 44), 'The wearing of the Muslim face covering ... has become increasingly vilified ... in the West. It is stereotypically seen as a "threat" to notions of national cohesion and public safety'. In an act of gross absurdity, five police officers swooped on an outdoor photo shoot in Sydney during a hijab fashion event, mistakenly identifying the clothing as 'Islamic flags' (Khalik, 2015).

Halal certification has also been elevated to a terrorism threat, through a well-orchestrated scare campaign. The fees charged in the certification process have been alleged (without evidence) to be used to fund terrorism, as well as obliging unwitting Christians to ingest 'the Muslim Other' (Hussein, 2015a). This campaign has been a major activity of the anti-Muslim Q Society, which metamorphosed into the ALA. Some social media associated with the campaign alleged that the Lindt cafe was chosen as a terrorism target because of Lindt Chocolates' ostentatious refusal of halal certification (Hussein, 2015a)!

The question remains as to who is constructed as terrorist. Certainly not the Hoddle Street murderer, the Port Arthur killer or Norwegian mass assassin Anders Breivik. The November 2015 conviction and imprisonment for a mere month and $5,000 fine for a member of the far-right Muslim hate group, Reclaim Australia, is illuminating. He had in his possession in his Melbourne home, five tasers and a quantity of mercury. The sentencing magistrate formed the view that he had possessed tasers for the purpose of 'an aggressive attack on others in the community with whom you have a disagreement'. Unlike reports on even alleged or suspected Muslim terrorism, the news item was granted minimal space on page 16 of *The Age* newspaper (Cooper, 2015).

How it all started: Australia's first War on Terror

As mentioned above, the Australian state passed draconian anti-terror laws in the immediate aftermath of 9/11. These have been added to ever since: a very good run-down is provided by George Williams (2011) who catalogues that between September 2001 and September 2011, the Australian parliament passed 54 distinct pieces of anti-terror legislation.

In 2003, Sydney Lebanese-background teenager Zaky Mallah became the first person to be charged under Australia's new anti-terrorism laws. His case illuminates the longevity of the climate of fear and moral panics. He spent two years in maximum security prison, but when finally tried in 2005, was acquitted of the terrorism charges.

Like Numan Haider, the 19-year-old Mallah had been denied an Australian passport on security grounds when he wanted to travel abroad. As with Haider, this had compounded mental turmoil that the young man was suffering. His mother had died when he was thirteen. A lonely young man, Mallah had wished to travel to Lebanon to be married. The denial of the travel document wrecked his plans. He placed silly, posturing menaces online, and threatened to kill a federal police officer by phone whom he blamed for his predicament. If his intention to do so had been real, this would hardly have helped him to achieve his goal. In the light of Numan Haider's fate, the now 31 year old can be thankful he is still alive, though he has little to be grateful for about the two years he spent in prison on remand.

Mallah should never have been charged with terrorism offences; the fact that he was so charged demonstrated how keen federal police and security services were to crow that they had caught a terrorist and to obtain a scalp under their new laws. Mallah had originally been sent for trial on only one charge of preparing a terrorist act, to wit selling a videotape supposedly to be played in the event of his death in an act of martyrdom. The Director of Public Prosecutions submitted a further charge before the trial, namely threatening to cause serious harm to an undercover federal police officer who entrapped him, while posing as a journalist, into boasting that he would take hostages at ASIO headquarters. That charge was proven, and Mallah was sentenced to two and a half years in jail.

The trial judge, Justice Wood, found that Mallah was:

an idiosyncratic, and embittered young man, who was to all intents something of a loner, without significant prospects of advancing himself. While I accept that the Prisoner enjoyed posing as a potential martyr, and may from time to time, in his own imagination, have contemplated creating a siege and taking the lives of others, I am satisfied that in his more rational moments he lacked any genuine intention of doing so. (R v Mallah [2005] NSWSC 317)

The case, buried from public consciousness after the terrorism acquittal, was to be reprised twice in the events of 2014 and 2015. In 2011, Mallah had travelled to Syria to support the Free Syrian Army in its struggle against Bashar Assad. This would not be possible today. He posted video of his sojourn there, claimed that his efforts were peaceful and not of a military nature, and declared his implacable opposition for ISIS (Islamic State in Iraq and Syria – another translation of ISIL). Ironically, during the Lindt cafe siege when Monis was demanding an ISIS flag, ASIO (with whom Mallah now claims good relations) asked him to lend them one – something they should have known was rather unlikely.

Secondly, there was something of a moral panic when Zaky Mallah appeared on the Australian Broadcasting Commission's (ABC's) Q&A programme in June 2015 (Meade, 2015). He asked a pre-approved question on air of the conservative Liberal Party MP Steve Ciobo: 'As the first man in Australia to be charged with terrorism under the harsh Liberal Howard government in 2003 … what would have happened if my case had been decided by the minister himself and not the courts?' When Ciobo replied that he'd be happy if Mallah were out of the country, Mallah replied: 'The Liberals have just justified to many Australian Muslims in the community tonight to leave and go to Syria and join ISIL because of ministers like him' (Griffiths, 2015). The compere panicked and distanced Q&A from the remark, and with good reason, since the ABC came under savage ideological attack in the wake of the programme (Meade, 2015). Prime Minster Abbott predictably complained, 'What our national broadcaster has done is give a platform to a convicted criminal and terrorist sympathiser' (Griffiths, 2015).

Countering Islamophobia in Australia

Academic research and broader social movements have by and large been relatively absent in challenging Islamophobia. There has been some academic research literature that examines ways to counter Islamic extremism, for example, Aly (2014). There has been little popular challenge to anti-terrorism measures or policing practices and the construction of moral panic has arguably allowed official Islamophobia to take hold.

Although anti-racist groups exist in Australia they have not been as strong as in the UK, for example, where Hope Not Hate has garnered massive support. Sometimes they can be spontaneous and short-lived, such as the 'I'll ride with you' hashtag that followed the Martin Place siege described above, to offer safe companionship to Muslim women commuters. Muslim organisations express concern at the rising tide of Islamophobia but their voices are largely invisible in the public domain. An Islamophobia register initiated by lawyer and community activist Mariam Veiszadeh has attracted some media attention and sympathy (Islamophobia Register Australia, n.d.; Price, 2016), but its operation is small-scale and perilously under-resourced (Feldman and Littler, 2014). Campaigning, then, remains predominantly the domain of government which has financial and propaganda resources so powerful that contestation by civil society does not effectively compete. Furthermore, disproportionate media attention is given to right-wing groups as they conduct their visible campaigns such as protesting the building of mosques (Dunn, 2005). The formation of such groups as Reclaim Australia has helped push expressions of Islamophobia from the political margins to a central position (Akbarzadeh, 2016).

Governments perpetuate fear and loathing under the guise of community safety. The terror threat in Australia is now designated as 'probable', with the presumed Islamic terror threat prompting this assessment. Also aligned to a discourse of community safety, the general public experiences government campaigning that becomes normalised in everyday existence. After the 9/11 attacks in the US, all Australian households received fridge magnets from the government that said, 'be alert, not alarmed'. More recently in 2014, insidious signs around railway stations in Melbourne stated: 'If you see something, say something' (Briskman, 2015). The 15-year-old 'War on Terror' thus continues in Australia, a war that is without justifiable cause and without apparent end.

Conclusion

In this chapter we have argued that Islamophobia has become increasingly integral to the Australian political landscape, with local and global factors – ideologies and policies – enabling this to occur. Pessimistically, it seems that the series of Islamophobic moral panics exemplified by the case studies has no end in sight. Although the replacement of Prime Minister Abbott with the less aggressively conservative Malcolm Turnbull in 2015 appeared to signal reform, little has changed on the ground. After the

March 2016 attacks at the airport and metro station in Brussels, Turnbull had the audacity to proclaim that Europe (unlike Australia) was weak on security (Sandhu, 2016). His comments are an indication that War on Terror-footing national security and policing will not diminish 'downunder'. Although Turnbull has built some bridges with Muslim communities, discriminatory policing appears unstoppable, the media remain unhinged and right-wing extremist groups continue to parade their Islamophobic wares, including, for example, the 2016 display of anti-Mosque banners during matches of the nation's iconic Australian Rules Football (Nicholson, 2016).

Terror attacks create fear and ignite hatred, especially after an assault on Western soil. We conclude that it is not merely questionable as to who is deemed a terrorist but also whose lives matter. In both imagination of what Muslim 'folk devils' are planning and through solidarity with those affected by actual events, usually far away from Australia, there is an interplay. The clash of civilisations paradigm extends to empathy and worthiness. Faisal Kutty (2016: 6) describes the deafening silence over terror attacks in the Ivory Coast, Turkey, Pakistan, Nigeria, Syria and Egypt. With 'people like us' from France, Belgium or other 'civilised' countries being indiscriminately targeted, selective compassion emerges. In the Australian context, those deemed sympathetic to terrorists or 'radicalised' are collectively punished through unsubstantiated claims, with the populace convinced by government rhetoric that excessive security has saved Australian lives: those lives that matter. And the cycle then continues with irrational imputation that we are increasingly at risk. With the terror alert level in Australia hovering at 'probable', it becomes an undisputed truth that Australians are in imminent danger.

It is our view that until we confront Australian racism that has beset this country from the time of European invasion, little more than 200 years ago, we will continue to target, stereotype and blame in the interest of holding on to white privilege and appease those with hatred in their hearts, often for electoral favour. With attacks on Muslims from multiple directions – politics, media and those charged with implementing the law – we are indeed in danger of creating a disenfranchised category of Australians, as we have done before with Indigenous peoples and different waves of migrants and refugees. Now those at risk of rhetorical and political exclusion are mainly young Muslims, who may react in a variety of ways to hostility and hatred, including in ways most feared.

This unnecessary cycle, we posit, can be halted and reversed through rational policies, fair media reporting and a wider community educated about Islam and Muslim lives. We need a discourse of goodwill and trust towards Muslims, and appreciation of the gifts they offer to our societies rather than allegations of threat and clashes of values.

On a global scale, Islamophobia is entrenched, institutionalised and now apparently acceptable in the mainstream. No matter how much governments proclaim that it is only a minority of Muslims that create terror problems, their actions speak louder than words as we have suggested above. If such aggressive tactics were targeted at other minority religions, it is likely that there would be zero tolerance for this. The fact that Islamophobia is now a globalised phenomenon in the West reassures Islamophobic governments that they are acting in unity with their kindred allies. Nowhere is this clearer than in the case of remote and marginally significant Australia, which adopts 'me too' policies to align itself with the centre of world politics, rather than being independent but isolated on the periphery.

Regrettably few and small are the 'people movements' challenging the hegemony of Islamophobic discourses, which might provide a counter-voice to dominant anti-terrorism narratives, revealing the power of the security discourse and the silencing of those daring to oppose this. This allows political leaders in Western countries to present their counter-terrorist responses as logical and rational, rather than populist and harmful.

Note

1. www.bbc.com/news/world-europe-34832512.
2. For example, the Melbourne 'Hoddle Street Massacre' of 1987 where assailant Julian Knight gunned to death seven people in their vehicles and the 'Port Arthur Massacre' of 1996 in Tasmania, where Martin Bryant shot dead 35 men, women and children at a popular historical tourist venue.

Bibliography

Abu-Raya, H. and White, F. (2010), 'Acculturation orientations and religious identity as predictors of Anglo-Australian attitudes towards Australian Muslims', *International Journal of Intercultural Relations*, 34, 592–9.

Akbarzadeh, S. (2016), 'The Muslim question in Australia: Islamophobia and Muslim alienation', *Journal of Muslim Minority Affairs*, doi: 10.1080/13602004.2016.1212493.

Aly, A. (2014), 'Walk away from violent extremism: a campaign to address violent extremism online', *Journal Exit-Deutschland: Zeitschrift fuer Deradikalisierung und demokratische Kultur*, 3, 64–77.

Aly, W. (2011), 'Monoculturalism, Muslims and myth making', in R. Gaita (ed.), *Essays on Muslims and Multiculturalism*. Melbourne: The Text Publishing Company, pp. 47–92.

Banks, L. (2016), 'Teen jihadi's Hyde Park hate', *Daily Telegraph*, 14 October, 2–3.

Bourke, L. (2014), 'Terror raids: attack feared within days, Tony Abbott says', *Sydney Morning Herald*, 19 September. www.smh.com.au/federal-politics/political-news/terror-raids-attack-feared-within-days-tony-abbott-says-20140918-10j337.html. Accessed 22 April 2016.

Briskman, L. (2015), 'The creeping blight of Islamophobia in Australia', *International Journal for Crime, Justice and Social Democracy*, 4 (3), doi: 10.5204/ijcjsd.v3i2.244.

Briskman, L. and Mason, G. (2015), 'Abrogating human rights responsibilities: Australia's asylum seeker policy at home and abroad', in M. Clark and J. Pietsch (eds), *Migration Flows and Regional Integration in Europe, South East Asia and Australia*. Amsterdam: Amsterdam University Press, pp. 137–59.

Byrne, M. (2015), 'Jesting verged on obsession', *The Age*, 10 January. www.theage.com.au/comment/jesting-verged-on-obsession-20150109-12lone.html. Accessed 26 April 2016.

Cohen, S. (2002), *Folk Devils and Moral Panics*, 3rd edn. London and New York: Routledge.

Cooper, A. (2015), 'Prison for Reclaim man', *The Age*, 21 November, 16.

Crane, E. (2015), 'This monster should not have been on our streets', *Daily Mail Australia*, 22 February. www.dailymail.co.uk/news/article-2963436/I-wanted-talk-Monis-police-said-make-things-worse-Tony-Abbott-reveals-ready-talk-siege-monster-report-cafe-terror-attack-released.html#ixzz3sZQ5a031. Accessed 28 April 2016.

Dagistanli, S. and Poynting, S. (2017, forthcoming), 'Terrorism and anti-terrorism laws in Australia', in A. Deckert and R. Sarre (eds), *The Australian and New Zealand Handbook of Criminology, Crime and Justice*. Basingstoke: Palgrave Macmillan.

Deen, H. (2011), *Ali Abdul v The King: Muslim Stories from the Dark Days of White Australia*. Crawley: UWA Publishing.

Department of Immigration and Border Protection (2015), 'Border clearance advice – Hajj pilgrims'. www.border.gov.au/News/Pages/border-clearance-advice-hajj-pilgrims. (No longer available at this site on 25 August 2015. Copy in possession of the authors.)

Donnelly, K. (2015), 'Singing the national anthem at schools should be compulsory', *The Age*, 28 October. www.theage.com.au/comment/tolerance-of-diversity-cannot-exist-without-common-values-20151026-gkja8z.html. Accessed 28 April 2016.

Dunn, K.M. (2005), 'Repetitive and troubling discourses of nationalism in the local politics of mosque development', *Environmental Planning: Society and Space*, 23 (1), February, 29–50.

Feldman, M. and Littler, M. (2014), *Tell MAMA Reporting 2013/14 Anti-Muslim Overview, Analysis and 'Cumulative Extremism'*. Centre for Fascist, Anti-fascist and post-fascist Studies, Teeside University, July.

Feneley, R. (2014), 'Sydney siege: Man Haron Monis, "humanitarian" and terrorist"', *Sydney Morning Herald*, 20 December. www.smh.com.au/nsw/sydney-siege-man-haron-monis-humanitarian-and-terrorist-20141219-12ajn5.html. Accessed 28 April 2016.

Gormley, J. and Callan, S. (2015), Opening Address for Second Segment. Counsel Assisting's Opening Remarks made on 17 August 2015. Inquest into the deaths arising from the Lindt cafe siege. www.lindtinquest.justice.nsw.gov.au/Pages/documents.aspx. Accessed 28 April 2016.

Griffiths, E. (2015), 'Q&A: PM Tony Abbott labels program a "lefty lynch mob" as ABC admits error in judgement over former terrorism suspect Zaky Mallah's appearance', ABC News, 24 July. www.abc.net.au/news/2015-06-23/abc-to-review-acquitted-former-terror-suspect-qa-appearance/6565886. Accessed 28 April 2016.

Hage, G. (2003), *Against Paranoid Nationalism*. Sydney: Pluto Press.

Hall, L. (2015), 'Judge questions why terrorism accused Omarjan Azari is on remand in Supermax', *Sydney Morning Herald*, 20 August. www.smh.com.au/nsw/judge-questions-why-terrorism-accused-omarjan-azari-is-on-remand-in-supermax-20150820-gj3g03. Accessed 22 April 2016.

Henderson, A. and Borello, E. (2015), 'Australia confirms air strikes in Syria, announces 12,000 additional refugee places', ABC News, 9 September. www.abc.net.au/news/2015-09-09/australia-to-accept-additional-12,000-syrian-refugees/6760386. Accessed 27 April 2016.

Henderson, A. and Uhlmann, C. (2015), 'Syrian migrant crisis: Christians to get priority as Abbott faces pressure to take in more refugees', ABC News, 8 September. www.abc.net.au/news/2015-09-08/christians-to-get-priority-in-syrian-refugee-intake/6757110. Accessed 27 April 2016.

Henderson, G. (2002), 'Terrorists don't come via detention centres', *The Age*, 19 November. www.theage.com.au/articles/2002/11/18/1037599359073.html. Accessed 27 April 2016.

Hirsi Ali, A. (2015), 'Why Islam needs a reformation', *The Australian*, 21 March. www.theaustralian.com.au/opinion/why-islam-needs-a-reformation/news-story/8fe4eb9dc1d7d90428b48ff5fc7a18bb. Accessed 28 April 2016.

Hocking, Jenny (2004), *Terror Laws: ASIO, Counter-Terrorism and the Threat to Democracy*. Sydney: UNSW Press.

Hockey, J.B. (2015), Budget Speech 2015. 12 May. www.budget.gov.au/2015-16/content/speech/html/speech.htm. Accessed 26 April 2016.

Hoerr, K. (2015), 'Tony Abbott released information about case against terrorist suspect Omarjan Azari, court told', ABC News, 24 February. www.abc.net.au/news/2015-02-24/tony-abbott-accused-misinformation-omarjan-azari-terror-case/6249890. Accessed 22 April 2016.

Houston, C., Mills, T., Silvester, J. and Wroe, D. (2014), 'Terror suspect Numan Haider: heightened alert before grand final weekend', The Age, 24 September. www.theage.com.au/victoria/terror-suspect-numan-haider-heightened-alert-before-afl-grand-final-weekend-20140924-10lk5b.html. Accessed 22 April 2016.

Huntington, S. (1993), 'The clash of civilizations?', Foreign Affairs, Summer, 72 (3), 22–49.

Hussein, S. (2015a), 'Not eating the Muslim Other: halal certification, scaremongering, and the racialisation of Muslim identity', International Journal for Crime, Justice and Social Democracy, 4 (3), 85–96.

—— (2015b), 'The myth of the lying Muslim: "taqiyya" and the racialization of Muslim identity', Religion and Ethics, 28 May. www.abc.net.au/religion/articles/2015/05/28/4244447.htm. Accessed 26 March 2017.

Hutchinson, F. and Myers, F. (1885), The Australian Contingent: A History of the Patriotic Movement in New South Wales and an Account of the Despatch of Troops to the Assistance of the Imperial Forces in the Soudan, Sydney: Thomas Richards, Government Printer.

Islamophobia Register Australia (n.d.), www.islamophobia.com.au/. Accessed 28 November 2016.

Kabir, N.A. (2004), Muslims in Australia: Immigration, Race Relations and Cultural History. London, New York and Bahrain: Kegan Paul.

Khalik, J. (2015), 'Police swoop as hijab fashion shoot flags trouble', The Australian, 2 November. www.theaustralian.com.au/in-depth/community-under-siege/police-swoop-as-hijab-fashion-shoot-flags-trouble/news-story/d6b3eb7df2bd50170ace108a0e53401d. Accessed 28 April 2016.

Kutty, F. (2016), 'Do western lives matter more?', Jakarta Post, 9 April, 6.

Latham, S. and Briskman, L. (2015), 'Anti-Muslim sentiment reaches fever pitch as ministers channel their inner Howard', Crikey, 10 June. www.crikey.com.au/2015/06/03/anti-muslim-sentiment-reaches-fever-pitch-as-ministers-channel-their-inner-howard/. Accessed 27 April 2016.

Lean, N. (2012), The Islamophobia Industry: How the Right Manufactures Fear of Muslims. London: Pluto Press.

Levey, G.B. and Moses, A.D. (2009), 'The Muslims are our misfortune', in G. Noble (ed.), Lines in the Sand: The Cronulla Riots, Multiculturalism and National Belonging. Sydney: The Institute of Criminology Series 28, pp. 95–109.

Lewis, B. (1990), 'The roots of Muslim rage', Atlantic Monthly, September, 47–60.

Lillebuen, S. (2014), 'Numan Haider: from teenager to terror suspect', Dominion Post, 25 September. http://i.stuff.co.nz/world/australia/61484985/numan-haider-from-teenager-to-terror-suspect. Accessed 22 April 2016.

Macmillan, J. (2016), 'Amira Droudis found guilty of murdering ex-wife of Man Haron Monis', ABC News, 3 November. www.abc.net.au/news/2016-11-03/amirah-droudis-guilty-murder-man-haron-monis-wife-2013/7991620. Accessed 22 November 2016.

McNeill, S. (2015), 'Government set to focus Syrian refugee program on Christians in wake of Paris attacks: Scott Morrison', ABC News, 18 November. www.abc.net.au/news/2015-11-18/morrison-expects-christians-to-be-focus-of-refugee-program/6952854. Accessed 27 April 2016.

Meade, A. (2015), 'How Zaky Mallah ended up on live TV: Q&A producers took a calculated risk', Guardian, 23 June. www.theguardian.com/australia-news/2015/jun/23/how-zaky-mallah-ended-up-on-live-tv-qa-producers-took-a-calculated-risk. Accessed 28 April 2016.

Meiksins Wood, E. (2003), Empire of Capital. London: Verso.

Monis & Droudis v The Queen [2014] HCATrans 280.

Morgan, G. and Poynting, S. (eds) (2012), Global Islamophobia: Muslims and Moral Panic in the West. Farnham: Ashgate.

Nicholson, L. (2016), 'Anti-Muslim banner: AFL disappointed names not taken', The Age, 2 April. www.theage.com.au/afl/afl-news/antimuslim-banner-afl-disappointed-names-not-taken-20160402-gnwy16.html. Accessed 28 April 2016.

Noble, F., Lee, S., Piotrowski, P., Cheer, L. and AAP (2014), 'Was he a lone wolf?', Mail Online, 23 September. www.dailymail.co.uk/news/article-2766539/BREAKING-Man-shot-dead-counter-terrorism-police-making-threats-against-Tony-Abbott.html . Accessed 22 April 2016.

Olding, R. (2015), 'Counter-terrorism adviser: Abbott's "death cult" label is counter-productive', Sydney Morning Herald, 12 May. www.smh.com.au/federal-politics/political-news/counterterrorism-adviser-abbotts-is-death-cult-label-is-counterproductive-20150510-ggyl4i.html. Accessed 27 April 2016.

Owens, J. (2015), 'Paris attacks: Grand Mufti must condemn Paris killings, say Libs', The Australian, 18 November. www.theaustralian.com.au/in-depth/paris-terror-attacks/paris-attacks-grand-mufti-must-condemn-paris-killings-say-libs/news-story/0193672f84f5f5b40deedec4884bfaed. Accessed 28 April 2016.

Poynting, S. (2002), '"Bin Laden in the suburbs": attacks on Arab and Muslim Australians before and after 11 September', Current Issues in Criminal Justice, 14 (1), July, 43–64.

Poynting, S. and Noble, G. (2004), Living with Racism: The Experience and Reporting by Arab and Muslim Australians of Discrimination, Abuse and Violence since 11 September 2001. Sydney: Human Rights and Equal Opportunities Commission.

Poynting, S., Noble, G., Tabar, P. and Collins, J. (2004), Bin Laden in the Suburbs: Criminalising the Arab Other. Sydney: Institute of Criminology.

Price, J. (2016), 'How Muslim Australians are being terrorised every single day', Sydney Morning Herald, 17 August. www.smh.com.au/lifestyle/

news-and-views/opinion/how-muslim-australians-are-being-terrorised-every-single-day-20160721-gqax4w.html. Accessed 28 November 2016.

R v Mallah [2005] NSWSC 317.

Ralston, N. (2014), '"Spiritual healer" Man Haron Monis charged with an extra 40 sexual offences', *Sydney Morning Herald*, 13 October. www.smh.com.au/nsw/spiritual-healer-man-haron-monis-charged-with-an-extra-40-sexual-offences-20141013-115epb.html. Accessed 27 April 2016.

Reclaim Australia (2015), www.reclaim-australia.com/. No longer available online (apparently hacked) but cited at http://mamcrae-author.blogspot.com.au/2015/07/reclaim-australia-is-not-racist.html. Accessed 26 April 2016.

Sandhu, S. (2016), 'Australian Prime Minister Malcolm Turnbull says "weakness in European security" to blame for Brussels attacks', *Independent*, 23 March. www.independent.co.uk/news/world/australasia/australian-prime-minister-malcolm-turnbull-says-weakness-in-european-security-to-blame-for-brussels-a6947821.html. Accessed 28 April 2016.

Schliebs, M. and Taylor, P. (2014), 'Sydney siege: Iran claims it warned about mad Man Haron Monis', *The Australian*, 18 December. www.theaustralian.com.au/in-depth/sydney-siege-iran-claims-it-warned-about-mad-man-haron-monis/story-fnqxbywy-1227159953719. Accessed 27 April 2016.

Seccombe, M. (2015), 'Farhad Jabbar shooting sees a change in the failed language of terror', *The Saturday Paper*, 10 October. www.thesaturdaypaper.com.au/news/politics/2015/10/10/farhad-jabar-shooting-sees-change-the-failed-language-terror/14443956002485. Accessed 27 April 2016.

Sentas, V. (2014), *Traces of Terror: Counter-Terrorism Law, Policing and Race*. Oxford: Oxford University Press.

Silvester, J. (2014), 'Melbourne terror shooting: Numan Haider "planned to behead Victoria Police officers, drape bodies in IS flag"', *The Age*, 24 September. www.theage.com.au/victoria/melbourne-terror-shooting-numan-haider-planned-to-behead-victoria-police-officers-drape-bodies-in-is-flag-20140924-10lb4i.html. Accessed 22 April 2016.

Tlozek, E. (2015), 'Tony Abbott says Islamic State "coming after us" after spate of terror attacks overseas', ABC News, 27 June. www.abc.net.au/news/2015-06-27/abbott-condemns-spate-of-terror-attacks/6577786. Accessed 27 April 2016.

The Australian (2015), 'Reflections on a Muslim community under siege' (editorial), 23 May. www.theaustralian.com.au/opinion/editorials/reflections-on-a-muslim-community-under-siege/news-story/d5b71920f459ee5ecd73bbba3d3ae004. Accessed 22 April 2016.

UNHCR (2014), *Syrian Refugees: Inter-Agency Regional Update*, 4 November. United Nations High Commissioner for Refugees.

Williams, G. (2011), 'A decade of Australian anti-terror laws', *Melbourne University Law Review*, 35, 1136–76.

Wroe, D. (2015), 'Julie Bishop: smashing people smuggling the priority due to terrorism links', *Sydney Morning Herald*, 23 May. www.smh.com.au/

federal-politics/political-news/julie-bishop-smashing-people-smuggling-the-priority-due-to-terrorism-links-20150522-gh7oez.html. Accessed 27 April 2016.

Xinhua, (2015), 'Aussie counter-terror agents question 400 travellers each day at airports', 16 March. http://news.xinhuanet.com/english/2015-03/16/c_134070419.htm. Accessed 28 April 2016.

Zempi, I. and Chakraborti, N. (2015), 'They make us feel like we're a virus: the multiple impacts of Islamophobic hostility towards veiled Muslim women', *International Journal for Crime, Justice and Social Democracy*, 4 (3), 44–56.

8

Islamophobia, Counter-extremism and the Counterjihad Movement

Hilary Aked

Though there is little evidence that the War on Terror has been effective in achieving its stated goals, counter-terrorism policies have legitimised Islamophobia and institutionalised discrimination. In the process, this chapter argues, counter-extremism policies in particular have helped to foster the 'counterjihad' movement, a section of the far right distinguished by its hostility to migrants, Muslims and Islam. The chapter begins by situating the counterjihad movement within the changing face of the far right. It explains the flaws in research that fails to do so, and why studies which deal with counterjihadists as if in a vacuum – ignoring the state's central role in Islamophobia – are both analytically and politically inadequate. The claim that counter-extremism policies merely need to be applied more consistently, so as not to neglect the far right, is then challenged. It is argued that there is in fact a symbiotic relationship between Islamophobic counter-extremism policies and the Islamophobic far right, which reveals in-built biases in counter-extremism frameworks.

Detailed analysis of the under-researched interactions between counter-jihadist and counter-extremism actors shows that not only are certain far-right ideas being 'mainstreamed', but liberal counter-extremism rhetoric used by state actors is also being appropriated by counterjihad actors. At times, the two currents overlap considerably or work in synergy, as the chapter illustrates with examples from the UK, and to a lesser extent Germany, France, the US and elsewhere. It highlights examples of counterjihadists presenting themselves as counter-extremism bodies and points to the close links between a number of officially recognised counter-extremist groups and the Islamophobic far right. It is argued that counterjihad actors are able to present themselves as centrist or 'moderate' only in relation to an enemy dubbed 'Islamofascism', a term which obfuscates the far right's own fascistic politics but can be accommodated by ahistorical counter-extremism frameworks. Finally, the chapter draws attention to elite support for the counterjihad movement in several countries, which allows it to work through and with state power, contributing to the continued dangerous growth of Islamophobia and the rightward shift of the political mainstream.

Situating the counterjihad movement:
the changing face of the far right

As older biological forms of racism have increasingly been superseded by essentialist conceptions of culture, sections of the far right have been transformed. Some analysts have begun to speak of 'two fascisms' in contemporary politics: one traditional faction committed to anti-Semitism, and another, newer, bloc – nurtured by the War on Terror – focused on Islamophobia (Fleischer, 2014). Despite the similarities between these two ideologies, while the anti-Semitism of the old far right is widely understood as racism, the Islamophobia of the emerging counterjihad movement is less commonly recognised as such. A number of scholars have invested time in explaining how processes of racialisa-tion work (Meer, 2013; Sayyid and Vakil, 2011). Attention also needs to be paid to the specific actors at the vanguard of this new front, and their interactions with the most powerful actor in the field, the state.

The counterjihad movement, a strand of the far right which has developed in the last decade in numerous Western countries, particularly the US and Northern Europe, ostentatiously disavows racism, as it is conventionally understood. Indeed, the emergence and popularity of new movements like PEGIDA (Patriotische Europäer Gegen die Isla-misierung des Abendlandes, Patriotic Europeans Against Islamisation of the West), in Germany and beyond, has rested on their lack of obvious neo-Nazi associations. Counterjihad actors claim that their support for Israel differentiates them from the 'real' (old) far right and demonstrates their abhorrence of anti-Semitism (Shroufi, 2015). In its place, however, vehement Islamophobia is twinned with virulent anti-immigration sentiment, a combination best illustrated by the movement's preoccupation with a perceived process of 'Islamisation', a myth popularised by counterjihad author Bat Ye'or (Carr, 2006).

After Anders Behring Breivik committed mass murder in Norway, on 22 July 2011, there was an upsurge of interest in the counterjihad ideology to which his 'manifesto' showed he was deeply committed (Fekete, 2011). While the attention paid to this previously overlooked current is welcome, much existing scholarship suffers from conceptual weaknesses. Some otherwise useful analyses such as Bangstad (2014) remain focused on discourse, at the expense of examining concrete practices. More problematically, research that situates the movement within the broader study of 'radicalisation' and 'extremism' tends to misrepresent the nature of the problem and downplay its severity. The International Centre for the Study of Radicalisation (ICSR), for example, fails to even use the word 'Islamophobia' in its 72-page report on the counterjihad movement. It rejects the racialisation literature (discussed elsewhere in this book), claiming that while an essentialist view of Islam 'can lead to' cultural racism, 'terms such as racist ... should generally be avoided' (Meleagrou-Hitchens and Brun, 2013: 39). ICSR also takes pains to uphold some of the counterjihad movement's key ideas, saying that 'national pride ... does not always have to translate into far right fascism' and adding that there are 'genuine concerns about Islamic extremism' and 'Saudi-Wahabi control of European mosques' (Meleagrou-Hitchens and Brun, 2013: 55). As a UK-based research institute that has received Home Office funding it is perhaps unsurprising that ICSR would support counterjihad ideas where they echo government counter-extremism priorities. This chapter begins from the premise that we need to explore and unpack these overlaps.

When the ICSR laments that 'it becomes awkward to categorise a group positioning itself in defence of liberal enlightenment values as far right' (Meleagrou-Hitchens and Brun, 2013: 1), it reveals a fundamental failure to grasp the changing face of far-right politics. The actors who self-identify as constituting the counterjihad movement do indeed claim to be defending 'liberal' values. For instance, Bürgerbewegung Pax Europa, a German counterjihad pressure group founded in 2008 which describes itself as a 'human rights organisation', says it opposes ideologies that pose a threat to 'liberal democratic societies'. Such appeals to the macro-nationalist politics of 'enlightenment' – or, more often, 'Western values' (as in the blog Western Resistance or the International Centre for

Western Values in the Netherlands) – are in part a means to overcome the parochial nature of the nationalist politics with which counterjihad activism remains strongly associated. This enables transnational collaboration and replication; examples of counterjihad movements which have spawned copycats traversing state boundaries include Stop the Islamisation of Denmark, the English Defence League (EDL) and most recently PEGIDA. Yet, it is also consistent with the exclusionary and racist politics of the broader far right today. Islamophobia increasingly provides common ground for deepening the unity and solidarity of European far-right political parties (Hafez, 2014: 479), just as it serves as a vehicle for linking largely decentralised counterjihad networks. Despite professed liberalism, the counterjihad movement should in fact be situated within the far right, which itself occurs against a backdrop of economic crisis, declining trust in mainstream political parties and increasing hostility to multiculturalism.

The organised Islamophobia of the far right, however, operates within a still wider spectrum. State racism – in particular, discriminatory rhetoric and practices associated with the 'War on Terror' – is *the* primary force structuring Islamophobia today (as noted in the introductory chapter of this collection). Yet, most research on the counterjihad movement examines it in isolation, excluding the state (or indeed the wider conservative movement) from analysis and thus inevitably producing a narrow account in which the problem of Islamophobia is relegated to a fringe spectacle. The reality, on the contrary, is that due to its common thread running from the fringes to the mainstream, Islamophobia 'threatens to become the defining condition of the new Europe' (Bunzl, 2007: 4).

The analysis here proceeds from an important observation made by Arun Kundnani. He notes that a large body of work studies the relationship between government and jihadist narratives – and asks how governments can deploy effective 'counter-narratives' (Kundnani, 2012). Likewise, researchers have grappled with the interaction between right-wing extremism and militant Islamism – and the idea of 'cumulative radicalisation', itself problematic (Fekete, 2013), has emerged to explain the perceived relationship. However, the third dimension of this triad – the relationship 'between official security narratives and counter-jihadist narratives' – has rarely been interrogated (Kundnani, 2012: 11). Few scholars have asked how government narratives could undermine the far right; fewer still have inquired as to 'whether counter-terrorism policy narratives, claiming to tackle jihadism, in practice reinforce far-Right counter-jihadist narratives' (Kundnani, 2012: 11).

This chapter juxtaposes official counter-extremism policies and the counterjihad movement, examining both narratives and practices. It illustrates the symbiotic relationship between counter-extremism and counterjihadists and argues that it is sometimes also appropriate to speak of synergies between the two, in the sense that they work together – and in interaction with three other social movements which collectively make up the 'five pillars of Islamophobia' (explained in the first chapter of this volume, neoconservatism, Zionism and liberal/left currents) – to collectively reproduce and deeply ingrain Islamophobia in society. Though it should be emphasised that anti-immigration sentiment is equally fundamental to the counterjihad movement, examining its interactions with border regimes is beyond the scope of this chapter.

In-built biases of counter-extremism

It is significant that the counterjihad movement 'became visible and vocal after September 11' (Fekete, 2012: 43). As its name suggests, the movement takes its cue directly from the War on Terror, positioning itself in opposition to the Islamic concept of jihad, which has come to be seen as synonymous with political violence (though counterjihadists also suffix the term to all manner of imagined phenomena supposedly related to Islam, such as 'welfare jihad', 'rape jihad' and 'demographic jihad'). Why has the counterjihad movement flourished in the era of counter-extremism?

Firstly, it is vital to understand the history of counter-extremism ideas and practices and the context in which dominant understandings of concepts like 'radicalisation' have evolved and been operationalised. The dichotomous terms 'extremist' and 'moderate' in British political discourse originated in colonial India in the early twentieth-century era (Kundnani, 2014: 68). Contemporary government definitions were also formulated with specific – apparently foreign – threats in mind; 'extremism' in the UK today is to be defined by way of reference to deviation from so-called 'British values' (Home Office, 2011). Given the genealogy of official counter-extremism thinking and practice, the notion that these policies merely need to be applied more consistently should be challenged. We find this suggestion in a number of contexts. After the Breivik massacre, for example, Norwegian security services were criticised for having been 'blind in the right eye' (Bangstad, 2014: 14). In the UK, one academic has called for the government to 'get tough' on extremism 'in all its forms' (Goodwin, 2013). But counter-extremism programmes like the UK's Prevent strategy are a product as well as a progenitor of Islamophobia. Viewed in this way, de-sensitivity towards far-right threats can be seen as systemic rather than an imbalance to be corrected. Illustrating this dynamic – and the overlap between the various pillars of Islamophobia – is the fact that the same year neoconservative intellectual Douglas Murray welcomed the emergence of the EDL as a grassroots response to Islamism (Pitt, 2011), his Centre for Social Cohesion think tank was repeatedly cited in the revised 2011 Prevent strategy (Home Office, 2011). Paying attention to the ways that actually existing counter-extremism practices have been helpful to the far right makes it questionable whether a more even-handed approach is even possible.

Jihadist terrorism is widely viewed as a strategic threat to the West. In contrast, the far right tends to be seen merely as a public order issue (Kundnani, 2012). ICSR claims, for example, that the counterjihad movement 'has not expressed any real desire for a revolutionary overthrow of the current government' (Meleagrou-Hitchens and Brun, 2013: 33). Yet this is inaccurate: in fact, Breivik claimed to have been part of a small group of counterjihadists who refounded the Knights of Templar, a medieval crusading Christian military order; their purpose, he wrote, was 'to seize political and military control of Western European countries and implement a cultural conservative agenda' (Lean, 2012: 161). That said, it is broadly true that while advocating more radically authoritarian and exclusivist policies, the counterjihad movement does not fundamentally oppose the state and could not be said to be counter-hegemonic. While one of its central tenets is that violent civil war is likely or indeed inevitable, such a conflict would not be revolutionary in character but waged against Muslims and migrants in defence of perceived national identity; counterjihadist terrorism is more likely to take the form of pro-state violence at the expense of ethnic and religious minorities. Far-right violence is frequently dismissed as 'lone wolf', often inaccurately – as in the case of Breivik (Berntzen and Sveiung, 2014). Despite clear patterns of growing Islamophobic violence, few governments have taken serious practical action to oppose it. In the UK, for example, the bulk of the Extremism Task Force's 2013 policy recommendations were geared towards policing rather than protecting the Muslim community, regardless of the wave of Islamophobic attacks in mid 2013 (Cabinet Office, 2013).

It is instructive to compare this lacuna to the sprawling surveillance regime established in the UK through the aforementioned Prevent policy, the primary stimulus for which has been fear of 'Islamic extremism' – dubbed by former UK Prime Minister David Cameron as the 'struggle of a generation' (Perraudin, 2015). From the outset, the implementation of Prevent treated Muslims as an officially 'suspect community': funding was originally distributed according to a crude algorithm which used the size of a region's Muslim population as a proxy for the threat of extremism (Kundnani, 2009). The move towards rooting out so-called 'non-violent extremism' ushered in policies designed to catch would-be terrorists 'upstream' in the 'pre-criminal space'. Cameron declared the country needed to 'drain the swamp' that extremists inhabit (Wintour, 2013). In practice, the Counter-Terrorism and Security Act 2015 which requires public sector bodies to 'have due regard to the need to prevent people from being drawn into terrorism' (HM Government, 2015) has meant that doctors, lecturers, teachers, prison officers, social workers and even librarians are trained to be vigilant for signs of 'radicalisa-tion'. In the unprecedented climate of suspicion and mistrust that these policies have fostered, disproportionate numbers of Muslims have been referred through Prevent and its associated programme, Channel, as Chapter 1 explained.

Just as the secondary importance of the far right is clear from its description by the UK government as 'other forms of extremism' (Home Office, 2011: 57), even in Germany – a country which has experienced very few jihadist attacks but does have an entrenched problem of far-right violence – it is the Islamist threat which is emphasised by authorities as the most grave (Federal Ministry of the Interior, n.d.). Germany's Federal Bureau for the Protection of the Constitution (n.d., a) groups extremism into three categories: right wing, left wing and Islamist. Conscious of modern history, the German government places more emphasis than many other European governments on opposing the far right. It has run a far-right dropout programme since 2001 and financially supports a similar project run by the not-for-profit group EXIT-Deutschland, co-founded by former neo-Nazi Ingo Hasselbach. That this is, nonetheless, still inadequate was demonstrated by the National Socialist Underground scandal which emerged in 2011. Furthermore, such initiatives have been criticised for their lack of accountability (Fekete, 2014) and more pertinent to this discussion are focused on combating neo-Nazism while mostly neglecting counterjihadists. There are notable contrasts, too, in how the far right and those described as Islamists are treated. For instance, a German government 'deradicalisation' programme focused on Muslims called Hayat (Arabic for 'life') was modelled on EXIT-Deutschland, whose stated aim is 'to help anyone who wants to break with right-wing-extremism' (EXIT-Deutschland, n.d.). However, whereas individuals self-refer to the latter programme, Hayat almost exclusively works through other informants – the families, friends, teachers or employers of potentially 'radicalised' Muslims (Brenner, 2015).

The French government, too, has recently intensified its efforts to counter 'radicalisation'. In January 2015, a propaganda campaign explicitly focused on Muslims, with a name echoing that of the counterjihad movement – 'Stop Djihadism' – was launched. Soon afterwards, an anonymous hotline – *Numero Vert* (Green Number) – was introduced, which families, friends and neighbours of suspected 'extremists' were encouraged to call. Francesco Ragazzi of Sciences Po, in Paris, argues that, as in the UK and Germany, the initiative is 'creating an atmosphere of suspicion' (McHugh, 2015).

It is this climate of fear and mistrust, generated by governments' counter-extremism policies, that has provided fertile ground for the paranoid conspiracy theories of the far-right counterjihad movement.

Cometh the swamp drainers:
counterjihad synergies with counter-extremism

It is now well established that rather than being opposed with counter-narratives, aspects of counterjihad ideology and language are being 'mainstreamed' (Townsend, 2015). But influence is not only one-way. Sensing the 'racial subtext to the entire discourse of counterterrorism' (Kundnani, 2014: 23), the counterjihad movement is increasingly borrowing, adapting and utilising elements of official counter-extremism rhetoric and ideology too. In other instances, the targets and rationale of counterjihadists overlap with official counter-extremism perspectives and governmental concerns.

PEGIDA is perhaps the most notable group to have packaged its message in the language of liberal counter-extremism. Its leaders have declared their movement opposed to 'preachers of hate, regardless of what (sic) religion' and 'radicalism, regardless of whether religiously or politically motivated' (Dearden, 2015). In a clear nod to the German government's approach – rejection of Islamist, left-wing and right-wing (predominantly neo-Nazi) extremism – PEGIDA's logo depicts the ISIL flag, the Communist hammer and sickle, the Anti-Fascist Network logo and the Nazi Swastika being thrown in a dustbin together; the accompanying slogan reads, 'Away with all the radical trash!'

Speaking at a PEGIDA protest in Dresden in February 2015, René Stadtkewitz, leader of the far-right German party Die Freiheit (Freedom), said: 'I call on all Muslims: Stand up and tear the violence and the hatred out of the Koran. Write a new Koran 2.0. Only then can there be peaceful co-existence. Only you can do that!' This comment neatly illustrates the way 'anti-Muslim racism is typically articulated in an inductive way by generalising the behaviour of individuals, claiming that this behaviour is determined by "Islam" and that it is emblematic for all persons coming from a Muslim background' (Fleischer, 2014: 56). Though worded more stridently, Stadtkewitz's insinuation that Islam and/or Muslims in general are responsible for causing – and can therefore also prevent – acts of violence was not original. Following the Paris attacks the previous month (January 2015), UK government minister Eric Pickles had delivered a not dissimilar message, writing to more than 1,000 Muslim leaders (unconnected to the attacks), telling them they had 'more work to do'. It was not outlandish, therefore, for a spokesperson from the Muslim Council of Britain to compare Pickles's actions to those of 'members of the far right' (Wintour, 2015).

A similar parallel between government and far-right thinking can be illustrated using the words of EDL founder and ex-leader, Stephen Lennon (aka Tommy Robinson). In December 2015, he told a newspaper that the city of Birmingham, home to the UK's biggest Muslim population, had been chosen as the site of a protest by his new outfit, PEGIDA UK, because it was 'where most of the terrorists have been from' (Wright, 2015). This type of logic mimicked, albeit more bluntly, government assessments. As noted, the British government has used the size of a city's Muslim population as a proxy for the threat of political violence when allocating Prevent funding (Kundnani, 2009). It also appears to have made much the same diagnosis about Birmingham, five years earlier than Lennon. In 2010, a unique project code-named Project Champion – according to police sources, 'the first of its kind in the UK that seeks to monitor a population seen as "at risk" of extremism' – saw the installation of hundreds of cameras in two Muslim areas of the city, secretly financed with £3 million from police counter-terrorism (Lewis, 2010). Thus, when Lennon declared Birmingham 'the continued epicentre for terrorism', he was only making explicit the rationale implicit in the authorities' own surveillance operations.

While both counterjihadists and government have eyed Muslim communities with suspicion, the far right has also been watching government. In December 2013, the UK Prime Minister called for an end to the practice of gender segregation by university Islamic societies and Education Secretary Michael Gove asserted a link to 'extremism' (Young, 2013). Their statements followed a report about alleged instances of the practice by a pressure group called Student Rights, a project of the neo-conservative Henry Jackson Society think tank (Aked, 2017). By May 2014, members of the counterjihad group Britain First had begun a series of 'mosque invasions' and – though not normally women's rights advocates (the party opposes abortion, for instance) – its leaders filmed themselves demanding 'the removal of sexist mosque signs' designating separate entrances for men and women. This was not the first time that the Islamophobic far right had taken its cue from government, with right-wing think tanks and media acting as intermediaries. In early 2013, following several years of messaging from government and media about universities being 'hotbeds of extremism' hosting 'hate preachers', counterjihad groups decided to help 'drain the swamp'. When Student Rights alleged that several 'extreme' events were due to take place at universities, 'concerned patriots' from the football hooligan-linked Casuals United and the EDL took matters into their own hands, demonstrating outside one university and turning up on campus at another; several events were cancelled for fear of violence (Erfani-Ghettani, 2013).

Underlining the way counter-extremism agendas have proved amenable to the far right, some counterjihad groups have even styled themselves as 'counter-extremism' bodies. Examples include the Stresemann Stiftung (in Germany) and Stand for Peace and VOICE (both in the UK, discussed later). Their self-declared mandate allows these groups to attack Muslims with a high degree of impunity, while simultaneously distracting from the extreme views of their own personnel. Meanwhile, some counter-extremism organisations have links to the counterjihad movement. Several UK groups, for instance, have ties to the US Gatestone Institute, a major clearing house for counterjihad viewpoints. Both the ICSR's Shiraz Maher and Alexander Meleagrou-Hitchen have written articles for Gatestone (though each has at times criticised Islamophobia and the latter co-authored ICSR's counterjihad movement report); Sam Westrop of Stand for Peace is a 'distinguished senior fellow'; and the Quilliam Foundation's Usama Hasan and Maajid Nawaz signed a statement placed in the *New York Times* by Gatestone following the January 2015 Paris attacks. The Henry Jackson Society – and by extension its university watchdog arm Student Rights – has received funding from the Abstraction Fund, the main funder to Gatestone and run by its president, Nina Rosenwald (Aked, 2015).

The state is also intertwined in some of the relationships between counter-extremists and counterjihadists. For instance, the counter-extremist Quilliam Foundation received millions in government funding in its early years. After state funding had dried up, it wrote to the Department of Communities and Local Government in 2013, requesting more financial support in order to facilitate Stephen Lennon's departure from the EDL, which it presented as a major counter-extremism coup (Political Scrapbook, 2014). The money was not forthcoming, but it later emerged that Quilliam had paid Lennon approximately £8,000 (Hopkins, 2015). Although not a significant sum, it soon became clear that Lennon's views were unchanged and he later established PEGIDA UK. Thus, an organisation funded by government to challenge extremism instead channelled money to a far-right activist – and put the government just one degree of separation away from the UK's most notorious counterjihad activist.

Counterjihadists as 'centrist' vanguard of resistance to 'Islamofascism'

It took little more than for Lennon to declare himself tired of EDL street protests and 'opposed to extremism at both ends of the spectrum' for him to suddenly be considered a liberal (Pai, 2016: 193). The ease with which counterjihad activists feign 'moderate' credentials by borrowing counter-extremist rhetoric is also apparent elsewhere. For example, VOICE (Victims Of Islamic Cultural Extremism), set up in 2015 by UK counterjihad activist Anne Marie Waters, declared itself opposed to 'left and right wing extremists' (VOICE, 2016). In Germany, the Stresemann Stiftung states that its namesake Gustav Stresemann (leader of the German People's Party, 1918–29) understood the need to protect the country 'from extremist forces from the left as well as from the right' (Stresemann Stiftung, 2016).

This positioning is of course strategic. On leaving the EDL in 2013, Lennon complained that 'what we've been saying was criticised, or ignored and pushed to the margin because of [the] far right extremist tag they managed to give us', and declared his desire to 'take this [movement] mainstream' (Shevardnadze, 2013). So, when he launched PEGIDA UK in 2016 – with Waters and others – the group said explicitly that their organisation aimed to be 'something that is possible (sic) for Middle England to follow' (PEGIDA UK, 2016). In order to gain mainstream credibility, they understood the need to shake off the 'far-right' label. Similarly, French intellectual Renaud Camus declared – shortly before announcing that he planned to vote for the far-right Front National (FN) party – 'there is nothing right wing about me' (Schofield, 2014). In the same spirit, the leader of Germany's Alternative für Deutschland (AfD) party, Frauke Petry, also sought to resituate her party by rejecting the 'far-right' tag, claiming instead: 'It's to do with politicians that either recognise that we need concepts that lead to solutions or not. Right and left are terms that haven't fitted for a long time' (Connolly, 2016).

This rebranding has been facilitated by official counter-extremism frameworks. These schema invite us to see any ideology besides liberalism as merely one expression of a single phenomenon of 'extremism' (while remaining, in practice, hyper-sensitive to Islamist threats). Not only is a false equivalence drawn between a range of opposing political ideologies, the role of right-wing extremism is invariably occupied by the traditional neo-Nazi far right, providing the newer counterjihad strand of the far right with an opportunity. By aligning itself with liberal counter-extremism agendas and condemning not only the left and 'Islamic extremism' but also 'right-wing extremism' (meaning the anti-Semitic right), counterjihadists manoeuvre themselves into a position apparently beyond reproach.

The authorities have taken approving note. As early as September 2009, Metropolitan Police Commissioner Sir Paul Stephenson had concluded that the EDL and Stop the Islamisation of Europe were *not* themselves extreme right-wing groups – but expressed concern that such groups might be 'exploited by very extreme right-wing groups like the National Front' (Boxell, 2009). Little has changed; in 2016, the National Domestic Extremism Unit still did not categorise the EDL as 'far right' (Pai, 2016: 208). Therefore, while successive incarnations of Anjem Choudary's Islamist groups – al-Muhajiroun, Al-Ghurabaa and Islam4UK – have all been proscribed (Pai, 2016: 8), groups like the EDL have not been banned. The complacency runs so deep that one British Conservative prospective parliamentary candidate, Afzal Amin, directly colluded with Stephen Lennon in 2015. Amin plotted with the EDL so that a planned march on a Mosque was cancelled, for which Amin could take the credit. In the discussion Amin promised to be an 'unshakeable ally' to the EDL at Westminster (Wright, 2015; Wyatt and Taylor, 2015).

Similarly, in Germany, some elements of the state have downplayed the threat of PEGIDA. While Chancellor Merkel herself strongly condemned the movement, her Vice-Chancellor, Social Democrat leader Sigmar Gabriel, admitted he had attended a Dresden forum and spoken with PEGIDA supporters. Saxony Interior Minister Markus Ulbig meanwhile declared: 'We cannot label 10,000 people as right-wing extremists ... there are many middle-class citizens among them ... and you can't toss them all into the same Neo-Nazi pot' (Der Spiegel, 2014). However, neither the class position of its followers nor its widespread popularity detracts from PEGIDA's deep Islamophobia and xenophobia. The official line of the Federal Bureau for the Protection of the Constitution (n.d., b) is that right-wing extremism in Germany is declining but this seems misplaced; in fact, in line with the broader transformation of the far right, outlined at the start of this chapter, it is merely changing shape.

Counterjihadists have been able to present themselves as benign and even centrist by comparison to an enemy they call 'Islamofascism'. The emergence of this term may have been facilitated by ahistorical counter-extremism frameworks which, as Liz Fekete (2013) notes, dislocate far-right actors from their lineages and abstracts political violence from its context. It also relies on the collapsing of boundaries between left and right engendered by counter-extremist thinking. That is to say, while there is a certain historical logic to the 'rummaging [of] the national past for an evocative warrior against "Islam'" (Bhatt, 2012) – an exercise which has produced counterjihad blogs named after the likes of Richard the Lionheart, Vlad 'the Impaler' Tepes, Charles 'the Hammer' Martell and the Gates of Vienna – the notion of Islamofascism, by contrast, turns history on its head. Just as the concept of 'Islamisation' rests on what French sociologist Raphaël Liogier calls a 'fantasy of reverse colonialism' (Henni-Moulai, 2015), Islamofascism, too, relies on a distorted reinterpretation of history. As well as demonising the Islamic 'threat' as nothing less than a new fascism, it perversely allows the new far right to usurp the language and legacy of anti-fascism.

The boldest example of this role reversal comes from Germany, where counterjihad activist Conny Axel-Meier, national secretary of Bürgerbewegung Pax Europa, claimed in 2012 to have revived the White Rose movement – which resisted the Nazis – for the purposes of 'resisting Islamofascism'. Meier asserted that 'today through historical misrepresentation' the original White Rose movement was 'being pushed into proximity with so-called anti-fascists' and was actually 'a national-conservative, liberal movement' (Bodissey, 2014). Especially when combined with the distancing act of ostentatiously condemning the traditional, 'real' far right, the counterjihad movement's invention of 'Islamofascism' adroitly works to conceal its own fascistic tendencies. In addition, it provides a tool with which to attack the left: those denying the threat of 'Islamofascism' are guilty of 'appeasement', or else submission to a life of 'Dhimmitude' under Islamic rule (Carr, 2006). The term 'red-green alliance' puts radical left anti-racism campaigners allied with Muslim groups into the same category.

Why, then, would France's Socialist Prime Minister Manuel Valls pointedly use the word 'Islamofascism' himself in 2015? His rhetoric was a gift to the Front National, whose leader Marine Le Pen has herself used the phrase 'green fascism' to indict Islam. Valls's participation in legitimising this terminology suggests a coincidence of interests between the French government (and Western states more broadly) and the counterjihad movement. All stand to gain power as a result of the 'fundamental fear' of Islamism (Sayyid, 1997). The extensive abuses of civil liberties by the French authorities, documented under the prolonged état d'urgence, are indicative of this. So while we should be wary of counterjihadists' attempts to pose as a somehow centrist vanguard of resistance to 'Islamofascism', we should also be alert to the way in which extremism frameworks that treat the government as neutral can obscure the increasing authoritarianism of state power in the era of the War on Terror (Fekete, 2013).

Working through the state:
waging counter-extremism with elite support

Unlike any Islamist (or, at least in Western Europe, any neo-Nazi party), the counterjihad movement not only influences the mainstream, and is influenced by it, but also exists *within* the mainstream political and media establishment. The movement is 'best described as a spectrum – with street fighting forces at one end and cultural conservatives and neoconservative writers at the other' (Fekete, 2012: 43). This hybridity is a key strength. Militant street-based elements (such as the EDL) are complemented by an intellectual wing. Counterjihad ideas are not only disseminated via the blogosphere but also through publishing houses like Encounter Books, newspapers such as *Dispatch International* and films, for instance, *Fitna* and *Obsession*. As several studies show, organised Islamophobia is a multi-million-dollar business (Ali et al., 2011; Lean, 2012; Saylor, 2014). Yet, the counterjihad movement's elite elements – the well-educated, middle-class Islamophobes – are sometimes overlooked.

Numerous elite actors sympathetic to or active within the counterjihad movement can be cited. They include those who formerly held, or retain, influential positions within governments. In France, General Christian Piquemal, a former commander of the French Foreign Legion, joined a PEGIDA Calais demonstration. The country's *nouveaux réaction-naires* (new reactionaries), including figures like Eric Zemmour, Renaud Camus and Alain Finkielkraut, brought counterjihad ideas into the intellectual mainstream with books like *The Great Replacement* and *The Unhappy Identity*. In Germany, Thilo Sarrazin, a former senator of finance for the State of Berlin who then served on the Executive Board of Deutsche Bundesbank, published his best-selling *Germany Abolishes Itself* in 2010, similarly articulating counterjihad themes. In the UK, two peers of the realm, Baroness Cox and Lord Pearson, have twice invited another leading European counterjihad figure, Dutch Party for Freedom (Partij voor de Vrijheid, PVV) leader Geert Wilders, to speak in Parliament. Meanwhile, Cox and former US Ambassador to the UN John Bolton sit together on the board of the Gatestone Institute, the New

York body mentioned earlier which publishes the writing of Wilders, Bat Ye'or and Peder Jensen aka 'Fjordman' – a Norwegian blogger heavily cited in Breivik's manifesto whose writing contains 'many of the tropes of fascism' (Jackson, 2013: 247). Though Jensen could not be characterised as a member of the elite, he has nonetheless embedded himself in the mainstream public sphere to such an extent that he has received funding from the respectable Fritt Ord Foundation, which also supports freedom of speech group Index on Censorship (Bangstad, 2014: 216).

Wilders and Pearson were among those to attend the Defeat Jihad Summit in the US in 2015, organised by the Center for Security Policy's Frank Gaffney. Gaffney himself formerly served in the Reagan administration and was more recently appointed as a political advisor to senior Republican Ted Cruz. When Donald Trump pipped Cruz to the Republican presidential nomination and went on to win the election, it was reported that Gaffney had advised his transition team (Bump, 2016). Trump's campaign manager and later chief strategist Steve Bannon also had close links to the counterjihadists, running Breitbart News which promotes the likes of Geert Wilders, and praising Islamophobic blogger Pamela Geller (Woodruff and Resnick, 2016). Prior to Trump's ascent to power in the US, perhaps the most striking elite show of support for the counterjihad movement in Europe was Czech President Miloš Zeman's speech at a Bloc Against Islam rally in Prague in November 2015 – a rally also attended by EDL and PEGIDA UK founder Stephen Lennon. It bears repeating that the proximity to power evidenced by these connections is a feature of the counterjihad movement that stands in stark contrast to the relative dearth of political influence enjoyed by Islamist actors in Europe.

Given the counterjihad movement's hybridity and its significant elite connections, while the threat posed by some actors is of an immediately violent nature, large sections of the movement can pursue their goals through official channels. Counterjihadists work in concert with other actors on the right, especially neoconservatives (see Chapter 10 in this volume), in order to 'put in place legal and administrative structures that discriminate against Muslims' (Fekete, 2006: 2). Parliamentarians across the West with allegiances to the counterjihad movement have been at the forefront of advocating discriminatory legislation. In sharp contrast to most other forms of racism, Islamophobia has been officially sanctioned by many governments with the passage of anti-Islam legislation related to mosque or minaret construction, the hijab, niqab and burqa, halal (and kosher) slaughter, and Sharia law in Switzerland, France, Denmark, Spain, Italy, Austria, the US and beyond.

While some scholars have suggested that the counterjihad movement eschews electoral politics (Goodwin et al., 2014), this is a mischaracterisation. Some groups that come from a recognisable counterjihad persuasion, or have a close affinity to it, have had considerable success engaging in the political process, despite the deeply anti-democratic nature of their racist ideas. Although they style themselves as 'anti-parties' (Meyer and Storck, 2015), several have become key players in government: in 2014, Geert Wilders's PVV came third in European elections in the Netherlands; in 2015, the populist radical right Danish People's Party became the second biggest in the country; in 2016, the Austrian Freedom Party (Freiheitliche Partei Österreichs, FPÖ) narrowly lost the presidential election.

The so-called pressure valve hypothesis – the view that the presence of radical right parties in democratic elections will prevent the rise of extreme right movements (Bangstad, 2014: 179) – is commonly asserted. But it is far from clear that the growth of street-based movements and radical right parties are mutually exclusive, as demonstrated by the rise of the AfD in Germany, alongside – rather than in place of – the PEGIDA movement. Even if far-right parties do undercut grassroots organisations, this is not necessarily a preferable option for democracy. Though politics focused on the ballot box is more appealing to managerial mindsets, a far-right party such as the FPÖ or FN with its hands on the levers of state power – even if acquired through theoretically legitimate electoral means – could produce far more violence than any non-state actor, including the small number of violent Islamists with whom governments and the media remain preoccupied.

Another possibility is that such currents may serve to amplify and reinforce each other. Importantly, the grassroots wing of the counterjihad movement is not disconnected from the intellectual wing, or from political parties. For instance, AfD figures and PVV leader Wilders have attended PEGIDA rallies. The establishment arm gives the grassroots wing access to important arenas of power, such as the European Parliament, where counterjihad events have been held, or the House of Lords, where Baroness Cox has given a platform to a handful of UK counterjihad groups including Sharia Watch UK and Stand for

Peace (Aked, 2015). These imprimaturs of legitimacy strengthen the movement. Vertical links even cross state boundaries: the UK's Alan Ayling (aka Alan Lake), reportedly an EDL funder – though he denies this (Bartholomew, 2011; Lowles, 2009; Townsend and Traynor, 2011) – has cultivated close links with key figures in the Sweden Democrats party; Daniel Pipes, of the Philadelphia-based Middle East Forum (MEF), has participated in a counterjihad demonstration organised by French groups Résistance Républicaine and Riposte Laïque (Pipes, 2014). US funding has also been vital to the European movement; MEF alone has provided financial assistance to Geert Wilders in the Netherlands, Christine Tasin of Résistance Républicaine in France, Peder Jensen and Bruce Bawer in Norway, the Discourse Institute in the UK, and the Stresemann Stiftung in Germany (Powerbase, n.d.). The increasing power of Islamophobic actors in the US suggests Europe's counterjihad movement may also continue to flourish.

The combined effect of these top-down and bottom-up actors enables the counterjihad movement to exert a radicalising influence on the mainstream. For example, the US Defeat Jihad Summit was deliberately timed to coincide with President Obama's Countering Violent Extremism summit, an attempt to pull the centre to the right by acting as an unofficial fringe or shadow event promoting an even more hard-line approach. In some countries, as the counterjihad-oriented far right rebrands itself as respectable while governments become increasingly authoritarian, a degree of convergence is visible. In France, for instance, the FN's rise to apparent respectability has been carried out all the more smoothly of late thanks to a 'rapid shift in French public opinion' that is both a symptom of and contributor to the movement of the political centre ground (Nardelli, 2015). When Nicolas Sarkozy declared that the FN was now 'compatible with the Republic', this undoubtedly 'said more about the drift of Republican values than any progressive evolution on the part of the FN' (Wolfreys, 2015).

Conclusion

Bearing in mind that 'fascism acquired respectability as a counterweight to Bolshevism' (Kundnani, 2014: 101), we should pay more attention to the way in which far-right movements are being empowered by the War on Terror. Tugging on the thread of Islamophobia that runs from the fringes to the establishment, the counterjihad movement is exerting a radicalising influence on the mainstream, engineering a degree of convergence by aligning itself with official counter-extremism. Counter-extremism has proved amenable to the counterjihad movement's agenda, by providing it with a respectable vocabulary with which to express its racism. The flexibility and slipperiness of concepts like 'extremism' is such that some counterjihad groups now present themselves as 'counter-extremists', appropriation which suggests an alarming depth of compatibility. It suggests that counter-extremism policies have created space for this strand of the far right to advance while posing as 'moderate' or 'centrist' and speaking the language of liberalism. Governments cannot play firefighter as well as arsonist; they are not in a position to oppose the counterjihad movement effectively since their counter-extremism policies helped produce it, and remain part of the wider problem of Islamophobia.

Bibliography

All websites accessed 3 February 2017.

Aked, H. (2015), 'One of America's most dangerous think tanks is spreading Islamophobic hate across the Atlantic', Alternet, 23 November. https://tinyurl.com/gmg48sf.

—— (2017, forthcoming), 'Student rights, the Henry Jackson Society and the "campus extremism" debate', in D. Miller, L. Brown, W. Dinan and L. Stavinoha (eds), *Researching the Powerful: Public Sociology in Action*, London: Routledge.

Ali, W., Clifton, E., Duss, M., Fang, L., Keyes, S. and Shakir, F. (2011), *Fear, Inc. The Roots of the Islamophobia Network in the US*. Washington, DC: Center for American Progress.

Bangstad, S. (2014), *Anders Breivik and the Rise of Islamophobia*. London: Zed Books.

Bartholomew, R. (2011), 'Alan Lake: "I have given some money to help some EDL things happen"', Bartholomew's Notes, 10 April. https://tinyurl.com/jhgtgou.

Berntzen, L. and Sveiung, S. (2014), 'The collective nature of lone wolf terrorism: Anders Behring Breivik and the anti-Islamic social movement', *Terrorism and Political Violence*, 26 (5), 759–79.

Bhatt, C. (2012), 'The new xenologies of Europe: civil tensions and mythic pasts', *Journal of Civil Society*, 8 (3), 307–26.

Bodissey, B. (2014), 'Heilbronn: once again, a penal order against an Islam critic – video transcript: revival of the White Rose, Conny Axel Meir', Gates of Vienna, 12 February. https://tinyurl.com/zcqrrx9.

Boxell, J. (2009), 'Police play down threat from far right', *Financial Times*, 24 September.

Brenner, Y. (2015), 'How Germany is attempting to de-radicalise Muslim extremists', *Forward*, 16 January. https://tinyurl.com/gouh76j.

Bump, P. (2016), 'Meet Frank Gaffney, the anti-Muslim gadfly reportedly advising Donald Trump's transition team', *Washington Post*, 16 November. https://tinyurl.com/jkmgahf.

Bunzl, M. (2007), *Anti-Semitism and Islamophobia: Hatreds Old and New in Europe*. Chicago, IL: Prickly Paradigm Press.

Cabinet Office (2013), *Tackling Extremism in the UK: Report from the Prime Minister's Task Force*. HM Government. https://tinyurl.com/kcv7ok2.

Carr, M. (2006), 'You are now entering Eurabia', *Race & Class*, 48 (1), 1–22.

Connolly, K. (2016), 'Frauke Petry: smiling face of Germany's resurgent right', *Guardian*, 7 February. https://tinyurl.com/j7b4365.

Dearden, L. (2015), 'PEGIDA in London: British supporters of anti-'Islamisation' group rally in Downing Street', *Independent*, 4 April. https://tinyurl.com/jadqulx.

Der Spiegel (2014) 'The end of tolerance? Anti-Muslim movement rattles Germany', *Der Spiegel International Online*, 21 December. https://tinyurl.com/nwyssg6.

Erfani-Ghettani, R. (2013), 'Far right targets Islamic events', Institute of Race Relations, 4 April. https://tinyurl.com/zaae6sy.

EXIT-Deutschland (n.d.), 'Home page'. www.exit-deutschland.de/english.

Federal Bureau for the Protection of the Constitution (n.d., a), 'Fields of work', Federal Bureau for the Protection of the Constitution. https://tinyurl.com/zqtogcq.

—— (n.d., b) 'Right wing extremism following (general survey)', Federal Bureau for the Protection of the Constitution. https://tinyurl.com/zmtqzmg.

Federal Ministry of the Interior (n.d.), 'Counter-terrorism', Federal Ministry of the Interior. https://tinyurl.com/jpx2w36.

Fekete, L. (2006), 'Enlightened fundamentalism? Immigration, feminism and the right', *Race & Class*, 48 (2), 1–22.

—— (2011), 'The Muslim conspiracy theory and the Oslo massacre', *Race & Class*, 53 (3), 30–47.

—— (2012), *Pedlars of Hate: The Violent Impact of the European Far Right*. London: Institute of Race Relations.

—— (2013), 'Anti-extremism or anti-fascism?', Institute of Race Relations, 21 November. https://tinyurl.com/z9k798g.

—— (2014), 'Exit from white supremacism: the accountability gap within Europe's de-radicalisation programmes', *European Research Programme Briefing*. London: Institute of Race Relations.

Fleischer, R. (2014), 'Two fascisms in contemporary Europe? Understanding the ideological split of the radical right', in M. Deland, M. Minkenberg and

C. Mays (eds), *In the Tracks of Breivik: Far Right Networks in Northern and Eastern Europe*. Berlin: Lit Verlag, pp. 53–70.

Goodwin, M. (2013), 'We need to get tough on extremism – in all its forms', *Guardian*, 5 December. https://tinyurl.com/zsvjudc.

Goodwin, M., Cutts, D. and Janta-Lipinski, L. (2014), 'Economic losers, protesters, Islamophobes or xenophobes? Predicting public support for a counter-jihad movement', *Political Studies*, 64 (1), 4–26.

Hafez, F. (2014), 'Shifting borders: Islamophobia as common ground for building pan-European right-wing unity', *Patterns of Prejudice*, 48 (5), 479–99.

Henni-Moulai, N. (2015), 'INTERVIEW: Raphael Liogier condemns Europe's identity politics of decline', *Middle East Eye*, 13 November. https://tinyurl.com/jkhyfsj.

HM Government (2015), *Prevent Duty Guidance*, HM Government. https://tinyurl.com/jrm9h9g.

Home Office (2011), *Prevent Strategy*, HM Government. https://tinyurl.com/0xz5uzy.

Hopkins, S. (2015), 'Tommy Robinson, former EDL leader, claims Quilliam paid him to quit far-right group', *Huffington Post*, 4 December. https://tinyurl.com/gnvmpd3.

Jackson, P. (2013), 'The license to hate: Peder Jensen's fascist rhetoric in Anders Breivik's Manifesto 2083: a European declaration of independence', *Democracy and Security*, 9 (3), 247–69.

Kundnani, A. (2009), *Spooked! How Not to Prevent Violent Extremism*. London: Institute of Race Relations.

——(2012), *Blind Spot? Security Narratives and Far-Right Violence in Europe*. The Hague: International Centre for Counter-Terrorism.

——(2014), *The Muslims are Coming! Islamophobia, Extremism and the Domestic War on Terror*. London: Verso.

Lean, N. (2012), *The Islamophobia Industry: How the Right Manufactures Fear of Muslims*. London: Pluto Press.

Lewis, P. (2010), 'Surveillance cameras in Birmingham track Muslims every move', *Guardian*, 4 June. https://tinyurl.com/otctlc9.

Lowles, N. (2009), 'Businessman bankrolls "street army"', Searchlight. https://tinyurl.com/zc76z4e.

McHugh, J. (2015), 'Can France's new "Stop Jihadism" counterterrorism program prevent Westerners from joining ISIS?', *International Business Times*, 10 July. https://tinyurl.com/zpy8gjx.

Meer, N. (2013), 'Racialisation and religion: race, culture and difference in the study of antisemitism and Islamophobia', *Ethnic and Racial Studies*, 36 (3), 385–98.

Meleagrou-Hitchens, A. and Brun, H. (2013), *A Neo-Nationalist Network: The English Defence League and Europe's Counter-Jihad Movement*. London: International Centre for the Study of Radicalisation and Political Violence.

Meyer, H. and Storck, U. (2015), 'Understanding Pegida – an introduction', in *Understanding PEGIDA in Context*. Berlin: Social Europe/Friedrich Ebert Stiftung, pp. 1–3.

Nardelli, A. (2015), 'From margins to mainstream; the rapid shift in French public opinion', *Guardian*, 8 January. https://tinyurl.com/zoa7eqk.

Pai, H. (2016), *Angry White People: Coming Face to Face with the British Far Right*. London: Zed Books.

PEGIDA UK (2016), 'PEGIDA UK leadership announcement', YouTube, 5 January (at 3 min 23 sec. https://tinyurl.com/jkaan7s.

Perraudin, F. (2015), 'David Cameron: extremist ideology is "struggle of our generation"', *Guardian*, 20 July. https://tinyurl.com/hz99q53.

Pipes, D. (2014), 'Conservatives rally on the streets of Paris', *National Review Online*, 2 April. https://tinyurl.com/m4w4nv6.

Pitt, B. (2011), 'Douglas Murray welcomes EDL as a grassroots response from non-Muslims to Islamism', *Islamophobia Watch*, 30 January. https://tinyurl.com/h9k8lzq.

Political Scrapbook (2014), 'Quilliam Foundation wanted taxpayer cash for Tommy Robinson', Political Scrapbook, 3 February. https://tinyurl.com/jjegt4z.

Powerbase (n.d.), 'Middle East Forum', Powerbase. http://powerbase.info/index.php/Middle_East_Forum.

Saylor, C. (2014), 'The US Islamophobia Network: its funding and impact', *Islamophobia Studies Journal*, 2 (1), 99–118.

Sayyid, S. (1997), *A Fundamental Fear: Eurocentrism and the Emergence of Islamism*. London: Zed Books.

Sayyid, S. and Vakil, A. (eds) (2011), *Thinking Through Islamophobia: Global Perspectives*. London: Hurst.

Schofield, H. (2014), 'France shaken up by Zemmour and "new reactionaries"', BBC News Online, 14 December. https://tinyurl.com/lsa2gur.

Shevardnadze, S. (2013), '"Islam-leaning UK politicians openly forecast complete takeover of British politics" – ex-EDL leader' (interview transcript), Russia Today, 25 October. https://tinyurl.com/jyxgatc.

Shroufi, O. (2015), 'The gates of Jerusalem: European revisionism and the populist radical right', *Race & Class*, 57 (2), 24–42.

Stresemann Stiftung (2016), 'Home page'. www.stresemann-foundation.org.

Townswend, M. (2015), 'Anti-Muslim prejudice is moving to the mainstream', *Guardian*, 5 December. https://tinyurl.com/hb8tsn3.

Townsend, M. and Traynor, I. (2011), 'Norway attacks: how far right views created Anders Behring Breivik', *Guardian*, 30 July. https://tinyurl.com/javc2lg.

VOICE (2016), 'Events'. www.voiceuk.org/events.

Wintour, P. (2013), 'Cameron vows to "drain the swamp" creating Islamic extremism', *Guardian*, 3 June. https://tinyurl.com/gqve39k.

——(2015), 'Muslim Council of Britain objects to Pickles letter to Islamic leaders', *Guardian*, 19 January. https://tinyurl.com/jyu7enp.

Wolfreys. J. (2015), 'The Republic of Islamophobia', Hurst Books, 12 January. https://tinyurl.com/z79kooh.

Woodruff, B. and Resnick, G. (2016), 'Alt-right rejoices at Donald Trump's Steve Bannon hire', *Daily Beast*, 17 August. https://tinyurl.com/hecduz3.

Wright, O. (2015), 'Afzal Amin: Tory candidate told to "fess up" over alleged plot to stop fake EDL mosque protest', *Independent*, 22 March. https://tinyurl.com/mzlh8lb.

Wright, P. (2015), 'PEGIDA UK: Tommy Robinson says "terrorist epicentre" of Birmingham will be location of far-right march, *International Business Times*, 4 December. https://tinyurl.com/z2maqnz.

Wyatt, N. and Taylor, M. (2015), 'Tory candidate accused of EDL plot expected to be forced out within days', *Guardian*, 22 March. https://tinyurl.com/z7zf6ey.

Young, S. (2013), 'Segregated audiences not acceptable at UK universities, PM says', *Reuters*, 13 December. https://tinyurl.com/j858s6d.

9

The Transatlantic Network: Funding Islamophobia and Israeli Settlements

Sarah Marusek

Introduction

Islamophobia has somehow become a more acceptable form of racism in the West. In the US, billionaire businessman Donald Trump won the 2016 presidential election after promising to ban Muslims from entering the country (Diamond, 2015). Across the Atlantic, far-right politician Marine Le Pen stands a chance in 2017 of winning the French presidency (Chrisafis, 2016; Nossiternov, 2015), after a spate of horrible attacks in the country were committed by individuals widely described as Muslim fundamentalists, even though they hardly practised their religion (Davies and Allen, 2016). The electoral gains of the far right in Germany and in the UK indicate that the Islamophobic fringe is increasingly becoming mainstream, often displacing (although not at all replacing) the vicious anti-Semitism of the past (Al Jazeera, 2016).[1] Hafez (2014) has argued that this shift from overt anti-Semitism to overt Islamophobia goes beyond European borders and enables Europe's far right to connect to extremist Israeli parties and the far right in the US, creating a well-funded transatlantic movement. This chapter examines some of the key funders and relationships sustaining the transatlantic Islamophobia network and the extent to which significant funding agencies also support Israeli settlements and the infrastructure of occupation.

Two things are important to stress at the start. Firstly, this is not a claim that all supporters of Israel are part of the transatlantic Islamophobia network; this is certainly not the case. The individuals and groups specifically examined here are exceptional, albeit politically powerful. Secondly, narrowing in on those right-wing individuals and groups within the pro-Israel lobby that are peddling Islamophobia qualifies neither as a conspiracy theory nor anti-Semitism (Mughal, 2016). This chapter is based upon empirical evidence (tax filings) as the primary source to try to shed light on a powerful political force, not a religion. The chapter examines the funding and relationships that sustain hatred towards Islam by focusing on a narrow group of activists mostly on the extreme end of the pro-Israel movement. Furthermore, the Americans involved in this network are overwhelmingly Republican. While a 2016 survey found that 79 per cent of Democrats held favourable views of Muslims and 64 per cent of Islam, favourability among Republicans was 42 per cent for Muslims and 24 per cent for Islam (Telhami, 2016).

Meanwhile, although Western support for Israel's policies in the occupied territories is declining, this is not true among Republicans, who have further moved to the right. This shift was visible in January 2017 when Republican senators Ted Cruz and Lindsey Graham set in motion a bill that would defund the United Nations after the Security Council approved resolution 2334 condemning Israeli settlements (Tibon, 2017). While the US has long protected Israel from criticism at the UN, censuring its settlement expansion was previously standard American policy. Furthermore, Republican senators Marco Rubio, Ted Cruz and Dean Heller introduced another bill to cut the funding for embassy security globally (except in Tel Aviv) if the US did not move its Israeli embassy to Jerusalem, in line with Trump's campaign promise (Jilani, 2017). Again, while the House and Senate have long called for moving the embassy, if enacted, this law would put American lives at risk. The combination of all these developments has inspired strategic new alliances between anti-Islam Republicans and supporters of Israeli expansion into historical Palestine not only in the US, but also in Europe, Israel and the occupied territories.

While none of the organisations in the transatlantic Islamophobia network are required to publicly list their donors, searching through the annual tax documents of registered charities and foundations in the US and UK reveals to whom they send funds. I focus on the US, where philanthropy has always played an important role because the government has a weaker influence on society than in European countries. Thus, private American donors inevitably play an oversized role in giving, whether domestically or abroad. Ostrower's (1995) study of New York philanthropists illustrates that the elites who fund charities are actually quite heterogeneous; there are various social pressures at work alongside different moral and political agendas. Nevertheless, philanthropy generally works to reproduce the class hierarchies that it depends on. While considerable scholarly attention has been paid to the important role that liberal American foundations have historically had in the reproduction of global capitalism and forms of cultural imperialism (see Roelofs, 2007), despite the good intentions they may have (Arnove and Pinede, 2007; for a critique of this literature, see Berndtson, 2007), less consideration has been paid to their conservative counterparts. Furthermore, meaningful studies on the specific elite networks that foundations help to propagate are thin on the ground (for an analysis of their historical role both within the US and in pushing American hegemony abroad, see Parmar, 2012).

Focusing particularly on a group of right-wing anti-Islam organisations based in the US, Europe and Israel, this chapter looks at the main American personalities that are funding them. Instead of centring on one group of elites or selected charities/foundations, the originality here is to first make an empirical connection by finding out who is donating money to the Islamophobic network. In doing this, it quickly becomes apparent that significant numbers of the foundations are also funding Israeli settlements. Of course, this approach also has its limitations: sending donations does not necessarily mean that all donors are in full agreement with the groups in question, let alone fully aware of their agenda. However, since the donations do have political consequences, it is imperative to follow the money. This research draws on a series of projects undertaken by Public Interest Investigations on neoconservatism, the transatlantic Islamophobia network and the Zionist movement, examining the various connections between them (Cronin et al., 2016; Griffin et al., 2015; Marusek and Miller, 2015; Mills et al., 2011; Mills et al., 2013). Based on investigative research of media, NGOs, policy reports and Internet archives, we follow the money to engage in social network analysis, highlighting the relationships between people, organisations and power (see Cronin et al., 2016: 11–12). Data in this chapter is drawn particularly from annual reports lodged by charities, foundations, think tanks and other groups with regulators in the US and UK. In the US, we examined annual tax filings with the Internal Revenue Service; and in the UK, annual reports and accounts lodged with the Charity Commission.[2] The data includes documents associated with those organisations that we are interested in but, more importantly, also with the charities and foundations that pass money to such anti-Islam groups.

Key organisations peddling Islamophobia

We looked first at the key American organisations overtly promoting an anti-Islam agenda as identified from previous research (Ali et al., 2011; CAIR, 2013; SPLC, 2016a). The Center for American Progress names the heads of the Center for Security Policy, David Horowitz Freedom Center, Investigative Project on Terrorism and Middle East Forum as 'the leading lights of the Islamophobia network' in the US (Ali et al., 2011: 7). The Southern Poverty Law Center also lists the heads of these four organisations, in addition to Robert Spencer, head of Jihad Watch, a project of the David Horowitz Freedom Center, as anti-Muslim extremists (SPLC, 2016a). A subsequent report by the Council on American-Islamic Relations (CAIR, 2013) adds the Clarion Project and MEMRI to this list. Furthermore, the Southern Poverty Law Center lists the Center for Security Policy as a hate group, saying that: 'For the past decade, [its] main focus has been on demonising Islam and Muslims under the guise of national security' (SPLC, 2016b); as well as the David Horowitz Freedom Center, calling the latter 'the premier financier of anti-Muslim voices and radical ideologies, as well as acting as an exporter of misinformation that seeks to increase popular appeal for Horowitz's fears and phobias' (SPLC, 2017). The data shows that both the Center for Security Policy and David Horowitz Freedom Center share at least one funder with all of the above organisations. Furthermore, the Center for Security Policy's director, Steve Emerson, is also a director of MEMRI, while his wife sits on the board of NGO Monitor. As this chapter shows, there are many other organisational and financial linkages that justify grouping them together as a network to be interrogated.

These include (in alphabetical order): Center for Security Policy; Clarion Project; Committee for Accuracy in Middle East Reporting in America (CAMERA); David Horowitz Freedom Center; Foundation for Defense of Democracies (FDD); Investigative Project on Terrorism (IPT); Gatestone Institute; Middle East Forum; Middle East Media Research Institute (MEMRI); and Washington Institute for Middle East Policy (WINEP). While there are many other groups in the US promoting Islamophobia, we focus primarily on these ten organisations as the most active and influential in the media and in policy debates. In addition to the above, there are other groups outside the US, in Israel and Europe that are promoting a range of issues that include Islamophobia, and which, the data shows, share many of the same funders as the more overt organisations highlighted above. We therefore look at an additional four (in alphabetical order): European Foundation for Democracy in Brussels; Henry Jackson Society (HJS) in London; NGO Monitor in Jerusalem; and UN Watch in Geneva.

So, while not every organisation above is explicitly peddling an Islamophobic agenda, their shared funders suggests a shared milieu. Indeed, a careful examination of their relationships, activities and publications backs up this claim. Public Interest Investigations' research shows that each of these groups appears to be prominent in what we call the transatlantic Islamophobia network. Table 9.1 provides some background on each organisation, including key people.

Table 9.1   Foundations identified with the transatlantic Islamophobia network

Organisation	Location	Key people	Comments
Center for Security Policy	Washington, DC	Frank Gaffney	Gaffney argues that 'nearly every major Muslim organisation in the US is actually controlled by the [Muslim Brotherhood] or a derivative organisation. Consequently, most of the Muslim-American groups of any prominence in America are now known to be, as a matter of fact, hostile to the US and its Constitution' (Ali et al., 2011: 30).
Clarion Project	Washington, DC	Robert Shore	Initially linked with Aish HaTorah,[a] the Clarion Project produces virulently anti-Muslim films, including *Obsession: Radical Islam's War Against the West* and *The Third Jihad: Radical Islam's Vision for America*. Robert is the brother of Ephraim Shore, who heads the pro-Israel media watchdog HonestReporting.[b]
Committee for Accuracy in Middle East Reporting in America (CAMERA)	Boston, MA	Andrea Levin	Monitors both the American and British media for alleged anti-Israeli bias, as well as US college campuses.[c] Its website has an extensive database of journalists that it has targeted over the years, including many prominent Israelis.[d]

Organisation	Location	Key people	Comments
David Horowitz Freedom Center	Sherman Oaks, CA	David Horowitz and Peter Collier	The Anti-Defamation League charges that the centre has 'consistently [vilified] the Islamic faith under the guise of fighting radical Islam' and 'introduced a growing number of Americans to its conspiratorial anti-Muslim agenda'.[e] The anti-Muslim author and activist Robert Spencer currently serves as its 'Jihad Watch Director'.[f]
European Foundation for Democracy	Brussels	Roberta Bonazzi, Nicola Dell'Arciprete and Miguel Papi Boucher	Dell'Arciprete previously worked as an assistant to an MEP with the far-right Italian party Lega Nord (Northern League),[g] during which time she participated in a tour of occupied East Jerusalem hosted by Ateret Cohanim, an organisation affiliated with Israeli settlers.[h] The foundation has adopted a number of political campaigns that echo policies advocated by the Israeli establishment; for example, proposing a European ban on television channels linked to Hamas and Hizbullah.[i]
Foundation for Defense of Democracies	Washington, DC	Clifford May and R. James Woolsey	Eli Clifton of Salon news website has called the foundation 'Washington's premiere hawkish think tank'.[j] It has organisational and financial ties to the European Foundation for Democracy.
Gatestone Institute	New York	Nina Rosenwald and John Bolton	Among the writers it has published are Robert Spencer and Peder Nøstvold Jensen (who previously wrote under the pseudonym of Fjordman), a far-right blogger 'idolised' by Norwegian mass murderer Anders Breivik.[k]
Henry Jackson Society	London	Alan Mendoza and Douglas Murray	Murray once infamously said that 'conditions for Muslims in Europe should be made harder across the board' and that all immigration from Muslim countries 'should be stopped'.[l] After the brutal attack on 7 January 2015 against *Charlie Hebdo* newspaper, he blamed Islamists for being behind anti-Semitic hate crime in Europe, asking, 'Why do they always target the Jews?', this question following a reference to the Muslim 'population who came to Europe since the Holocaust'.[m]

Organisation	Location	Key people	Comments
Investigative Project on Terrorism	Washington, DC	Steve Emerson	Emerson once presented the Associated Press with a purported FBI dossier showing ties between Muslim American organisations and radical Islamist groups. The agency's reporters 'concluded [that] the dossier was created by Emerson and that [Emerson] had edited out all phrases, taken out anything that made it look like his' (Ali et al., 2011: 49). In January 2015, Emerson falsely told Fox News that Birmingham is a 'Muslim-only city' where non-Muslims 'don't go'. The subsequent public outcry forced him to apologise.[n]
Middle East Forum	Philadelphia, PA	Daniel Pipes	Lean (2012: 5) has called Pipes 'the grandfather of Islamophobia'. He created widespread controversy in 2002 when he launched a website called Campus Watch, which posted dossiers on academics critical of Israel and encouraged students to report comments or behaviour that might be considered hostile to Israel (Mearsheimer and Walt, 2006: 47). The dossiers were removed after only two weeks, but the website continues to solicit student complaints of academics deemed anti-Israel.
Middle East Media Research Institute (MEMRI)	Washington, DC	Yigal Carmon, Meyrav Wurmser and Steve Emerson	Distributes free English language translations of Arabic, Persian, Urdu, Pashto and Turkish media reports. Carmon is a former Israeli military intelligence officer. Brian Whitaker, a journalist for the *Guardian*, has argued that it poses 'as a research institute when it's basically a propaganda operation'.[o] Robert Spencer hails MEMRI as 'a goldmine of translated material' (Ali et al., 2011: 94).
NGO Monitor	Jerusalem	Gerald Steinberg	Exists in partnership with the Institute for Zionist Strategies, led by Israel Harel, a founder of the Gush Emunim settler movement.[p] Israeli journalist Didi Remez says that NGO Monitor 'is a partisan operation that suppresses its perceived ideological adversaries through the sophisticated use of McCarthyite techniques – blacklisting, guilt by association and selective filtering of facts'.[q]

Organisation	Location	Key people	Comments
UN Watch	Geneva	Morris Abram	Under the control of the American Jewish Committee since 2001, its mission is to campaign against United Nations officials critical of Israel.[r] Former chess champion Garry Kasparov, a UN Watch board member, penned an editorial in the *Wall Street Journal* arguing that Islamists were waging a 'global war on modernity', setting 'the time machine to the Dark Ages'.[s]
Washington Institute of Near East Policy	Washington, DC	Martin Indyk and Barbi Weinberg	Sometimes referred to as the American Israel Public Affairs Committee's (AIPAC) think tank,[t] its board of advisors include formerly high-ranking US security officials, such as Richard Perle, former US Assistant Secretary of Defense, and Robert McFarlane, former US National Security Advisor.[u]

Notes:

a. Meg Laughlin, 'Senders of Islam movie "Obsession" tied to Jewish charity', *Tampa Bay Times*, 26 September 2008. www.tampabay.com/news/politics/national/senders-of-islam-movie-obsession-tied-to-jewish-charity/827910. Accessed 25 March 2015.

b. Robert Shore, TV.com, n.d. www.tv.com/people/david-shore/biography/. Accessed 7 December 2015.

c. 'About CAMERA', Committee for Accuracy in Middle East Reporting, n.d. www.camera.org/index.asp?x_context=24. Accessed 14 January 2017.

d. 'Names in the news', Committee for Accuracy in Middle East Reporting in America, n.d. www.camera.org/index.asp?x_context=8. Accessed 8 July 2015.

e. Anti-Defamation League, 'Stop Islamization of America', Anti-Defamation League, 19 September 2012. www.adl.org/civil-rights/discrimination/c/stop-islamization-of-america.html. Accessed 31 October 2015.

f. 'About', Jihad Watch, n.d. www.jihadwatch.org/about-robert. Accessed 21 January 2017.

g. Documents registering European Foundation for Democracy, Belgium Justice Ministry, 24 May 2006. www.ejustice.just.fgov.be/tsv_pdf/2006/06/06/06092519.pdf. Accessed 7 November 2015.

h. 'EU rep tours with Ateret Cohanim in the heart of Jerusalem', American Friends of Ateret Cohanim, n.d. www.jerusalemchai.org/contents/read.cfm?categoryID=115&cID=1202. Accessed 7 November 2015.

i. Alexander Ritzmann, 'Germany bans Hezbollah's al-Manar TV', European Foundation for Democracy, 24 November 2008. http://europeandemocracy.eu/2008/11/germany-bans-hezbollahs-al-manar-tv/. Accessed 7 November 2015.

j. Eli Clifton, 'Home Depot founder's quiet $10 million right-wing investment', *Salon*, 5 August 2013. www.salon.com/2013/08/05/home_depot_founder%E2%80%99s_quiet_10_million_right_wing_investment/. Accessed 2 July 2015.

k. 'Experts', Gatestone Institute, n.d. www.gatestoneinstitute.org/experts/. Accessed 1 July 2015.

l. Paul Goodman, 'Letters', *The Spectator*, 15 October 2011.

m. Douglas Murray, 'The siege in a kosher shop in Paris proves why Israel needs to exist', *The Spectator*, 9 January 2015. http://blogs.spectator.co.uk/douglas-murray/2015/01/the-siege-in-a-kosher-shop-in-paris-proves-why-israel-needs-to-exist/. Accessed 13 January 2015.

n. 'Apology for "Muslim Birmingham" Fox News claim', BBC News, 12 January 2015. www.bbc.co.uk/news/uk-england-30773297. Accessed 2 July 2015.

o. 'Email debate: Yigal Carmon and Brian Whitaker', *Guardian,* 23 January 2003. www.theguardian.com/world/2003/jan/28/israel2. Accessed 3 November 2015.

p. Didi Remez, 'Bring on the transparency', *Haaretz*, 26 November 2009. www.haaretz.com/print-edition/opinion/bring-on-the-transparency-1.3326. Accessed 2 July 2015.

q. Remez, 'Bring on the transparency'.

r. 'UN Watch, AJC seal partnership', American Jewish Committee, 4 January 2001. www.ajc.org/site/apps/nlnet/content2.aspx?c=7oJILSPwFfJSG&b=8479733&ct=12487775. Accessed 26 March 2017.

s. Garry Kasparov, 'The global war on modernity', *Wall Street Journal,* 20 January 2015. www.wsj.com/articles/garry-kasparov-the-global-war-on-modernity-1421800948. Accessed 3 July 2015.

t. M.J. Rosenberg, 'Who funds Muslim-baiting in the US?', Al Jazeera, 27 August 2011. www.aljazeera.com/indepth/opinion/2011/08/201182713537929189.html. Accessed 2 July 2015.

u. 'Board of Advisors', Washington Institute for Near East Policy, n.d. www.washingtoninstitute.org/about/board-of-advisors/. Accessed 21 January 2017.

The transatlantic Islamophobia network's key figures and funders

As noted above, overlapping relations are not uncommon in the transatlantic Islamophobia network. For example, in addition to chairing FDD (2015), R. James Woolsey, former director of the CIA, is also an advisor to HJS (2017), MEMRI (Powerbase, 2016), NGO Monitor (2017) and WINEP (2017). In 2010, Woolsey co-authored a book on the perceived threat of Sharia (Islamic) law in the US, with, amongst others, retired military general William Boykin and Frank Gaffney, head of the Center for Security Policy. Then there is Nina Rosenwald, head of the Gatestone Institute, who is also affiliated with the Center for Security Policy, CAMERA and Middle East Forum (Gatestone Institute, 2017). Furthermore, her Abstraction Fund finances nine of the 14 organisations highlighted above. The journalist Max Blumenthal has argued that she uses 'her millions to cement the alliance between the pro-Israel lobby and the Islamophobic fringe' (M. Blumenthal, 2012). And finally, Elliott Abrams, a former US national security advisor, and leading neocon, has been a member of the Center for Security Policy, a director of MEMRI (Powerbase, 2015a), an author at the Gatestone Institute (2015) and an outside expert at WINEP (2015a). Figure 9.1 provides a clearer idea of how some of the key figures of the transatlantic network are connected not only to each other, but also to the Israeli government and institutions like the Interdisciplinary Center (IDC) Herzliya, Israel's only private university, which has connections to Israeli intelligence and military (Powerbase, 2015b). For example, Woolsey is a frequent speaker at the annual conference of the International Institute for Counter-Terrorism (ICT),[3] housed at the IDC. Matthew Levitt, who sits on the advisory board of FDD (2017), and is director of WINEP's Stein Program on Counterterrorism and Intelligence (WINEP, 2015b), is also on the advisory board of the ICT (IDC, 2015).

As noted in Table 9.1, Daniel Pipes heads the Middle East Forum. The Center for American Progress argues that both Pipes and the Middle East Forum are part of a network of 'misinformation experts' that 'peddle hate and fear of Muslims and Islam' (Ali et al., 2011). He once wrote that 'Western European societies are unprepared for the massive immigration of brown-skinned peoples cooking strange foods and maintaining different standards of hygiene ... All immigrants bring exotic customs and attitudes, but Muslim customs are more troublesome than most' (Whitaker, 2001). In a similar anti-Islam vein, Douglas Murray (2006), the associate director of HJS, has stated that 'conditions for Muslims in Europe should be made harder across the board'. On the Israeli side, Dore Gold, head of the Jerusalem Centre for Public Affairs – which lists *NGO Monitor* as one of its online publications (JCPA, 2015a) – is a former advisor to Israeli Prime Ministers Benjamin Netanyahu and Ariel Sharon (JCPA, 2015b). While he is not vocal about Muslims in Europe, Gold has argued that East Jerusalem must be under Israeli sovereignty because 'Muslim Palestinians are looking to obliterate other faiths' in the city (Cline, 2008).

However, human resources are not the only thing that this network has in common; it also shares funders. Although none of these organisations publish their list of donors, it was possible to track down a number of their backers through online searches and piecing together the wider network of related organisations. In total, we discovered that 60 US-based charities donated almost $41 million to the 14 organisations outlined above promoting a right-wing anti-Islam agenda between 2009 and 2013. A complete listing of all the known funders of these groups and the total amount that they granted during this time can be accessed online at Powerbase, an online wiki project of Public Interest Investigations. It is noteworthy that the majority of these funders, indeed over 80 per cent, support multiple organisations that collectively make up the Islamophobia industry. Table 9.2 focuses on the top ten donors, along with the total they granted and their grantees, while Figure 9.2 illustrates the interconnectedness of this financial network. For the purposes of the figure, I connected all those that donated to the American Jewish

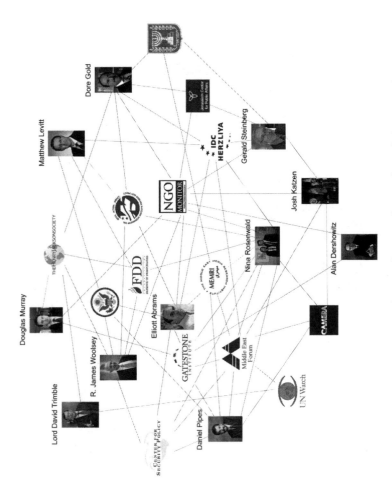

Figure 9.1   Key personalities in the transatlantic Islamophobia network

Table 9.2 Top ten donors to the transatlantic Islamophobia network between 2009 and 2013

Charity/foundation	Amount (US$)	Grantees
Abstraction Fund	3,439,130	CAMERA, Center for Security Policy, Clarion Project, David Horowitz Freedom Center, Foundation for Defense of Democracies, Henry Jackson Society, Investigative Project on Terrorism, Middle East Forum and MEMRI
Middle East Forum	4,876,434	NGO Monitor, CAMERA, Center for Security Policy, David Horowitz Freedom Center, Gatestone Institute, Investigative Project on Terrorism and MEMRI
Klarman Family Foundation	2,600,000	NGO Monitor, Center for Security Policy, CAMERA, Foundation for Defense of Democracies, Middle East Forum, MEMRI and WINEP
Koret Foundation	1,840,000	NGO Monitor, CAMERA, Center for Security Policy, David Horowitz Freedom Center, Foundation for Defense of Democracies, Henry Jackson Society, Investigative Project on Terrorism, Middle East Forum and MEMRI
Lynde and Harry Bradley Foundation	2,832,150	Center for Security Policy, David Horowitz Freedom Center, Foundation for Defense of Democracies, Middle East Forum and MEMRI
Marcus Foundation	12,155,000	CAMERA, Foundation for Defense of Democracies, European Foundation for Democracy and MEMRI
Newton and Rochelle Becker charities	5,409,775	UN Watch, CAMERA, Center for Security Policy, Clarion Fund, David Horowitz Freedom Center, Foundation for Defense of Democracies, Investigative Project on Terrorism, MEMRI, Middle East Forum and WINEP
Paul E. Singer foundations	1,475,000	NGO Monitor, European Foundation for Democracy and MEMRI
Russell Berrie Foundation	1,620,000	Investigative Project on Terrorism and MEMRI
Sarah Scaife Foundation Inc.	2,600,000	Center for Security Policy, David Horowitz Freedom Center and Foundation for Defense of Democracies

Committee to UN Watch, since they jointly file taxes, to show the full extent of the network.

The largest donors include familiar names like Daniel Pipes' Middle East Forum (giving $4,876,434) and Nina Rosenwald's the Abstraction Fund (giving $3,439,130). Of the other top donors, several are notable for being key funders of Republican and Zionist causes. For example, the largest funder of Islamophobia is billionaire pharmacist, retail entrepreneur and philanthropist Bernard Marcus. Marcus donated almost $13.5 million to the Republicans in 2016 (Open Secrets, 2017), while his Atlanta-based foundation provided more than $12.1 million to the transatlantic network between 2009 and 2013. Marcus sits on the board of directors of the Republican Jewish Coalition (RJC), the most significant Republican pro-Israel lobbying group in the US, alongside Paul E. Singer (RJC, 2017), whose affiliated foundations are another major donor to Republicans and the transatlantic network (giving the latter almost $1.5 million). Another billionaire businessman and philanthropist, Singer is currently the second largest conservative donor in the US, giving $23.5 million to Republican causes in 2016 (Open Secrets, 2017). And finally, businessman turned philanthropist Seth Klarman gave almost $3 million to Republican causes in 2016 (Open Secrets, 2017), while his Klarman Family Foundation gave $2.6 million to the transatlantic network. During the 2016 election, however, Klarman publicly denounced the Republican candidate Donald Trump (Reuters, 2016). As Klarman, Marcus and Singer are also key funders of the settlements, they are discussed in more detail below, alongside other major donors.

Connections to the settlements

Although the international community is almost uniform in its condemnation of Israeli settlements, Israel's expansion of illegal blocs is financed obliquely through community organisations that receive funding from abroad – mostly from the US (often 'American Friends of' organisations), but also from other places such as the UK. In recent years, scholars and the media have increasingly been paying attention to the funding of Israeli settlements via American charitable donations. Several (2011) has provided background on the opacity of some of the key organisations funding the occupation; and in their extensive report on private American financial contributions to Israel, Fleisch and

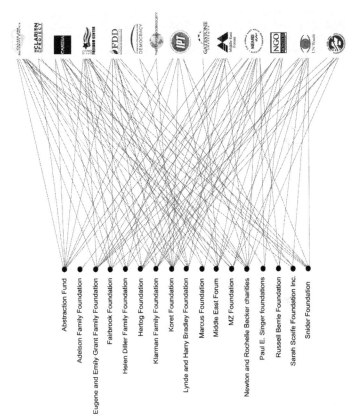

Figure 9.2 Donors who provided more than $700,000 to the transatlantic Islamophobia network between 2009 and 2013

Sasson (2012) included over 40 registered charities in the US that fund the settlements. More recently, Israel's *Haaretz* newspaper published an in-depth report on this subject (Blau, 2015). While conducting research on this issue, it became apparent that there was a significant overlap between the funders of Islamophobia and Israel's occupation of Palestine. In 2012, the Israeli government passed a new law to grant tax breaks for donations to organisations that promote pro-Zionist causes and the settlements (Hever, 2013: 20); but in the US, these donations are also tax-deductible when steered through a registered charity.

Of the 60 known charities/foundations that fund the transatlantic Islamophobia network, the data shows that 45 also finance organisations identified as supporting Israel's occupation and/or settlements, giving almost $169 million over five years (2009–13). The 2015 *Haaretz* report found that American donors gave over $220 million to Israeli settlements during the same time (Blau, 2015). While our research is still a work in progress, our own figures for the total funding are likely higher, as we have included groups that further both the occupation and the settlements, as well as several organisations that are supporting them to some degree, and have only focused on the funders of the Islamophobia network. That said, the majority of 'pro-settler organisations' that we have identified overtly and/or uniformly fund Israel's occupation and/or settlement enterprise. However, it is also important to point out that there are many pro-settler organisations that do not share any funding ties to the charities/foundations affiliated to Islamophobia. Here, we have identified 38 pro-settler organisations that share funders with the transatlantic Islamophobia network (the 14 organisations outlined above), 30 of which overtly and/or uniformly fund Israel's occupation and/or settlements. The charities/foundations that contributed more than $1 million each to them between 2009 and 2013 are included in Table 9.3.[4]

Table 9.3 Donors of Israel's occupation/settlements giving at least $1 million between 2009 and 2013

Charity/foundation	Amount (US$)	Grantees
Abramson Family Foundation	1,984,265	Birthright Israel
Adelson Family Foundation	83,078,844	Birthright Israel, Christians United for Israel, Jewish National Fund and Zionist Organization of America

Charity/foundation	Amount (US$)	Grantees
Goldhirsh family foundations	1,300,000	Birthright Israel, Friends of Ir David, International Christian Embassy Jerusalem and Jewish National Fund
Hertog Foundation	4,605,683	American Friends of Beir Orot, American Friends of the College of Judea & Samaria, American Friends of Hebrew University, Birthright Israel, Central Fund of Israel, Friends of Ir David, Friends of the IDF and Israel Independence Fund
Hochberg Family Foundation	1,217,259	Birthright Israel, Friends of the IDF, Jewish National Fund, One Israel Fund, Proclaiming Justice to the Nations, StandWithUs and Zionist Organization of America
Jacobson Family Foundation Trust	8,495,000	Central Fund of Israel, Friends of the IDF, Friends of Ir David and Jerusalem Foundation
Klarman Family Foundation	7,510,000	Central Fund of Israel, Friends of Ir David, Friends of the IDF, Jewish National Fund and StandWithUs
Koret Foundation	15,400,000	American Friends of the Hebrew University, Birthright Israel, Friends of the IDF, Jewish National Fund, StandWithUs and Zionist Organization of America
Marcus Foundation	11,321,800	Birthright Israel, Christians United for Israel, Friends of the IDF and Jewish National Fund
Milken family foundations	2,203,000	Aish HaTorah, American Friends of Ariel, Ariel University Center of Samaria, Central Fund of Israel, Friends of the IDF, Jewish National Fund, StandWithUs and Zionist Organization of America
Moskowitz family foundations	20,917,300	American Friends of Ateret Cohanim, American Friends of Beit Orot, American Friends of Bet El Yeshiva, American Friends of Old City Charities, American Friends of Shiloh, American Friends of the College of Judea & Samaria, American Friends of the Everest Foundation, American Friends of Yeshiva High School in Kiryat Arba, American Friends of Bimad Alon Moreh, Americans for a Safe Israel, Central Fund of Israel, Friends of Ir David, Friends of Itamar, Friends of the IDF, Friends of Yeshivat Nir, Kiryat Arba, Gush Etzion Foundation, Haztalah Yehuda and Shamron, Hebron Fund, Israel Allies Foundation, Israel Independence Fund, One Israel Fund, Proclaiming Justice to the Nations, Shavei Hevron Institutions, Shilo Israel Children's Fund, Shuva Israel, StandWithUs and Zionist Organization of America
Newton and Rochelle Becker charities	1,351,000	Christians United for Israel, Friends of the IDF, Israel Allies Foundation, StandWithUs and Zionist Organization of America
Paul E. Singer foundations	2,062,000	Aish HaTorah, Birthright Israel, Friends of the IDF and Israel Independence Fund
Shillman Foundation	1,428,150	Christians United for Israel, Friends of the IDF, Jewish National Fund and Zionist Organization of America

As noted, not every organisation above is entirely focused on funding the occupation and/or settlements. For example, one of the organisations that we identified as supporting the occupation is the New York-based Friends of the Israel Defense Forces (IDF), the US fundraising arm of the Israeli military – including its occupation forces. Friends of the IDF is the largest known international donor to the Israeli military, giving over $72 million in 2013 alone. Another organisation, Birthright Israel, is a pro-Zionist organisation based in West Jerusalem that arranges and finances trips to Israel for Jewish young adults from around the world, aiming to strengthen their relations with the state of Israel. However, this includes trips to settlements in the occupied territories without acknowledging them as such (Wedgle and Carter, 2015). In 2013, the Birthright Israel Foundation in New York reported an income of over $74 million. Other organisations that have a wider mission, but also still provide material support to the occupation and/or settlements, include: Aish HaTorah; American Friends of Hebrew University; Christians United for Israel; Jerusalem Foundation; Jewish National Fund; StandWithUs; and Zionist Organization of America.

Otherwise, the remaining 30 organisations either run projects overtly supporting the colonisation of Palestine, focus on individual settlements or on the ethnic cleansing of Jerusalem. One that falls into the first group is the New York-based Central Fund of Israel, which supports a Jewish state in all of historical Palestine. The *New York Times* reported in 2010 that the Central Fund of Israel had 'raised tens of thousands of dollars to help erect temporary structures' in an Israeli settlement in the occupied West Bank to keep 'the community going until officials lifted the building ban' on further construction (Rutenberg et al., 2010). It channels donations to Palestinian Media Watch (PMW, 2015), and extremist Israeli groups like Im Tirtzu (Ravid, 2010), a far-right extra-parliamentary youth movement that has campaigned against universities, NGOs and peace groups (Felsen, 2013). Then there is the One Israel Fund, also based in New York, which was initially established in 1994 as the American Friends of Yesha. This refers to the Yesha Council, the umbrella organisation of municipal councils of Jewish settlements in the occupied territories. Other organisations give to a particular settlement in the occupied territories, for example, American Friends of Ariel, American Friends of Beir Orot, American Friends of Bet El, American Friends of Kedumim, Gush Etzion Foundation and the Hebron Fund, among others. And finally, others focus exclusively on ethnically cleansing East Jerusalem, like Ir David and Friends of Ateret Cohanim. Ir David, also known as Elad, uses archaeology to stake exclusively Jewish claims over the land. The Israeli government granted it management of the national park in the East Jerusalem neighbourhood of Silwan, which Hever (2013: 23) says: 'is used by Ir David to try and prove that the biblical King David was an historical figure, and that his kingdom in ancient Jerusalem justifies the Israeli occupation of the region and efforts to Judaise it (and to expel the indigenous Palestinian population through various means)'. Ateret Cohanim, on the other hand, is known for appropriating Palestinian homes in East Jerusalem. It also runs a *yeshiva* (a centre for the study of religious scripture) in the Old City, where its students have sported sweatshirts calling for the destruction of Jerusalem's Al-Aqsa Mosque, the third holiest site in Islam (Silverstein, 2012).

Main funders of Islamophobia and the occupation/settlements

Both the organisations funding the occupation and/or settlements and the transatlantic Islamophobia network are considerable in numbers and scope; however, there are several large donors who repeatedly appear, making the core of the network much tighter than its outlying elements. Indeed, among the largest funders of both Islamophobia and the settlements are the following charities/foundations: Adelson Family Foundation; Marcus Foundation; Moskowitz family foundations; Koret Foundation; Newton and Rochelle Becker charities; Klarman Family Foundation, Paul E. Singer foundations; and Hertog Foundation. This section provides more information on the wealthy financiers behind them.

Sheldon Adelson, a conservative casino billionaire, is by far the largest donor to the occupation and/or settlements, the Adelson Family Foundation giving over $83 million between 2009 and 2013. Adelson and his wife Miriam also granted $25 million to Ariel University in the occupied West Bank (JNS, 2014). Adelson has claimed that the Palestinians are 'an invented people' whose 'purpose ... is to destroy Israel' (Zengerle, 2015). He sits on the board of the Republican Jewish Coalition and owns the right-wing Israeli daily *Israel Hayom*, which is so closely associated with Israeli Prime Minister Benjamin Netanyahu that it is typically referred to as *Bibiton* – '*Bibi*' is Netanyahu's nickname; *iton* is Hebrew for 'newspaper' (Zengerle, 2015). His foundation funded the transatlantic network through MEMRI (giving $750,000); however, in previous years, Adelson reportedly donated more than $1.5 million to the Foundation for Defense of Democracies (Clifton, 2013), as well as over $300,000 to CAMERA (Blau, 2016). He is currently the top US donor to Republican causes, giving almost $78 million in 2016 (Open Secrets, 2017). Indeed, during the lead-up to the 2016 presidential campaign, potential Republican candidates all competed in what is known as the 'Adelson primary' to secure access to his vast fortune (Zengerle, 2015). When it became obvious that outsider Donald Trump was ahead, Adelson was one of the few Republican donors to back him, later taking 'an honorary position as a member of Trump's inauguration committee' (Guttman, 2017). According to *Forbes* (2017a), he is currently worth $31 billion.

The second largest donor is the above-mentioned Marcus Foundation, giving almost $23.5 million to Islamophobia and the occupation and/or settlements combined. A co-founder of the American retailer Home Depot, its founder Bernard Marcus serves as director of the Foundation for Defense of Democracies, which he also generously funds (he gave it almost $11 million between 2009 and 2013). Alongside Israeli Ayre Carmon, in 1991 Marcus co-founded the Israel Democracy Institute, described by one writer at the *Jerusalem Post* as being extremely well financed, secular, on the Israeli left and having 'close links to unelected [Israeli] elites, chiefly in the legal establishment, the media and academia, who determine so much of public policy' (Klein, 2009). Marcus was a vocal critic of the Obama administration, calling it 'amateurs in the White House' and 'amateurs surrounded by amateurs' (Clifton, 2013).

The third largest donor is California-based casino magnate Irving Moskowitz, giving almost $21 million to the occupation and/or settlements and over $500,000 to Islamophobia (all to MEMRI). Moskowitz has been buying property in occupied East Jerusalem for decades (Silverstein, 2009); more recently, he acquired Palestinian farmland in the occupied West Bank for a new settlement, a move that was embraced by Israel but condemned by American officials (Ravid, 2016). A long-time Republican donor, in 2012 he gave his largest donation yet: $1 million to a super PAC linked to the neoconservative Karl Rove (P. Blumenthal, 2012). Moskowitz has also reportedly funded groups that question the legitimacy of President Barack Obama's US citizenship, 'and others that stoke fears about the [former] president's alleged ties to "radical Islam"' (P. Blumenthal, 2012).

The Koret Foundation comes in fourth place, giving more than $17 million in total to both causes. Based in San Francisco, the foundation was established in 1978 by Russian-born Joseph Koret and his wife Stephanie, alongside Tad Taube, friend and chief executive officer of their women's sportswear company, Koret of California, Inc., which they sold to Levi Strauss Company in 1979. Joseph Koret's second wife, Susan, became chair for life of the foundation after his death in 1982, and Taube currently serves as its president (Koret Foundation, 2016). A personal friend describes Taube as 'a strong Republican, very right-wing' (May, 2011). In January 2016, he was embroiled in a scandal when it was reported that several women at Stanford University's Hoover Institution 'complained about Taube's "lewd" behavior as part of an investigation into the treatment of women at the conservative think tank' (Murphy, 2016). Taube is also locked in another legal battle with Joseph Koret's second wife Susan, who decided to sue him 'and other Koret board members in 2014, accusing them of steering the foundation's money to conservative causes and Taube's pet projects rather than helping the needy' (Murphy, 2016).

In fifth place is the the Klarman Family Foundation, which gave a total of over $10 million to Islamophobia and the settlements. As noted earlier, the foundation is run by billionaire Seth Klarman, whose worth *Forbes* (2017b) estimates to be about $1.38 billion. *Forward* newspaper describes Klarman as a 'wealthy American Jewish investor ... following in the footsteps of Sheldon Adelson and Ron Lauder [President of the World Jewish Congress and another close ally of Netanyahu] in acting on his belief that coverage of Israel within Israel itself is unbalanced and unjustifiably hostile – and that he can do something about it' (Nathan-Kazis, 2012). And indeed he did; he financed the right-wing Israel newspaper *The Times of Israel*. Klarman has publicly stated that he opposes the settlements, saying in 2012, 'We think it was a bad policy from the beginning and continues to be a bad policy' (Nathan-Kazis, 2012). Nevertheless, his foundation continued to funnel money to pro-settler organisations after this statement.

Other major donors include the late Newton Becker and his wife Rochelle. The Beckers have two foundations that support pro-settler and anti-Islam causes: the Newton and Rochelle Becker Foundation and the Newton and Rochelle Becker Charitable Trust. Together, they donated over $6.8 million. The 2011 report by the Center for American Progress names both charities as among the seven top contributors of Islamophobia in the US, contributing $1,136,000 to Islamophobic organisations between 2001 and 2009 (Ali et al., 2011: 19). According to the pro-settler group StandWithUs, Newton Becker 'shifted the paradigm of pro-Israel activism. Without him, the pro-Israel community would not be as strong and effective as it is today' (Benari, 2012). Another big donor is conservative businessman turned philanthropist Roger Hertog. His Hertog Foundation granted almost $5.5 million in total to both causes. Hertog is currently chairperson of the New York-based Tikvah Fund, which was first established by the late American billionaire Zalman Bernstein and finances settlement projects in the occupied territories. Its board members include: Elliot Abrams, national security advisor during the George W. Bush administration; William Kristol, founder and editor of the right-wing neoconservative magazine *The Weekly Standard*; and Sallai Meridor, former Israeli Ambassador to the United States (Tikvah Fund, 2017). Finally, the last major donor to highlight is Paul E. Singer, whose foundation spent more than $3.5 million. Singer's estimated worth is $2.2 billion, having earned his fortune as the CEO of Elliott Management Corporation, a hedge fund he founded in 1977 (Inside Philanthropy, 2016). During Israel's 2014 attack on the Gaza Strip, Singer characterised Palestine solidarity demonstrations in Paris as 'pogroms' and accused European governments of signalling that 'it is ok to be anti-Semitic' (ValueWalk, 2014).

Concluding comments

This chapter focuses only on selected key American funders of the transatlantic Islamophobia network. It is important to stress, once again, that not every donor is rich or Republican; nor do all of them finance Israel's occupation and/or settlements. However, the fact that 75 per cent of them do fund the latter, and that a small number of wealthy conservatives are funnelling tens of millions of dollars every year to both Islamophobia and the occupation and/or settlements, indicates that while the geographical reach of the transatlantic network is vast, it does not necessarily represent people on the ground. Indeed, a recent poll shows

THE TRANSATLANTIC NETWORK

that more Americans support UN resolution 2334 condemning the settlements than oppose it – 35 per cent approve, 28 per cent reject and 36 per cent hold no opinion or do not know (Cortellessa, 2017). A 2016 Pew Research Center survey found that only 17 per cent of American Jews think that continued settlement building helps the security of Israel, while 44 per cent say it hurts Israel (Stokes, 2016). And a 2015 survey found that 37 per cent of Americans support either economic sanctions against Israel over the settlements or more serious action, while 31 per cent prefer verbal sanction and only 27 per cent recommend doing nothing (Telhami, 2016).

The irony, as writer Jason Zengerle (2015) points out, is that most American Jews vote Democrat, and yet the Republican Party has become transformed into a pro-Israel stalwart by a small group of donors and activists, especially since the election of President Barack Obama. He reports one prominent Jewish member of the Grand Old Party (GOP) rhetorically asking: 'Long term, do more Jews become Republicans? Who gives a shit? What matters is that the Republican Party as a whole has become unapologetically and unflinchingly pro-Israel' (Zengerle, 2015). And being pro-Israel now appears to be more important than steering clear of anti-Semitism: the Republican Jewish Coalition, Zionist Organization of America and *Israel Hayom* – all affiliated with Sheldon Adelson – recently spoke out in defence of Steve Bannon, President Donald Trump's White House chief of strategy, who has been subject to widespread 'allegations that he peddled in anti-Semitism when he was chief of *Breitbart News*' (Guttman, 2017). As President Trump is sworn in at the time of writing, it is worth quoting Zengerle's (2015) article at length:

> Under the next Republican president, one neoconservative foreign-policy thinker predicts, the American Embassy in Israel will be moved from Tel Aviv to Jerusalem. American military aid to Israel, already substantial, will become even more substantial. 'They'll get whatever they want. They'll get shit they don't want. We'll arm them to the teeth.' And it won't just be Israel. On other national-security issues, ranging from domestic surveillance to Iranian nukes, the priorities of Adelson and his fellow Jewish Republicans are now the priorities of the GOP. 'Now, when the GOP ultimately does succeed and takes back the White House,' this neocon says, 'the hawks will have their way'.

This myopia is dangerous for the world. Indeed, it was reported that due to security concerns, the Israelis put a stop to Trump's plans to immediately move the US embassy to Jerusalem (Glasser, 2017). Although Republican politicians are increasingly out of step with the American public – not to mention the international community – on Israel, the peddling of Islamophobia has helped them to win a majority in the House and Senate, and now even the presidency. As long as these organisations do not have to reveal their funders, it is difficult to know for sure who is influencing politics anywhere, especially in relation to Israel.

Acknowledgements

I would like to acknowledge the research and advice of the following people, all of whom have been involved in projects on this and related issues with Public Interest Investigations: Hilary Aked, Tom Anderson, David Cronin, Alex Doherty, Tom Griffin, Melissa Jones, Azeezah Kanji, Freddie Mackereth, Narzanin Massoumi, David Miller, Tom Mills, Tom Pye, Luke Starr, Jamie Stern-Weiner and Karen from Corporate Watch.

Notes

1. Of course, this is not to argue that anti-Semitism has in any way been overcome, because it sadly has not. Indeed, today it has merely been pushed to the side, as evidenced by US President Donald Trump's prolonged delay in even addressing the alarming rise of anti-Semitic hate crimes across the US (Wildman, 2017).
2. Charity Commission documents were accessed at http://apps.charitycommission.gov.uk/showcharity/registerofcharities/RegisterHomePage.aspx; IRS documents were accessed at http://foundationcenter.org/find-funding/990-finder.
3. Woolsey spoke at the 2007, 2010, 2011, 2012, 2013 and 2014 annual IDC conferences.
4. A complete table of the donors that have funded the transatlantic Islamophobia network between 2009 and 2013 and their contributions to the occupation of Palestine can also be accessed online at Powerbase.

Bibliography

Al Jazeera (2016), 'Germany: Merkel's party suffers loss in Berlin election', Al Jazeera, 19 September. www.aljazeera.com/news/2016/09/germany-merkel-party-suffers-loss-berlin-election-160918185412444.html. Accessed 19 September 2016.

Ali, W. Clifton, E., Duss, M., Fang, L., Keyes, S. and Shakir, F. (2011), *Fear Inc.: The Roots of the Islamophobia Network in America*. Washington, DC: Center for American Progress.

Arnove, R. and Pinede, N. (2007), 'Revisiting the '"Big Three"' foundations', *Critical Sociology*, 33, 389–425.

Benari, E. (2012), 'Pro-Israel philanthropist Newton Becker dies at 83', *Arutz Sheva*, 2 September. www.israelnationalnews.com/News/News.aspx/151525. Accessed 22 January 2017.

Berndtson, E. (2007), 'Review essay: power of foundations and the American ideology', *Critical Sociology*, 33, 575–87.

Blau, U. (2015), 'U.S. donors gave settlements more than $220 million in tax-exempt funds over five years', *Haaretz*, 7 December. www.haaretz.com/settlementdollars/1.689683. Accessed 17 January 2017.

—— (2016), 'Times of Israel cofounder gave $1.5 million to right-wing media watchdog that routinely goes after news outlets', *Haaretz*, 5 September. www.haaretz.com/israel-news/1.740340. Accessed 20 January 2017.

Blumenthal, M. (2012), 'The sugar mama of anti-Muslim hate', *The Nation*, 13 June. www.thenation.com/article/168374/sugar-mama-anti-muslim-hate#. Accessed 29 March 2015.

Blumenthal, P. (2012), 'Irving Moskowitz, controversial backer of Israeli settlements, gives $1 million to anti-Obama super PAC', *Huffington Post*, 4 December. www.huffingtonpost.co.za/entry/irving-moskowitz-israeli-settlements-anti-obama-super-pac_n_1416041. Accessed 20 January 2017.

CAIR (2013), *Legislating Fear: Islamophobia and its Impact in the United States*. Washington, DC: CAIR.

Chrisafis, A. (2016), '"The nation state is back": Front National's Marine Le Pen rides on global mood', *Guardian*, 18 September. www.theguardian.com/world/2016/sep/18/nation-state-marine-le-pen-global-mood-france-brexit-trump-front-national. Accessed 19 September 2016.

Clifton, E. (2013), 'Home Depot founder's quiet $10 million right-wing investment', Salon, 5 August. www.salon.com/2013/08/05/home_depot_founder%E2%80%99s_quiet_10_million_right_wing_investment/. Accessed 2 July 2015.

Cline, E.H. (2008), 'Review: *The Fight for Jerusalem: Radical Islam, the West, and the Future of the Holy City* by Dore Gold', *Middle East Quarterly*, Fall. www.meforum.org/2023/the-fight-for-jerusalem. Accessed 26 March 2017.

Cortellessa, E. (2017), 'More Americans support UN resolution on Israel than oppose it – poll', *The Times of Israel*, 4 January. www.timesofisrael.com/more-americans-support-un-resolution-on-israel-than-oppose-it-poll/. Accessed 20 January 2017.

Cronin, D., Marusek, S. and Miller, D. (2016), *The Israel Lobby and the European Union*. Glasgow: Public Interest Investigations.

Davies, G. and Allen, P. (2016), 'Police question Bastille Day killer's 73-year-old male lover as it is revealed murderer was a "sex maniac" who searched for ISIS beheading videos online', *MailOnline*, 19 July. www.dailymail.co.uk/news/article-3697136/Mohamed-Lahouaiej-Bouhlel-s-73-year-old-male-lover-questioned-wake-Nice-Bastille-Day-attack.html#ixzz4KhSPE1ZN. Accessed 19 September 2016.

Diamond, J. (2015), 'Donald Trump: ban all Muslim travel to US', CNN, 8 December. http://edition.cnn.com/2015/12/07/politics/donald-trump-muslim-ban-immigration/. Accessed 19 September 2016.

FDD (2015), 'Our team: R. James Woolsey', Foundation for Defense of Democracies. www.defenddemocracy.org/about-fdd/team-overview/r-james-woolsey/. Accessed 3 July 2015.

—— (2017), 'Matthew Levitt', Foundation for Defense of Democracies. www.defenddemocracy.org/about-fdd/team-overview/matt-levitt/. Accessed 21 January 2017.

Felsen, M. (2013), 'Im Tirtzu's Zionism without democracy', *Haaretz*, 7 January. www.haaretz.com/opinion/im-tirtzu-s-zionism-without-democracy.premium-1.492403. Accessed 2 July 2015.

Fleisch, E. and Sasson, T. (2012), *The New Philanthropy: American Jewish Giving to Israeli Organizations*. Waltham, MA: Brandeis University.

Forbes (2017a), 'Sheldon Adelson', *Forbes*. www.forbes.com/profile/sheldon-adelson/. Accessed 20 January 2017.

—— (2017b), '#1367 Seth Klarman', *Forbes*. www.forbes.com/profile/seth-klarman/. Accessed 17 January 2017.

Gatestone Institute (2015), 'Authors', Gatestone Institute. www.gatestoneinstitute.org/authors/. Accessed 3 July 2015.

—— (2017), 'Nina Rosenwald', Gatestone Institute. www.gatestoneinstitute.org/biography/Nina+Rosenwald. Accessed 21 January 2017.

Glasser S.B. (2017), 'Can a "wrecking ball" of a president evolve?', *Politico Magazine*, 13 February. www.politico.com/magazine/story/2017/02/bob-corker-committee-foreign-relations-trump-214773. Accessed 25 February 2017.

Griffin, T., Aked, H., Miller, D. and Marusek, S. (2015), *The Henry Jackson Society and the Degeneration of British Neoconservatism*. Glasgow: Public Interest Investigations.

Guttman, N. (2017), 'How Sheldon Adelson's bet on Trump made him 2016 election's biggest winner', *Forward*, 9 January. http://forward.com/news/national/356644/how-sheldon-adelsons-bet-on-trump-made-him-2016-elections-biggest-winner/. Accessed 21 January 2017.

Hafez, F. (2014), 'Shifting borders: Islamophobia as common ground for building pan-European right-wing unity', *Patterns of Prejudice*, 48 (5), 479–99.

Hever, S. (2013), 'Private funding of right wing ideology in Israel', *The Economy of the Occupation: Socioeconomic Bulletin*, No. 29–30, Alternative Information

Center, Jerusalem, Israel and May Beit Sahour, Palestine. www.aurdip.org/EOO29-30.pdf. Accessed 22 February 2017.

HJS (2017), 'International patrons', Henry Jackson Society. http://henry jacksonsociety.org/about-the-society/international-patrons-2/. Accessed 21 January 2017.

IDC (2015), 'Professional Advisory Board', IDC Herzliya. www.ict.org.il/Content.aspx?ID=30. Accessed 3 July 2015.

Inside Philanthropy (2016), '"Paul Singer"', Inside Philanthropy. www.insidephilanthropy.com/wall-street-donors/paul-singer.html. Accessed 19 September 2016.

JCPA (2015a), 'About the Jerusalem Center for Public Affairs', www.jcpa.org/about-jun04.htm. Accessed 3 July 2015.

——(2015b), 'Dore Gold articles', Jerusalem Center for Public Affairs. www.jcpa.org/publication/dore-gold-articles/. Accessed 3 July 2015.

Jilani, Z. (2017), 'Senators threaten to cut worldwide embassy security if US doesn't move its Israeli embassy to Jerusalem', The Intercept, 5 January. https://theintercept.com/2017/01/04/senators-threaten-to-cut-worldwide-embassy-security-if-u-s-doesnt-move-its-israeli-embassy-to-jerusalem/. Accessed 21 January 2017.

JNS (2014), 'Sheldon and Miriam Adelson to donate $25 million to Ariel University', The Algemeiner, 24 June. www.algemeiner.com/2014/06/23/sheldon-adelson-to-donate-25-million-to-ariel-university/. Accessed 20 January 2017.

Klein, Y. (2009), 'The strange case of the Israel Democracy Institute', The Jerusalem Post, 26 April. www.jpost.com/Opinion/Op-Ed-Contributors/The-strange-case-of-the-Israel-Democracy-Institute. Accessed 19 January 2017.

Koret Foundation (2016), 'Our legacy', Koret Foundation. http://koret.org/about/legacy/. Accessed 19 September 2016.

Lean, N. (2012), The Islamophobia Industry: How the Far Right Manufactures Fear of Muslims. London: Pluto Press.

Marusek, S. and Miller, D. (2015), How Israel Attempts to Mislead the United Nations: Deconstructing Israel's Campaign Against the Palestinian Return Centre. Glasgow: Public Interest Investigations.

May, M. (2011), 'Tad Taube escaped Nazis, created own empire', SFGATE, 13 March. www.sfgate.com/news/article/Tad-Taube-escaped-Nazis-created-own-empire-2389263.php. Accessed 19 September 2016.

Mearsheimer J. and Walt, S. (2006), 'The Israel lobby and US foreign policy', Middle East Policy, XIII (3), Fall, 29–87.

Mills, T., Griffin, T. and Miller, D. (2011), The Cold War on British Muslims: An Examination of Policy Exchange and the Centre for Social Cohesion. Glasgow: Public Interest Investigations.

Mills, T., Miller, D., Griffin, T. and Aked, H. (2013), The Britain Israel Communications and Research Centre. Giving Peace a Chance? Glasgow: Public Interest Investigations.

Mughal, Fiyaz (2016), 'Home Affairs Committee Oral evidence: Hate Crime and its violent consequences, HC 609', UK Parliament, 13 December. http://data. parliament.uk/writtenevidence/committeeevidence.svc/evidencedocument/ home-affairs-committee/hate-crime-and-its-violent-consequences/oral/ 44438.pdf. Accessed 5 February 2017.

Murphy, K. (2016), 'Sexual harassment claim: Stanford ignored Tad Taube's "lewd" behaviour, Hoover fellow alleges', *The Mercury News*, 20 January. www. mercurynews.com/2016/01/20/sexual-harassment-claim-stanford-ignored-tad-taubes-lewd-behavior-hoover-fellow-alleges/. Accessed 19 September 2016.

Murray, D. (2006), 'What are we to do about Islam? A speech to the Pim Fortuyn Memorial Conference on Europe and Islam', The Social Affairs Unit, 3 March. http://web.archive.org/web/20080201133647/http://www.socialaffairsunit. org.uk/blog/archives/000809.php. Accessed 3 July 2015.

Nathan-Kazis, J. (2012), 'The softspoken man behind Times of Israel', *Forward*, 29 February. http://forward.com/news/152169/the-softspoken-man-behind-times-of-israel/. Accessed 6 November 2015.

NGO Monitor (2017), 'James Woolsey', NGO Monitor. www.ngo-monitor.org/ about/boards/r-james-woolsey/. Accessed 21 January 2017.

Nossiternov, A. (2015), 'Marine Le Pen's anti-Islam message gains influence in France', *New York Times*, 17 November. www.nytimes.com/2015/11/18/ world/europe/marine-le-pens-anti-islam-message-gains-influence-in-france. html?_r=0. Accessed 27 March 2013.

Open Secrets (2017), '2016 top donors to outside spending groups', Center for Responsive Politics. www.opensecrets.org/outsidespending/summ.php?disp= D. Accessed 20 January 2017.

Ostrower, F. (1995), *Why the Wealthy Give: The Culture of Elite Philanthropy*. Princeton, NJ: Princeton University Press.

Parmar, I. (2012), 'Foundational networks and American hegemony', *European Journal of American Studies*, 1, 1–25.

PMW (2015), 'Support us', Palestinian Media Watch. http://palwatch.org/pages/ donate1.aspx. Accessed 2 July 2015.

Powerbase (2015a), 'Elliott Abrams', 5 March. http://powerbase.info/index.php/ Elliott_Abrams. Accessed 21 January 2017.

—— (2015b), 'Interdisciplinary Center Herzliya', 11 March. http://powerbase.info/ index.php/Interdisciplinary_Center_Herzliya. Accessed 20 January 2017.

—— (2016), 'Middle East Research Institute', 29 February. http://powerbase.info/ index.php/Middle_East_Media_Research_Institute. Accessed 21 January 2017.

Ravid, B. (2010), 'Foreign Ministry working with rightists against Palestinian incitement', *Haaretz*, 7 May. www.haaretz.com/print-edition/news/foreign-ministry-working-with-rightists-against-palestinian-incitement-1.288828. Accessed 2 July 2015.

—— (2016), 'US condemns Defense Minister Ya'alon's decision to expand settlement bloc', *Haaretz*, 8 January. www.haaretz.com/israel-news/.premium-1.696369. Accessed 20 January 2017.

Reuters (2016), 'Billionaire Klarman slams Trump, vows to work for Clinton', *Reuters*, 8 August. www.reuters.com/article/us-usa-election-klarman-idUSK CN10E2TR. Accessed 17 January 2017.

RJC (2017), 'RJC leadership', Republican Jewish Congress. www.rjchq.org/leadership. Accessed 25 February 2017.

Roelofs, J. (2007), 'Foundations and collaboration', *Critical Sociology*, 33, 479–504.

Rutenberg, J., Mcintire, M. and Bronner, E. (2010), 'Tax-exempt funds aid settlements in West Bank', *New York Times*, 5 July. www.nytimes.com/2010/07/06/world/middleeast/06settle.html?pagewanted=all&_r=0 Accessed 2 July 2015.

Several, M. (2011), 'The strange case of American tax-exempt money for settlements', *The Palestine-Israel Journal*, 17 (12). www.pij.org/details.php?id=1280. Accessed 26 March 2017.

Silverstein, R. (2009), 'Irving Moskowitz's bingo madness', *Guardian*, 6 August. www.theguardian.com/commentisfree/cifamerica/2009/aug/06/irving-moskowitz-israel-obama-settlements. Accessed 20 January 2017.

—— (2012), 'Ateret Cohanim Yeshiva students sport sweatshirts calling for destruction of Dome of Rock', Tikun Olam, 17 January. www.richardsilverstein.com/2012/01/17/ateret-cohanim-yeshiva-students-wear-sell-sweatshirts-calling-for-destruction-of-dome-of-rock/. Accessed 29 March 2015.

SPLC (2016a), 'A journalist's manual: a field guide to anti-Muslim extremists', Southern Poverty Law Center, 25 October. www.splcenter.org/20161025/journalists-manual-field-guide-anti-muslim-extremists. Accessed 21 January 2017.

—— (2016b), 'Center for Security policy', Southern Poverty Law Center. www.splcenter.org/fighting-hate/extremist-files/group/center-security-policy. Accessed 14 January 2016.

—— (2017), 'David Horowitz', Southern Poverty Law Center. www.splcenter.org/fighting-hate/extremist-files/individual/david-horowitz. Accessed 21 January 2017.

Stokes, B. (2016), 'Are American Jews turning away from Israel? Recent polling shows a growing divide', *Foreign Policy*, 10 March. http://foreignpolicy.com/2016/03/10/are-american-jews-turning-away-from-israel/. Accessed 20 January 2017.

Telhami, S. (2016), 'American attitudes toward Muslims and Islam', Brookings, 11 July. www.brookings.edu/research/american-attitudes-toward-muslims-and-islam/. Accessed 22 January 2017.

Tibon, A. (2017), 'Republicans move to defund UN over censure of Israeli settlements', *Haaretz*, 12 January. www.haaretz.com/us-news/1.764706. Accessed 13 January 2017.

Tikvah Fund (2017), 'Board members', Tikvah Fund. https://tikvahfund.org/about/board/. Accessed 21 January 2017.

ValueWalk (2014), 'Paul Singer notes rich irony of French riots', *ValueWalk*, 22 July. www.valuewalk.com/2014/07/paul-singer-politics/. Accessed 22 January 2017.

Wedgle J. and Carter, C. (2015), 'On "birthright," a checkpoint is called a tollbooth, and Jews have E-ZPass', *Mondoweiss*, 8 March. http://mondoweiss.net/2015/03/birthright-checkpoint-tollbooth/#sthash.a55xNjwB.dpuf. Accessed 9 January 2017.

Whitaker, B. (2001), 'US pulls the plug on Muslim websites', *Guardian*, 10 September. www.theguardian.com/technology/2001/sep/10/internetnews.worlddispatch. Accessed 4 October 2016.

Wildman, S. (2017), 'The epidemic of bomb threats against Jewish organizations, explained', *Vox*, 23 February. www.vox.com/2017/2/23/14691010/bomb-threats-jccs-jews-anti-semitism-trump. Accessed 24 February 2017.

WINEP (2015a), 'Outside authors: Elliott Abrams', Washington Institute for Near East Policy. www.washingtoninstitute.org/experts/view/elliott-abrams. Accessed 3 July 2015.

——(2015b) 'Fellows: Matthew Levitt', Washington Institute for Near East Policy. www.washingtoninstitute.org/experts/view/levitt-matthew. Accessed 3 July 2015.

——(2017) 'Board of Advisors', Washington Institute for Near East Policy. www.washingtoninstitute.org/about/board-of-advisors/. Accessed 21 January 2017.

Zengerle, J. (2015) 'Sheldon Adelson is ready to buy the presidency', *NY Magazine*, 9 September. http://nymag.com/daily/intelligencer/2015/09/sheldon-adelson-is-ready-to-buy-the-presidency.html. Accessed 20 January 2017.

10

The Neoconservative Movement: Think Tanks as Elite Elements of Social Movements from Above

Tom Griffin, David Miller and Tom Mills

The neoconservative movement has played a key role in the production of Islamophobia in the UK and elsewhere. We see neoconservatism as an example of a 'social movement from above', that is, an instance of 'the collective agency of dominant groups, which is centred on … maintain[ing] or modify[ing] a dominant structure' (Cox and Nilsen, 2014: 59–60). The particular trajectory of the neoconservatives and, in the particular case of Islamophobia, their alliances with other social movements is also the story of divisions or factions within 'dominant groups'. Neoconservatism, which emerged to some extent from sections of the left, was born as a coherent political force in response to the rise of the New Left in the 1960s and 1970s; and the neocons' bid for hegemony necessitated not only intellectually confronting the various 'movements from below' of that period, but also influencing, challenging or attempting to displace more traditional conservative forces, organisations and structures.

In this chapter, we examine the role of the neoconservative movement in contemporary Islamophobia. We discuss the movement's origins in the US, and then outline its more recent manifestations in the UK, where we focus in particular on two key British neoconservative think tanks: Policy Exchange and the Henry Jackson Society. We examine the broader political networks and milieu within which these think tanks operate, and we detail the neoconservative movement's alliances with other Islamophobic movements, notably the counterjihad movement and elements of the Zionist movement.

In examining neoconservatism as a 'social movement from above' we apply the framework set out in Chapter 1 that suggests a number of features to help analyse different movements, and distinguish movements 'from above' from movements 'from below' – not always an easy task. Some key questions to ask of particular movements relate to their emergence, their organisational form and political location, their strategies and goals, and the outcomes of their activities, as detailed further below.

1. Emergence: From what milieu, social and political struggles, crises did the movement emerge?
2. Organisational form and political location: Where in the system do they operate? A movement on the streets or in the corridors of power? Are their movement organisations membership organisations, or think tanks and policy groups? With which other groups or movements do they form alliances or develop antagonisms?
3. Strategy and goals: What ideas and political demands or policy prescriptions do they advance? What specific campaigns have they mobilised on?
4. Outcomes: What have been the intended or unintended outcomes of the movement?

The emergence of neoconservatism

The neoconservatives are best known for the strong influence they exerted on and in the administration of George W. Bush following the 9/11 attacks, and particularly for the role they played in pushing for the 2003 invasion of Iraq. They had though earlier exerted some significant influence on the US Republicans in the 1980s, especially earlier in that decade when Reagan publicly opposed detente with the Soviet Union and his administration announced an earlier War on Terror, claiming that 'international terrorism' was largely sponsored by the US's Cold War rival. In both cases, the neocons' policy perspective put them at odds with the weight of opinion amongst the US foreign policy elites, and much of the US military and intelligence apparatus. Over the years, though, the neocons developed a parallel set of experts and institutions able to disseminate alternative information, expertise and policy ideas – essentially propaganda built around their favoured policies and their distinctly militarist worldview. Indeed, it is notable in this regard that a number of the progenitors of the neoconservative movement were not only former leftists, but had been involved in US-sponsored anti-communist intelligence and propaganda networks, such as Melvin Lasky of the CIA-funded *Encounter* magazine, or Irving Kristol of the CIA's Congress for Cultural Freedom.

Intellectually, neoconservatism is often said to owe a debt to the pessimistic and elitist ideas of the Chicago-based political philosopher Leo Strauss and/or the Cold War liberalism of Albert Wohlstetter of the Rand Corporation, a contention which has some merit. But according to Blumenthal's influential early study, the neocons:

> are less coherent as an intellectual movement than a social group. Some are welfare-statists, others are free-marketeers; some proclaim the moral mission of America in global terms, others urge hardheaded realpolitik. What really binds them together is their common experience. (Blumenthal, 2008: 110)

This common experience includes in many cases a background in socialist groups, and then Cold War liberal anti-communism, as has been noted, but also a particular reaction to the trajectory of liberal/left politics in the US from the late 1960s onwards. In this sense, neoconservatism, like other forms of conservatism, is defined not so much by a shared set of political ideas, but a particular reaction against mobilisations 'from below'. As Robin (2011: 15–16) in his study, *The Reactionary Mind*, notes of conservatism more generally, it

> is not a commitment to limited government and liberty – or a wariness of change, a belief in evolutionary reform, or a politics of virtue. These may be the byproducts of conservatism, one or more of its historically specific and ever-changing modes of expression. But they are not its animating purpose. Neither is conservatism a makeshift fusion of capitalists, Christians, and warriors, for that fusion is impelled by a more elemental force – the opposition to the liberation of men and women from the fetters of their superiors.

In the late 1960s, and over the course of the 1970s, the US government, having implemented a programme of domestic reforms on civil and economic rights, drew back from Vietnam, and sought to ease geopolitical tensions with the Soviet Union. These moves were opposed by the nascent neoconservatives through a number of elite social movement organisations (ESMOs) (see Boies and Pichardo Almanzar, 1990, 1993–94; Sklair, 1997) that lobbied against them; first, the Committee to Maintain a Prudent Defence Policy, then Team B and the Committee on the Present Danger in the 1970s. It should be remembered, though, that as well as a strong focus on foreign policy, neocons were also deeply involved with, and concerned about, domestic issues. These, in fact, were the issues that provided the 'reality' by which they were famously 'mugged' – and, pertinently for the issue of this book, racism was of some importance. In the case of Daniel Patrick Moynihan, for example, who came to the neocons from the Democrats, it was the response to his writing about the 'negro family' that converted him. In a report written in 1965 while serving in the Johnson administration, Moynihan

deplored the collapse of the black family and its dependence on welfare, arguing that the rise of single-mother families could be traced back to Jim Crow and slavery. Ghetto culture was a product not simply of a lack of jobs but of a deeper cultural problem that had its origins in slavery. (Heilbrunn, 2009: 138)

Moynihan's thesis was quickly decried as victim blaming and he was denounced as a racist. He was 'embittered and scarred by the experience' (Heilbrunn, 2009: 139). A similar process affected Norman Podhoretz following his 1963 essay in the flagship neocon journal *Commentary*: 'My Negro problem – and ours'. Most Whites, even liberals, he said were 'twisted and sick in their feelings about Negroes' (cited in Hartman, 2015), Podhoretz said he had 'grown weary of black arguments for special treatment', and pointed to his 'childhood memories of the black children in his Brooklyn neighborhood: rather than focus on their studies as he and his Jewish friends did, they roamed the streets terrorizing Podhoretz and the other white children' (Hartman, 2015). While Podhoretz had never been a socialist of any sort, his Cold War liberalism gave way in part as a result of this encounter, during which he was, unsurprisingly, denounced as a racist. Podhoretz then 'distanced himself from New York intellectual life, where he had become persona non grata. He even took a hiatus from *Commentary* (Hartman, 2015) while he went through what he saw as a conversion experience.

> By the time he returned to his editorial desk in 1970, Podhoretz was an unapologetic neoconservative. He earnestly commenced an ideological offensive against the New Left, the counterculture, and all that he deemed subversive about the sixties. (Hartman, 2015)

A distinct neoconservative worldview and movement at this time began to take shape amongst intellectuals and policy experts, and it developed a strong presence at certain publications and think tanks, most notably *Commentary* magazine, as has been mentioned, and the *Weekly Standard*, and the American Enterprise Institute and the Heritage Foundation, respectively. More overtly neoconservative think tanks would subsequently be set up, including the Washington Institute for Near East Policy, which was an initiative of the pro-Israel lobby group AIPAC (American Israel Public Affairs Committee), and somewhat more marginal outfits like the Middle East Forum and the Center for Security Policy, both of which would play a central role in Islamophobic politics in the US. Perhaps the best known neoconservative think tank is the Project for a New American Century, which was set up in 1997 by leading neocons William Kristol and Robert Kagan, and which would achieve some notoriety in the Bush era. It brought together an organisationally disparate but closely networked group of elite policy experts and intellectuals who would seize the opportunity of 9/11 to push for a more aggressively militaristic and unilaterialist US foreign policy and an extremely close relationship with Israel, and increasingly the Israeli right. The neocons reached the nadir of their influence in the years immediately after the invasion of Iraq, with their worldview somewhat discredited by the strong resistance the US faced. They nevertheless remain a significant current within US policy-making circles.

British neoconservatism

Neoconservatism is often thought of as an exclusively American phenomenon, characterised in part by a deep-seated belief in the moral righteousness of US military power. But the movement has always been to some extent 'internationalist', if not transnational, by virtue of its origins in Cold War geopolitics and European left and social democratic politics. Moreover, in the context of the early 'War on Terror' the extraordinary influence of neocons in the top echelons of the Bush administration was paralleled by the emergence of like-minded figures in elite policy-making circles and opinion leaders across the Atlantic. Neoconservatism won a number of disciples across Europe at this time, and something like a distinctly British neoconservative movement emerged.

The British neocons, who for the most part were only publicly self-defined as neoconservatives for a relatively short period when their American counterparts were at the height of their political power, have been spread across the mainstream political spectrum, with the movement incorporating social democrats identifying with the 'liberal interventionism' espoused by Blair and his acolytes, and right-wing Atlanticist conservatives. The British neocons, then, have certainly disagreed on a number of issues. But on foreign policy their underlying vision is fundamentally the same. Even if the devotion to military might and interventionist foreign policies is somewhat tempered compared to their US counterparts by a greater emphasis on the role of certain international alliances, the neocons all have something of a shared vision in the belief that Western democracies are embroiled in a Manichean struggle against Islamist totalitarianism. This political struggle, it is claimed, is comparable with the struggle against the Soviet Union and the revolutionary left during the Cold War, when hardline anti-communist ideology helped forge transatlantic networks of militant 'Cold Warriors', many with roots on the radical left. 'Political Islam', according to the British neocons, represents a similar geopolitical threat, and defeating it requires the same sorts of ideological warfare and domestic counter-subversion (Griffin, 2009; Mills et al., 2011).

Neoconservatives in Britain, as in the US, see international organisa-tions and military alliances, NATO especially, as vehicles for pushing the agenda of the US and its close allies, and as instruments of global power, regime change, nation-building, and 'democratisation'. Intergovernmen-tal bodies in which rivals and enemies of the US wield somewhat more influence, however, like the United Nations, are regarded as illegitimate insofar as they attempt to check or curb Western power. This 'unilat-eralist' worldview is evident in the 2007 Prague Charter signed at the Democracy and Security International Conference, which was described by one observer (Lobe, 2007) as a 'neoconservative international' because of the presence of a number of key American neocons, along with the-then US President George W. Bush. That conference brought together a coalition of European neoconservatives, particularly from Southern and Eastern Europe. A number of neoconservative initiatives have since been established in Europe. One example is Realité EU, an organisation with covert links to the US-based Israel Project, which sought to pressurise the EU into adopting a more hardline position on Iran (Mills and Miller, 2009). Another example is the Brussels-based Transatlantic Institute, which was founded by the pro-Israel American Jewish Committee (AJC) and headed by *Commentary* contributor Emanuele Ottolenghi, who has called for Europe to 'use its mighty economic, financial, and commercial clout to squeeze Iran'. Another AJC-linked Brussels-based organisation is UN Watch.

In the UK, meanwhile, the two major neocon outfits have been the Henry Jackson Society (HJS), which in 2010 subsumed another neo-conservative think tank, the Centre for Social Cohesion, and Policy Exchange, a think tank with a broader neoliberal agenda that has strongly influenced the Conservative Party, but which has also served as an important hub of neoconservatism in the UK.

The Henry Jackson Society

The Henry Jackson Society for Democratic Geopolitics was formed in 2005 at Peterhouse College, Cambridge, with patronage from some of the leading lights in American neoconservatism including William Kristol and Richard Perle. A few years later it moved to London where it is now based. The Society was named after the hawkish US Democratic Party Senator Henry 'Scoop' Jackson, a liberal opponent of detente and strong supporter of Israel. In its early 'Statement of Principles', HJS expressed a commitment to 'the maintenance of a strong military, by the United States, the countries of the European Union and other democratic powers, armed with expeditionary capabilities with a global reach'. Amongst its signatories were figures from politics, academia and the defence and security establishment in the UK, including some liberals and left-wingers. The more liberal faction, however, would later be ejected as HJS shifted notably rightwards, and the think tank has arguably always had a reactionary core. Its initial base at Peterhouse College, Cambridge is home to a conservative tradition associated with the historian Maurice Cowling, known as the 'Peterhouse Right'. This subset of British conservatism was one faction of the broader New Right which cohered around Margaret Thatcher in the 1970s and 1980s, but was distinct from the neoliberal faction, concerning itself more with political history and philosophy, and displaying a more overtly elitist anti-liberal politics. Heading HJS since 2006 has been its Executive Director Alan Mendoza, a former Conservative councillor and parliamentary candidate. Mendoza has also served as director and trustee for the Israel Diaspora Trust, which has brought speakers to the UK from right-wing Zionist outfits like NGO Watch and Palestinian Media Watch (Israel Diaspora Trust, 2013: 2). The 'putsch' at HJS, when many of the more liberal elements were jettisoned from the think tank, was led by Mendoza, and the rightward shift this signalled was broadly contemporaneous with the incorporation into HJS of another British neoconservative think tank, the Centre for Social Cohesion (CSC). This saw the think tank's income increase markedly, from around £300,000 in 2010 to around £1.3 million in 2013.

The Centre for Social Cohesion was founded in 2007, initially as a project of the conservative think tank Civitas, which in turn had been spun off from the seminal neoliberal think tank, the Institute of Economic Affairs. Civitas, which was influenced by right-wing communitarian ideas more than neoliberal currents, had already produced material critical of Islam and multiculturalism, and CSC would from its beginning focus on Islam as the main threat to 'social cohesion'. This emphasis was in line with Civitas' previous work on the subject. A key example was 'The "West", Islam and Islamism: is ideological Islam compatible with liberal democracy?', a 2003 pamphlet whose authors Caroline Cox and John Marks would later become directors of the CSC. They argued that Islamist terrorism was only part of a broader ideological challenge comparable to communist propaganda efforts during the Cold War, stating:

Western societies must respond effectively to the challenge from ideological Islamists. To do so they need to use principles and analyses which have many parallels with the earlier conflict with ideological Marxism. The broad distinction between terrorists operating in the name of Islam and peaceable law-abiding Muslims must be respected, but it must not be allowed to cripple the effort that is needed to preserve the principles and institutions of Western societies.

In effect, this is two veterans of the cultural Cold War of the 1970s arguing that the ideological apparatus of the period can be dusted off and applied, in a very crude way, to a totally new set of circumstances in the twenty-first century, with a clear recognition that this means going beyond a focus on terrorism, to labelling a much wider range of people and their activities as potentially subversive.

Heading CSC was the young right-wing ideologue Douglas Murray, who would go on to become HJS' associate director. Before his appointment to CSC, Murray, the author of *Neoconservatism: Why We Need It*, had made a provocative speech advocating that: 'Conditions for Muslims in Europe must be made harder across the board.'

A majority of CSC's output focused on Islam, typically examining a particular area of Muslim engagement with wider civil society and portraying it as an example of Islamist subversion. Examples include the 2008 report, *Islam on Campus*, which included a highly questionable poll that served as the basis for media reports that 'one third of British Muslim students say it's acceptable to kill for Islam', and a report the following year, *A Degree of Influence*, that claimed there was censorship of British universities by Muslim donors on the basis of just two pieces of evidence, neither of which stood up to scrutiny.

Policy Exchange

Another centre of British neoconservatism has been the centre-right think tank Policy Exchange. Founded in 2002, Policy Exchange has been associated with the more liberal, modernising faction of the Conservative Party, and was often described as David Cameron's 'favourite think tank'. It was particularly influential on the Conservative-led Coalition government's public service reform agenda, but has also played host to some key players in British neoconservatism. The best known of these is Michael Gove, who served as Policy Exchange's first chair. Gove was a signatory to the Statement of Principles of the Henry Jackson Society and also co-hosted HJS' parliamentary launch. A long-standing right-wing Eurosceptic, and a leading figure in the 'Brexit' campaign, Gove is also Britain's foremost neoconservative who as a *Times* journalist was advocating 'total war' and writing of 'Saddam Hussein, and his weapons of mass destruction' just a week after the 9/11 attacks. In the same month that Policy Exchange published its first report on Islam and multiculturalism, it also hosted a book launch for Gove's neoconservative polemic *Celsius 7/7*. Amongst the people who Gove thanked in the acknowledgements section of that book were the HJS' Douglas Murray. Another was the American neoconservative Dean Godson, Policy Exchange's director of research who has overseen the think tank's output on Islam and multiculturalism. Godson has close family connections to the neoconservative movement, notably through his brother Roy, a key figure in the anti-detente movement of the 1970s (Sanders, 1983: 212).

Like HJS and CSC, Policy Exchange has published a number of reports purporting to show evidence of extremism amongst British Muslims and calling on the government to sever links with particular individuals or groups and to expand its surveillance of Muslims. In one report, published in 2007, Policy Exchange alleged that 'extremist material' was available in 25 per cent of British mosques, and called on mosques to be subject to 'greater regulation'. The BBC, which had been offered the findings as an exclusive, checked the story and discovered evidence that some of the receipts said to support the report's findings had been fabricated.

A common theme in Policy Exchange's output on Islam has been the argument that effective counter-terrorism measures should focus not solely on security threats, but on 'extremist' ideas and undemocratic or unpatriotic values which are said to influence the broader cultural climate in which terrorism emerges – an argument also central in Michael Gove's *Celsius 7/7*. In a 2009 report called *Choosing Our Friends Wisely*, Policy Exchange called on the government to shift its counter-terrorism policy to focusing on 'non-violent extremism', and explicitly advocated for the establishment of political counter-subversion operations by Britain's Secret Service. In a subsequent report on faith schools, Policy Exchange called on MI5's Joint Terrorism Analysis Centre to monitor schools for threats to 'democratic values'.

We have elsewhere referred to this push for political counter-subversion as a 'cold war on British Muslims' (Mills et al., 2011). Both Policy Exchange and HJS/CSC were part of a successful effort by conservative interests, neoconservatives especially, to reshape counter-terrorism policy around Cold War-inspired ideological warfare, focusing on political and cultural threats, rather than security and public safety.

Policy influence

The Conservative-led Coalition government's Prevent Strategy, which was published in June 2011, was clearly influenced by the kind of neoconservative ideas that have been propagated by Policy Exchange and CSC/HJS. It stated that: 'preventing terrorism will mean challenging extremist (and non-violent) ideas that are also part of a terrorist ideology', and later lamented that 'work to date has not recognised clearly enough the way in which some terrorist ideologies draw on and make use of extremist ideas which are espoused by apparently non-violent organisations very often operating within the law' (HM Government, 2011: 50). Indeed, the official Prevent strategy document cites the CSC on no less than five occasions (HM Government, 2011: 25, 67, 72, 73).

The Counter-terrorism and Security Act (2015), which put the 2011 policy on a statutory footing, was also consonant with the ideas of the British neoconservative think tanks, and there is further evidence of neoconservative influence on the Cameron government – which was first most clearly evident in the former prime minister's 2011 speech in Munich decrying multiculturalism. In July 2015, HJS' Douglas Murray praised David Cameron's Birmingham speech on 'radicalisation', saying it was his best yet (Murray, 2015), and in September that year, Cameron caused considerable controversy when he publicly named four universities that had allegedly hosted speakers with views 'contrary to British values'. Shortly thereafter, the *Times Higher Education* reported that the source for much of the data was Student Rights, an initiative of HJS (Grove, 2015). The allegations against each of the universities is contested and denied by the universities concerned, and the evidential basis of that and other reports by Student Rights has been called into question on a number of occasions (Aked, 2013a, 2013b, 2013c).

These examples show that neoconservative think tanks are attempting to influence government counter-terrorism policy and have, at least arguably, had some effect, with specific negative consequences for Muslims (and others) throughout the country.

The neocon nexus

Many of the political ideas that bind together British neoconservatives also have a clear resonance with those of the pro-war left, as seen, for example, in the Euston Manifesto discussed in Chapter 11; the right of the Zionist movement, which is similarly pitched against international law and multilateralism, and closely tied to American militarism; and, on the political fringes, with the counterjihad movement and some other elements of the far right, which share the notion of a cultural or civilisational struggle with Islam or Islamism. The ideological affinity, and occasional political affiliation, with the far right is most notable on the right of British neoconservatism. HJS' Douglas Murray praised leading counterjihad ideologue Robert Spencer in a speech in January 2011, and also defended the far-right Islamophobic street movement, the English Defence League (EDL), as 'a grassroots response from non-Muslims to Islamism'. This is not surprising given that Murray's notorious 2006 speech was heavily influenced by the idea of a Muslim demographic threat to Europe, and particularly by Bat Ye'or and her concept of 'Dhimmitude'. That speech also attacked the 'relativism' of the left, which Murray referred to as the 'primary disease' in Western political culture; a common theme in British neoconservatism which also has some affinity with the liberal and left currents detailed in Chapter 11.

The overlap between the neoconservative movement and the Zionist movement is also considerable. This is an intertwined history that goes back to the beginning of the neoconservative project. Indeed, the growth of opposition to Israel in the wake of the Six Day War was one of the issues which alienated neoconservatism from the New Left in the late 1960s. In the contemporary period, there are many connections between Zionism and neoconservative think tanks and policy groups. We note below some of the key financial connections, which are further explored in Sarah Marusek's chapter on the funding of Islamophobia and the overlap with the funding of settlement activity in the West Bank.

Funding networks

Our research on the neocons and their think tanks has involved examining the history of the movement, biographical data on the individuals involved, the networks within which they are embedded, the origin and development of their ideas and the ideational products think tanks produce – that is, the reports they publish and disseminate. However, we have also insisted that it is crucial to examine the funding of these think tanks.

It is sometimes suggested that discussing donors implies that think tanks' funding crudely determines their ideas and output, and that the people working in think tanks are no more than ciphers for wealthy donors. This is not our contention. But funding is a crucial factor in any adequate understanding of think tanks since it provides the conditions of existence that allow think tank intellectuals to do their work. To be clear, it is sometimes the case that think tanks act straightforwardly as agents for a client. But there is a continuum between those outfits where the research is subordinated to the funding agency and those where ideological tenacity is highly prized and the think tank itself plays a leadership role for a particular set of interests. On the question of Islam, think tanks like the CSC/HJS and Policy Exchange are more often nearer the latter pole. In either case though, think tanks need to present themselves as independent bodies for the sake of credibility – independence meaning both independence from particular financial interests (unlike lobbying companies) and in the sense that they are able to think freely in their tanks. One way to maintain that image of independence is for the think tanks to be opaque about their funding. Neither HJS nor Policy Exchange are transparent about their donors. Evidently they think it is not in their interests. Thus, in 2014 we complained that HJS was not abiding by parliamentary rules in its sponsorship of two All Party Groups. But rather than disclose the source of all funding over £5,000, as parliamentary rules require, HJS elected to withdraw from the groups, which promptly collapsed (Aked et al., 2015; Ramesh, 2014). This illustrates the importance of maintaining secrecy of funding to these think tanks, and underlines the importance of investigating funding networks.

Following the money does often lead to interesting funding sources. These tend to undermine the notion that the think tanks are independent of particular political ideologies or movements, and reveals useful information about the interests and forces on which the production of ideas depends. Although, as we have noted, the think tanks we discuss here are not transparent, our research has enabled us to trace a significant amount of funding by trawling the financial reports of UK and US charities and foundations. By doing so, we were able to track around 25 per cent of the funding of the HJS in the years immediately after it absorbed the CSC in 2011–13. The top three donors in that period show the role of prominent conservative business operatives in providing the necessary resources for the production of anti-Muslim ideas and policies.[1]

The most significant single donor to HJS in that period (we were able to trace) was the Atkin Charitable Foundation, which is headed by Conservative Party donors Edward and Celia Atkin. The Atkins, who made their money through the Avent baby feeding company, provided nearly 10 per cent of HJS' total funding in 2013. The Atkin Foundation also gives money to the neocon-connected International Centre for Research on Radicalisation (ICSR) at Kings College, where former Policy Exchange and CSC researchers are now based, as well as several Israel-related groups active in the occupied territories in breach of international law, like the Jerusalem Foundation and the Jewish National Fund.

The second major donor is the businessman and Conservative peer Stanley Kalms, a former treasurer of the Party, who in 2009 flirted with UKIP. A life president of DSG International (formerly Dixons), Kalms has supported the Henry Jackson Society and the CSC before its incorporation into HJS through his Traditional Alternatives Foundation and the Stanley Kalms Foundation. His links with more mainstream conservatism are illustrated by his financial backing for the Institute of Economic Affairs and the Centre for Social Justice. A prominent member of Conservative Friends of Israel, Kalms appears to have quite 'radical' views on Muslims and Islam. Tony Lerman, the writer and 'lapsed' Zionist, notes in his courageous memoir, *The Making and Unmaking of a Zionist*, that at a meeting he attended in November 2006, Kalms remarked: 'Most Muslims didn't want to integrate ... Ultimately they would line up behind the fundamentalists' (Lerman, 2012: 161).

The third largest donor to HJS is the enormously wealthy Lewis family. The Lewis brothers set up what is now known as the River Island clothing company in 1948, which has over 300 stores today. The *Sunday Express* referred to co-founder David Lewis in his obituary as a 'pioneering champion of Zionism'. He was a key supporter of the Centre for Social and Economic Progress, a neoliberal think tank in Israel, and of Conservative Friends of Israel in the UK, where David Cameron presented him with a picture of a Lancaster bomber shortly before his death in 2011 (*Daily Telegraph*, 15 August 2011). Founded by deed in 2008, the Bernard Lewis Family Charitable Trust is a London-based charity with Bernard Lewis at the helm. The Catherine Lewis Foundation, established by members of the same family, was registered by deed in 1972. Together, both these foundations funded Civitas, from which CSC emerged, Stanley Kalms's Traditional Alternative Foundation (which was used to set up the CSC) and HJS after it absorbed the CSC.

Policy Exchange has been another recipient of Lewis family funding. It received £10,000 from the Lewis Family Charitable Trust in 2007/08, £20,000 the following year and another £10,000 in 2009/10, as well as £15,000 from the Bernard Lewis Family Charitable Trust (for further details and full references, see Mills et al., 2011). Other funding from the family in that period went to conservative movement groupings like the Social Affairs Unit and the Politics of Economics Research Trust, which is associated with the Taxpayers Alliance. Amongst the pro-Israel groups the family has funded are the Jewish Leadership Council, the United Jewish Israel Appeal and the JNF Charitable Trust, which sends money to the Jewish National Fund, an organisation long accused of ethnic cleansing in Israel/Palestine (Lehn and Davis, 1988; Pappé, 2006). This pattern of funding wider conservative movement organisations and especially pro-Israel groups is likewise seen with a range of other funders to the HJS, which also regularly send money to Zionist causes including organisations implicated in supporting the occupation of the West Bank or settlement activity such as the Jerusalem Foundation, the Jewish National Fund and the Association for the Wellbeing of Israel's Soldiers.

Policy Exchange's funding, meanwhile, directly connects it to US neo-conservatives via the Rosenkranz Foundation, which is known to have given approximately £60,000 to Policy Exchange in recent years (though as with the Lewis family trusts, research has not tied it specifically to Policy Exchange's neoconservative output). The Rosenkranz Foundation is headed by Robert Rosenkranz, chair and CEO of Delphi Financial Group and a trustee of Policy Exchange since January 2010. His foundation's executive director is S. Dana Wolfe, a journalist who worked for Benjamin Netanyahu before becoming assistant managing editor of *The National Interest* (Rosenkranz Foundation, 2013), a US foreign policy journal for many years published by William Kristol. The Rosenkranz Foundation has funded the American Enterprise Institute and *Commentary*. Robert Rosenkranz also chairs American Friends of Policy Exchange, which raises funds for Policy Exchange in the US. Its vice-chair is the historical biographer Amanda Foreman, a member of the Advisory Council of HJS and its director is David Frum, who authored George W. Bush's notorious 'axis of evil' speech and who is now also a Policy Exchange trustee (Rosenkranz Foundation, 2013).

An elite social movement

Despite the considerable overlap with other anti-Muslim currents, the neoconservative movement is distinct in its organisational form and political location. Neoconservatism is an essentially elite and elitist social movement, operating in a space that is densely networked and close to power and centres of decision making, as almost every study of the neocons shows. The neoconservatives prefer the policy terrain to the street, the quiet word in elite ears to the megaphone or the mosque invasion, and the expensive offices in Whitehall or Washington, DC to the PO Box and back street HQ. The think tanks we focus on here are interested in moving elite opinion, or more precisely action. They haunt the corridors of parliamentary buildings, government departments and policy venues. This contrasts with the other Islamophobic movements that have at least some orientation towards popular support. The neocons, by contrast, lack any kind of non-elite constituency.

The elite orientation of the neoconservative movement is reflective not only of its political location, but also the circumstances of its emergence. The neocons have a history of connections to the US military industrial complex, and they originally emerged, in part, from a non-communist left that was entangled with Western intelligence agencies. Historians debate whether the non-communist left was used by the intelligence services or vice versa (Wilford, 2009). But what is not in doubt is that many of those who travelled the road from Marxist anti-Stalinism to liberal anti-communism did so while also maintaining a relationship of one sort or another with the CIA or MI5/6.

Many of these Cold War Atlanticist connections were originally forged in the struggle between liberal interventionists and paleoconservative isolationists over US entry into World War II. Current tensions between a distinctly paleoconservative Trump administration and institutions such as the CIA present neoconservatives with an unprecedented dilemma. Some of the more extreme outriders of neoconservativism, such as Frank Gaffney of the Center for Security Policy, have been key influences on Trump's brand of Islamophobia. More moderate figures may yet align themselves with the liberal Atlanticist opposition to Trump, especially if there is a sustained shift towards a pro-Russian foreign policy. In this respect, the conflicts within the Henry Jackson Society, noted above, may reflect the position of neoconservativism across a deepening fault line between liberal interventionism and populist paleoconservatism.

Goals and outcomes: the influence of think tanks

There have been a range of think tanks active on counter-terrorism and Islam in the UK and there are serious concerns over the quality and integrity of the evidence these organisations produce. The spreading of Islamophobic ideas in the public sphere is one effect of these think tanks' activities. Another appears to be influencing government policy in a more Islamophobic direction. When think tanks are discussed in academic or popular debate there is a current of opinion that views them as irrelevant to political outcomes. This is usually on the basis of a particularist approach that seeks to identify the specific impact of given think tanks on particular policies, or the 'climate of opinion', which often ignores specific evidence of influence as 'anecdotal'. In our view, this fails to understand that the think tanks are embedded within networks of money and power. Tracing the ways in which certain ideas become influential, and may make it into government policy, is somewhat broader than the more particularist approaches, but is also quite different to examining the effects of think tanks on public debate or opinion. The reason for this is simple: think tanks operate mostly at the level of elite debate, in which the public have little role.

Conclusions

The neoconservative movement has been extremely important in advancing Islamophobic ideas and practice. It has performed a specific role in relation to policy and public debate. In general, its arguments are more sophisticated than those of the far right or counterjihad, though the sentiments are often very similar. It can include liberal or high-minded statements about issues of moral principle and the spread of democracy, and the arguments are addressed to elite audiences rather than street armies, though of course they help to legitimise the Islamophobia on the street.

Note

1. This section draws on Griffin et al. (2015, part 6).

Bibliography

Aked, H. (2013a), 'Student Rights "Campus Extremism" study: dishonest pseudo-science in support of a toxic narrative', *Huffington Post*, 15 May. www.huffingtonpost.co.uk/hilary-aked/student-rights-campus-extremism-study_b_3277503.html. Accessed 15 February 2017.

——(2013b), 'How front group "Student Rights" undermines Palestine solidarity', *The Electronic Intifada*, 11 December. https://electronicintifada.net/content/how-front-group-student-rights-undermines-palestine-solidarity/12991. Accessed 15 February 2017.

——(2013c), 'Ironically named "Student Rights" group exposed by actual students', *Huffington Post*, 17 December. www.huffingtonpost.co.uk/hilary-aked/student-rights-campaign_b_4452823.html. Accessed 15 February 2017.

Aked, H., Miller, D. and Jones, M. (2015), 'Henry Jackson Society forced to quit Westminster role after Spinwatch complaint – APPGs discontinued', Spinwatch, 7 January. www.spinwatch.org/index.php/issues/politics/item/5706-henry-jackson-society-forced-to-quit-westminster-role-after-spinwatch-complaint. Accessed 15 February 2017.

Blumenthal, S. (2008), *The Rise of the Counter-Establishment: The Conservative Ascent to Political Power*, 2nd edn. New York: Union Square Press.

Boies, J. and Pichardo Almanzar, N.A. (1990), 'Elite social movements and the state: a case study of the Committee on the Present Danger', CRSO Working Paper No. 416.

——(1993–94), 'The Committee on the Present Danger: a case for the importance of elite social movement organisations to theories of social movements and the state', *Berkeley Journal of Sociology*, 38, 57–87.

Cox, C. and Marks, J. (2003), 'The "West", Islam and Islamism: is ideological Islam compatible with liberal democracy?', June, Civitas, London. www.civitas.org.uk/pdf/cs29.pdf. Accessed 20 February 2017.

Cox, L. and Nilsen, A.G. (2014), *We Make Our Own History. Marxism and Social Movements in the Twilight of Neoliberalism*. London: Pluto Press.

Griffin, T. (2009), 'Who are the "Eurocons"?', RightWeb, 4 December. http://rightweb.irc-online.org/who_are_the_eurocons/. Accessed 15 February 2017.

Griffin, T., Aked, H., Miller, D. and Marusek, S. (2015), *The Henry Jackson Society and the Degeneration of British Neoconservatism: Liberal Interventionism, Islamophobia and the 'War on Terror'*. Glasgow: Public Interest Investigations.

Grove, J. (2015), 'No 10's extremism report mirrors text of thinktank study: government urged to reveal source of claims about universities that allegedly hosted extremist speakers', *Times Higher Education*, 1 October. www.timeshighereducation.com/news/no-10s-extremism-report-mirrors-text-thinktank-study. Accessed 17 February 2017.

Hartman, A. (2015), 'The neoconservative counterrevolution', *Jacobin*, 23 April. www.jacobinmag.com/2015/04/neoconservatives-kristol-podhoretz-hartman-culture-war/. Accessed 14 February 2017.

Heilbrunn, J. (2009), *They Knew They were Right: The Rise of the Neocons*. New York: Anchor Books.

HM Government (2011), *Prevent* Strategy, June. www.gov.uk/government/uploads/system/uploads/attachment_data/file/97976/prevent-strategy-review.pdf. Accessed 15 February 2017.

Israel Diaspora Trust (2013), *Israel Diaspora Trust Report and Accounts for the Year Ended 31 December 2012*. http://apps.charitycommission.gov.uk/Accounts/Ends31/0000286131_AC_20121231_E_C.PDF. Accessed 17 February 2017.

Lehn, W. and Davis, U. (1988), *The Jewish National Fund*. London: Taylor & Francis.

Lerman, A. (2012), *The Making and Unmaking of a Zionist: A Personal and Political Journey*. London: Pluto Press.

Lobe, J. (2007), 'A neo-conservative international targets Iran', Lobelog.com, 9 June. https://web.archive.org/web/20070703020904/http://www.ips.org/blog/jimlobe/?p=27. Accessed 15 February 2017.

Mills, T. and Miller, D. (2009), 'Réalité-EU: Front group for the Washington-based Israel Project?', Spinwatch, 30 October. www.spinwatch.org/index.php/issues/lobbying/item/529-realite-eu-front-group-for-the-washington-based-israel-project. Accessed 15 February 2017.

Mills, T., Griffin, T. and Miller, D. (2011), *The Cold War on British Muslims: An Examination of Policy Exchange and the Centre for Social Cohesion*. Glasgow: Public Interest Investigations.

Murray, D. (2015), 'David Cameron has given his best speech yet on tackling Islamic extremism', *The Spectator*, 20 July. http://blogs.spectator.co.uk/2015/07/david-cameron-has-given-his-best-speech-yet-on-tackling-islamic-extremism/. Accessed 15 February 2017.

Pappé, I. (2006), 'The 1948 ethnic cleansing of Palestine', *Journal of Palestine Studies*, 36 (1), 6–20.

Ramesh, R. (2014), 'Rightwing thinktank pulls funds for Commons groups after disclosure row', *Guardian*, 30 December. www.theguardian.com/politics/2014/dec/30/rightwing-thinktank-pulls-funds-commons-groups-disclosure-rules. Accessed 15 February 2017.

Robin, C. (2011), *The Reactionary Mind: Conservatism from Edmund Burke to Sarah Palin*. Oxford: Oxford University Press.

Rosenkranz Foundation (2013), 'About us'. http://rosenkranzfdn.org/aboutus.html. Accessed 18 February 2017.

Sanders, J. (1983), *Peddlers of Crisis: The Committee on the Present Danger and the Politics of Containment*. Boston, MA: South End Press.

Sklair, L. (1997), 'Social movements for global capitalism: the transnational capitalist class in action', *Review of International Political Economy*, 4 (3), 514–38.

Wilford, H. (2009), *The Mighty Wurlitzer: How the CIA Played America*. Cambridge, MA: Harvard University Press.

11

Liberal and Left Movements and the Rise of Islamophobia

Narzanin Massoumi, Tom Mills and David Miller

Introduction

This chapter focuses on those liberal and left groups and movements that have played a key role in Islamophobic politics. It suggests that collectively these movements can be considered one of the key 'pillars' supporting the practice of Islamophobia in the UK and elsewhere. Just as with the other movements discussed in this book, we regard these left and liberal currents as social movements from above. This may seem counter-intuitive, but we suggest that in relation to Islamophobia, the organisations and movements we discuss here have ended up in positions, and undertaking activities, that fit this definition. As we will show in the body of this chapter, a number of the individuals and groups have travelled a long path to this point, beginning their political journeys in social movements from below. This is not terribly surprising. Members of other movements have gone through similar transitions, the best known of which are the neoconservatives, discussed in Chapter 10. Many of the early neocons previously belonged to Trotskyist organisations before moving on to liberal anti-Communism and social democracy, through to extremely reactionary politics. In what follows we focus on four overlapping liberal and left movements:

1. the pro-war left
2. the New Atheists
3. some secularist feminist currents
4. the New Secularists.

We analyse the origins and political trajectories of these distinct but overlapping currents, describing how they coalesced around particular analyses of, and political responses to, events and developments. There is a historical and international context and pre-history to these currents, including the Iranian revolution, the Palestinian intifada and the fall of the Berlin Wall. In the UK in particular, though, we suggest that there were four political conjunctures (though some have wider resonance) which were key in shaping the groupings we discuss below: (1) multi-culturalism as a response to anti-racism; (2) the Rushdie Affair; (3) the early 'War on Terror' and the 2003 Iraq War; (4) the domestic 'War on Terror' and the Prevent agenda following the London bombings of 2005.

In response to political events and developments such as these, existing networks and movements disintegrate or reconstitute, while new alliances are formed, with individuals and groups coalescing around shared political positions and priorities. In the case of Islamophobia, the relations of left/liberal and secular groups with other Islamophobic currents, most obviously with the neoconservatives and sections of the Zionist movement, but also elements of the far right, have been notable, and are to be expected. By offering an account of the ways in which the above actors and groups have orientated themselves in particular struggles, we show how over time individuals, groups and movements, even those originating in anti-racist struggles (from below), have come to adopt Islamophobic political positions, thereby becoming parts of social movements from above. We turn first to the pro-war left.

The pro-war left

The 2003 US-led invasion of Iraq saw unprecedented levels of public protest around the world, including the largest ever demonstration in British history in London on 15 February 2003. The UK anti-war demonstrations were organised by the Stop the War Coalition (StWC) in partnership with the Campaign for Nuclear Disarmament (CND) and the Muslim Association of Britain (MAB). Stop the War was formed two years earlier, in response to the invasion of Afghanistan, as an alliance between the Labour left, including Jeremy Corbyn and George Galloway, the Socialist Workers Party, which was the dominant political force in the coalition, and other radical left groups. By 2003, however, a host of more mainstream political organisations had affiliated to Stop the War, including the Liberal Democrats, Plaid Cymru and the Scottish National Party. Even a leading national tabloid, the *Mirror*, supported the demonstration of 15 February 2003 and provided placards on the day.

By that time, StWC and its affiliates could claim support from the majority of the UK public according to some polls, and certainly the overwhelming majority of liberal and left opinion in the UK, which strongly opposed the illegal invasion of Iraq. There were, however, a number of left dissenters who supported the war, and whose opposition to the anti-war movement gave rise to new reactionary political alliances. The pro-war dissenters included liberal proponents of 'humanitarian intervention', who hoped that a greater willingness by the US and its allies to use military force in the Global South might curtail political repression and human rights abuses there, and leftists who identified with a tradition of anti-totalitarianism and left internationalism, and who supported 'regime change' in Iraq for similar reasons. Two particularly influential left-wing supporters of the Iraq War in the UK were the journalist and author Nick Cohen, and the long-standing Trotskyist intellectual, Norman Geras.

Nick Cohen was then best known as a left-wing critic of Blairism who wrote a weekly column for the *Observer*. Through his opposition to New Labour's treatment of asylum seekers he had got to know London-based Iraqi Kurds, and he claims that it was this which led him to support the 2003 invasion, even while everyone he 'respected in public life was wildly anti-war'. Cohen subsequently came to believe that the lack of support by the rest of the left for the invasion and occupation of Iraq was a symptom of a profound political malaise that had set in in the wake of the defeats of the radical left as well as the substantive gains won by more 'mainstream liberal-leftists' on civil rights. This, Cohen claimed, led a disoriented and morally bankrupt left to advance 'apologies for militant Islam' and 'fascistic governments and movements', as well as 'post-modern' defences of repressive practices in 'traditional cultures' (Cohen, 2007).

Norman Geras, a Marxist academic who had served on the editorial board of *New Left Review* and the *Socialist Register* – the foremost journals of the anti-Stalinist New Left – went through a similar political transition as a result of his outspoken support for the 2003 Iraq War. In the run-up to the invasion, Geras found himself uncomfortably at odds with liberal and leftist friends and colleagues, and wrote that he had come to find the opinion pages of the *Guardian*, his 'newspaper of choice', 'repellent' (Geras, 2003a). At that time, with the left, and increasingly much broader publics, mobilising against the planned invasion, Geras found common cause with a small group of intellectuals similarly 'dismayed at the tenor of supposedly progressive opinion' who circulated amongst themselves ideas and online material (Geras, 2003b). Like Nick Cohen and Christopher Hitchens, whom he often quoted, Geras quickly became the classic political apostate – pertinacious, contrarian and moralistic. Shortly after the invasion, he gave a talk to a radical left conference condemning 'the marching, the petition-signing, [and] the oh-so-knowing derision of George Bush' as 'a calamitous compromise of the core values of socialism, or liberalism or both'. The 'opposition to the freeing of the Iraqi people' – which he assumed to be motivated by 'an uncontrollable animus towards George Bush and his administration' – was, he charged, 'as shameful a moral failure of liberal and left opinion' as the apologias for Stalinism (Geras, 2003a). Geras subsequently set up his own blog, which was to become a prolific and influential operation in pro-war left circles. New to the world of blogging, he was assisted by politically sympathetic bloggers, notably the financier Oliver Kamm, who later became a leader writer at *The Times*, and another influential pro-war left blogger using the pseudonym 'Hatchet Harry' (Geras, 2003c).

'Hatchet Harry' had earlier set up a blog, Harry's Place, in response to the 9/11 attacks. He claimed to be interested in developing 'democratic socialist politics' that would exhibit a 'progressive morality' and perhaps stake out a third way between Blairism and the radical left. A Marxist in his youth, 'Harry' introduced his blog by stating that he still considered historical materialism a preferable framework of analysis 'to any of the alternatives – especially religion', and lamenting that the 'old socialist left' had become 'essentially reactionary' ('Hatchet Harry', 2002). The Harry's Place blog, to which 'Hatchet Harry' was initially the sole contributor, quickly became a major hub for ostensibly liberal and left-wing supporters of the Iraq War. For a period, its regular contributors included the award-winning young political journalist, Johann Hari, who was later suspended from the *Independent* newspaper after allegations of plagiarism. Articles by other 'mainstream' writers also regularly featured, or were linked to, on the blog, amongst them pieces from Christopher Hitchens, Nick Cohen and the former Communist columnist David Aaronovitch, who like Kamm later joined *The Times*.

Harry's Place, along with Geras's 'Normblog', became something of a centre of gravity for a cluster of pro-war left blogs. A common theme for the many voices in this newly constituted online echo chamber was the idea that socialists and liberals had betrayed their universalist and/ or internationalist moral commitments in favour of a pathological anti-imperialism, anti-Americanism and anti-Semitism, and had formed morally dubious alliances with Muslim groups and movements that were not only reactionary, but invited comparison to European fascism. Insofar as the pro-war left displayed any political vision, it was a rather hackneyed blend of muscular liberalism and contrarian leftism, inevitably peppered with allusions to Orwell. Often, though, there was little politics of any substance. Harry's Place, in particular, rather than offering much in the way of an alternative political project, acted as something of a trailblazer in political trolling. Contributors, who were often anonymous, attacked the anti-war movement over its opposition to American, British and Israeli militarism, and focused particularly on the left's relationship with politically engaged Muslims. Behind the relentless and bitter trolling though there was some sort of political vision, or at least vendetta. In essence, the politics of the War on Terror had radicalised liberals and leftists who were in any case uncomfortable with the multiculturalist settlement, especially post-Rushdie, and who in the context of Iraq were propelled into a reactionary politics that still claimed continuity with left traditions and values. For the pro-war left, it was the rest of the left that had lost its way by embracing the multiculturalism and 'moral relativism' thought to characterise post-1980s racial politics, which had blinded them to the dangers of 'Islamism', which, they charged, animated much if not all of the involvement of Muslim groups in the anti-war movement.

'Hatchet Harry', a British 'ex-pat' originally from Burnley in the North of England, was – rather revealingly – critical of the notion that the riots in Oldham in 2001 were related to racism, explicitly rejecting comparisons to the urban riots of the 1980s, and apparently endorsing the idea that 'the police have been letting Pakistani youth get away with actions that white youths would be banged up for' (Powerbase, 2010). On another occasion, 'Harry' complained of 'no-go areas for whites' in his hometown, claiming that he was 'stoned for entering one at the age of 12' (Powerbase, 2010). As these remarks illustrate, significant sections of the pro-war left would indulge in plainly reactionary political rhetoric, and the movement would go on to quickly intersect with contemporary conservative movements similarly mobilised against the multicultural settlement.

The other major contributor to Harry's Place, alongside 'Hatchet Harry', was a corporate lawyer, David Toube, who like 'Harry' began blogging after the 9/11 attacks. Toube, a former friend of the tabloid 'Islamist' provocateur Anjem Choudary, was one of around 20 people who in May 2005 met to discuss the trajectory of left politics in the UK. Most, though not all, according to Norman Geras, who was a leading participant in that meeting, were supporters of the Iraq War. But all had found themselves 'out of tune with the dominant anti-war discourse' and shared a 'common sense of discord with much current left-liberal thinking' on 'terrorism and the fight against it, US foreign policy, the record of the Blair government, the Israeli-Palestinian conflict and, more generally, attitudes to democratic values and to movements that reject these' (Geras, 2006). The group included another corporate lawyer, Adrian Cohen, the Director of Labour Friends of Iraq, Gary Kent, and a handful of former Trotskyist intellectuals, notably the academics Jane Ashworth and Alan Johnson, and the American labour activist Eric Lee. It met twice more, subsequently producing a political declaration called the Euston Manifesto, which was published in the *New Statesman* along with an accompanying piece penned by Norman Geras and Nick Cohen.

The authors of the Euston Manifesto declared the need for a 'fresh political alignment' on the left in favour of democracy, equality and 'the liberal freedom of ideas', and in opposition to anti-Americanism, terrorism and tyranny (Powerbase, 2016a). Geras headed the group that produced the Manifesto, with support from fellow members of his pro-war 'Loop' group, pro-war left bloggers and several right-wing Labour MPs including Denis MacShane, John Mann and Gisela Stuart. Other notable Eustonites included John Lloyd, another former Communist amongst Britain's elite commentariat, the aforementioned Oliver Kamm, Marko Attila Hoare, who at one stage was a member of the neoconservative Henry Jackson Society, and the London-based sociologist, David Hirsh. Speaking at the launch event, the academic Alan Johnson, a co-author of the Manifesto with Geras, said it had

> emerged in part from campaigning activity of a new sort, developed by networks of a new sort – networks that bridge together cyberspace, the blogosphere and the 'real world' of parliament, trade unions

and civil society, and which might help to renew social democracy. For those willing to dig – at normblog, Harry's Place, Little Atoms; LabourStart, Labour Friends of Iraq and Engage; Unite Against Terror and Democratiya – that's where the real story is. These campaigns and networks are modest affairs. But they are growing by the day, they punch well above their weight and they signpost a future. (Johnson, 2006)

Johnson would reflect, two years after the Euston Manfesto launch event, that the leading signatories lacked enough of a shared political vision to emerge as a cohesive group. He noted, however, the ongoing work of the various groupings he had alluded to at the event, and observed that it was at 'the online political journal Democratiya, [that] many Eustonians now gather' (Johnson, 2008) – a journal of which he was founding editor. Johnson, like many in the neoconservative tradition, had been a Trotskyist, including in the Alliance for Workers Liberty, perhaps as late as 2003. Also like that tradition, he traversed the left to work for a time in propaganda for the government. He was a consultant and researcher for Home Office propaganda unit, the Research, Information and Communications Unit (2008–10) and subsequently (in 2011) joined the UK's leading pro-Israel lobby group BICOM.

As this tale of the pro-war left and its various iterations and outputs illustrates, the line between the left and the conservative, neoconservative or Zionist right is not always a clear one. The pro-war left was not so very left in the end, but it was more or less united on its suspicions of religion and in particular Islam. A pro-war position that saw the Saddam Hussein regime, Hamas or Hezbollah as 'fascist' or used such terms as 'Islamofascism' (Molyneux, 2016) was already racialising Muslims. A strong element of this current of opinion was the defence of abstract secularism in opposition to 'Islamism' or 'fundamentalism', and the tendency for this to veer into obvious racism as demonstrated in particular by the so-called New Atheists, as well as by sections of the formal secularist movement, and it is to these currents that we now turn.

The New Atheists

The 'New Atheists' is an initially pejorative term coined in late 2006 to refer to a handful of anti-theist public intellectuals who became prominent in the early period of the 'War on Terror'. The best known of these is the British evolutionary biologist Richard Dawkins, who that year published his best-selling book, *The God Delusion*, and who remains the best known intellectual of the contemporary atheist movement. After Dawkins, the two most influential New Atheists have been the late Christopher Hitchens, a British political commentator and essayist whose book *God is Not Great* was published in 2007, and the American writer Sam Harris, who found fame with his 2004 book, *The End of Faith*, and later trained as a neuroscientist. Along with the somewhat less well known American scholar, Daniel Dennett, the author of *Breaking the Spell* (2006), these men came to be known as the 'Four Horsemen of New Atheism'; the leading figures in a newly assertive atheist and secularist movement that came to the fore in the mid to late 2000s. Since then, a number of other atheist and humanist intellectuals have also become prominent, perhaps most notably the British humanist philosopher A.C. Grayling and the Harvard psychologist and linguist Steven Pinker. Together with a host of other less well-known figures, these men (the movement is mostly male and its intellectuals overwhelmingly so) lead a relatively privileged, well-educated Anglo-American social movement that coheres around atheist, secularist, humanist and rationalist organisations, societies and websites, holds conferences, and produces books, videos and blogs.

There is some dispute as to whether there is anything particularly new about the New Atheism. At the level of ideas there has been no notable innovation on display. Notwithstanding the utilisation of some new findings from the fields of genetics and neuroscience, there is little to distinguish the arguments advanced by Dawkins et al. from the Darwinian-inspired scientific atheism of the nineteenth century, which pitched modern science against anachronistic religious authority, and liberal freethinking against the superstitions and credulity of the faithful. Like the more strident of their Victorian antecedents, the New Atheists hold that religion is a malign influence in the world that should be challenged politically and intellectually. They regard it as a legacy of the pre-scientific age (and perhaps a by-product of some evolutionary adaptation) that encourages irrational thought, justifies illiberal ideas and practices, and leads to, or at least exacerbates, violent conflicts. In this respect, the New Atheists essentially offer a particularly forceful exposition of some assumptions that are latent in much liberal, and some leftist and conservative, thought. If there is some novelty to put the 'new' in 'New Atheism', it lies less in their ideas – their critiques of religion and religiosity are either rather crude or completely unoriginal – and more in the strident manner in which these ideas have been expressed, and the historical circumstances in which they have been mobilised.

The early secularists and atheists were particularly concerned to curtail any influence the churches exercised over the education system, and in doing so they opposed religious authorities with considerable social power. But while broadly in agreement as to the need to overcome repressive religious authority, these atheists were otherwise a politically heterogeneous group. Many identified with humanist and socialist ideals. But others saw the eradication of religion and the expansion of scientific authority as an end in itself, or at least as part of a less radical process of social transformation based upon individual liberal and freethinking. The New Atheists stand more in this latter tradition of atheism. Moreover, they operate in a context in which the social authority of the natural sciences is fairly well entrenched, even if religion has not been completely exorcised from primary and secondary education and public life. This context is obviously important in understanding the politics of the New Atheism. As a political and intellectual movement, it stands not in opposition to dominant ideas or powerful institutions, but against religious belief, and ideas considered irrational or unscientific more generally, and against relatively marginal, if not insignificant, politically mobilised religious movements. The latter principally includes both the Christian right in the US, and more significantly for our purposes the various religiously inspired Middle Eastern and Asian groups and movements, some of which have militarily opposed the US and its allies – movements which have come to symbolise a rise in religiosity and 'religious fundamentalism' in the late twentieth and early twentieth centuries, which has alarmed liberals.

As all accounts of the New Atheism note, the 9/11 attacks and the politics of the War on Terror were crucial to the emergence of the movement in the mid 2000s. Sam Harris's *The End of Faith* grew out of an essay he wrote in response to the 9/11 attacks and opens with an account of a suicide bombing. In that book, Harris devotes a whole chapter to 'the problem with Islam', noting, and then immediately dismissing, the political factors that have driven Middle Eastern political violence, such as the US-sponsored Israeli occupation of Palestine and the diplomatic support provided by the US and its allies to authoritarian regimes in the region. It is in fact, Harris insists in *The End of Faith*, an 'infatuation with Koranic eschatology' alone that explains 'terrorism', asserting that we are 'at war with Islam' (2004: 11, 109). He would subsequently go as far as remarking that those 'who speak most sensibly about the threat that Islam poses to Europe are actually fascists' (cited in LeDrew, 2015: 86).

The logic of Harris's pugnacious prose, as with countless others, is to depoliticise the analysis of 'terrorism' in the Middle East, and to morally legitimise policies feeding the cycle of violence there. But despite the strong emphasis Harris places on reason and evidence, his argument simply does not stand up. Robert Pape's work on the use of suicide terrorism, which examined attacks between 1980 and 2003, found that such attacks were not connected to Islam, or to religion more generally, but driven by a desire to expel foreign occupiers (Pape, 2003, 2005; for a discussion of subsequent trends and questions of causation and policy responses, see also Atran, 2006). While in purely statistical terms Pape's conclusions could arguably be challenged in the light of the extraordinary growth in suicide bombings that followed the 2003 invasion and occupation of Iraq – which skewed the data greatly in favour of ostensibly religiously motivated actors – later research, based on much more extensive analysis of the data on 'terrorism', has more definitively undermined the Harris thesis. In 2015, the Institute for Economics and Peace published the results of an extensive statistical analysis of the largest existing dataset on 'terrorist' incidents, comparing that data with over 5,000 datasets, indices and attitudinal surveys. The researchers found no significant correlation between 'terrorism' and religiosity, nor any significant correlation between 'terrorism' and the percentage of Muslims in a population. What they did find, however, was a strong correlation with ongoing armed conflict, state repression, political instability and a history of sectarian violence and hostility between religious or ethnic groups (Institute for Economics and Peace, 2015: 100–4). These findings are broadly in keeping with Krueger's less extensive statistical analysis, which suggested a link between 'terrorism' and political repression (Krueger, 2007). The best evidence, then, suggests that the actual drivers of 'terrorism' are precisely those that Harris dismisses. Religion obviously plays some role, but only insofar as social conflicts will often assume a sectarian character along religious fault lines. The attempts by Harris to afford causal primacy to religion – and Islam in particular – therefore flies in the face of the best evidence.

The same flawed arguments are also at work in the reactionary polemics of Christopher Hitchens, which won him such acclaim in the latter years of his life. The attacks of 9/11, Hitchens argued, could not be attributed to the contemporary geopolitics of the Middle East. Like another favourite intellectual of the Bush administration, the conservative Orientalist Bernard Lewis, he argued that the 'grievance and animosity' felt towards the US in the Middle East was attributable to historic civilisational animus between Islam and Europe, and to the failure and inability of Islam to undergo a Reformation and come to terms with modernity (Seymour, 2012: 70).

By the time Hitchens found his greatest fame as one of the 'Four Horseman of New Atheism', the former leftist had already established himself as an outspoken apologist for US imperialism. Weeks after the 9/11 attacks, he confessed to having felt 'exhilaration' that day, as he anticipated a 'battle' against 'theocratic barbarism' that he pledged he would '[prosecute] to the utmost' (Hitchens, 2001) – an effort that would involve advocating torture and displaying an almost gleeful celebration of violence (Seymour, 2005). In that same article, Hitchens recalled 'the last confrontation with clerical bloodlust in 1989'; a reference to the Rushdie Affair, during which he had come strongly to the defence of the threatened author. In his memoir, Hitchens would write: 'I don't think it's possible to overstate the importance of the Rushdie case', comparing his friend (Rushdie) to the victims of Stalinism and describing him as 'the lineal descendent of all those who have had to confront the totalitarian idea'. Hitchens referred to God as a 'celestial dictator' and seems to have regarded his own anti-theism as part of his supposed anti-totalitarian politics – which saw him move dramatically to the right in the 2000s. Richard Seymour, the author of *Unhitched: The Trial of Christopher Hitchens*, suggests that Hitchens's wholehearted embrace of atheist politics in 2007, while to some extent rooted in his earlier rather crude Marxist anti-theism, and his role in the Rushdie Affair, was at least in part an opportunistic response to the unravelling of the neoconservative project around that time (Seymour, 2012: 54).

The 'overall thrust' of Hitchens's writing on religion, Seymour notes, is 'to pin on it social evils that are the product of a much more complex set of determinations' (Seymour, 2012: 67).[1] As we have seen also with Harris, this is the basic problem at the heart of the New Atheism whenever it stumbles from evolutionary theory and metaphysics into politics. As LeDrew also notes, its proponents have tended to obscure 'social reality by making religion a scapegoat for social problems at the expense of a careful examination of the structure of modern society' (LeDrew, 2015: 90). In the case of Hitchens, Harris and other right-wing New Atheists, this has made their writings at times barely distinguishable from the most hysterical neoconservative polemics. The same observation, though, could also be made of the more measured Richard Dawkins, who is still the leading New Atheist intellectual. A world without religion, Dawkins claims, would have

> no suicide bombers, no 9/11, no 7/7, no Crusades, no witch-hunts, no Gunpowder Plot, no India partition, no Israeli/Palestinian wars, no Serb/Croat/Muslim massacres, no persecution of Jews as 'Christ-killers', no Northern Ireland 'troubles', no 'honour killings ... no flogging of female skin for the crime of showing an inch of it. (Dawkins, 2016: 23–4)

As this passage illustrates, Dawkins believes that patriarchal violence and political conflicts involving religious groups are in some straightforward way caused by religion. Shortly after 9/11, he wrote a piece describing religion as 'the underlying source of the divisiveness in the Middle East' and 'the elephant in the room that everybody is too polite – or too devout – to notice' (Dawkins, 2001). The article, however, was more measured than many contemporary commentaries, and since then Dawkins – who publicly opposed the 2003 invasion of Iraq – has generally been less willing than many other New Atheists to pronounce on the politics of the Middle East, or to attribute conflicts there to religion.[2] In contrast to Hitchens, who was a thoroughly political animal, and whose anti-theism was part of a lifelong political struggle, Dawkins is the quintessential liberal elitist who sees his atheism as stemming from his commitment to scientific truth. His major concern, and one ostensibly shared by the more right-wing New Atheists, is with confronting threats to scientific rationality, which is seen not just as a principle of education and research, but also political governance. For Dawkins, politics is not a sphere for deliberation and negotiation between conflicting ideas and interests, but a specialist field requiring particular knowledge and expertise. This is well illustrated by an interview with *The Times* in 2016 in which he remarked:

> If you are going to have an operation you want to have an elite surgeon, if you are going to board a plane you want an elite pilot. The same should be true of government. We need to be governed by the elite rather than by people like you and me. (Sylvester, 2016: 2–3)

This elitist conception of politics, combined with a faith in the inherently irrational and reactionary nature of religion, means that the more liberal Dawkins still vociferously opposes any encroachment into politics by religious groups, which are seen as a threat to a just and rational social order. Dawkins's politics, whilst some way from the histrionics and apologetics of Hitchens and Harris, respectively, is equally not defined by the sort of pluralism that has characterised much contemporary liberal thought. Multiculturalism is thought to too readily accommodate religious beliefs and practices, or facilitate political influence from religious groups. As LeDrew notes of the New Atheists, they perceive the modern scientific and liberal democratic order to be 'under threat by a swirling concoction of religious ignorance, epistemic relativism, identity politics, and cultural pluralism' (LeDrew, 2015: 2). In this respect, there is an affinity between the strident liberal elitism exemplified by Dawkins and much more reactionary political actors who have identified broadly the same political and intellectual currents as having eroded the self-confidence of Western civilisation, or as more immediately representing a threat to critical inquiry and freedom of speech. Islamophobia, from this perspective, is seen as a bogus concept that contributes towards an irrational and censorious culture. 'There's a tendency among liberals in the West,' Dawkins remarked in 2016, 'to bend over backwards because they're terrified of being called racist. Islam gets a free pass':

> There's an awful confusion in many people's minds. They think Islam is a race, which of course it isn't. If you're seen to criticise Islam you are often accused of racism, which is absurd. I'm all for offending people's religion. I think it should be offended at every opportunity. (cited in Sylvester, 2016: 2–3)

This distrust of, and impatience with, multiculturalism and 'political correctness' – both products, however imperfect, of social movements from below – in combination with considerable arrogance, ignorance and political naivety, has brought Dawkins and other purported defenders of scientific rationality into the orbit of more committed reactionaries.

As the preceding discussion illustrates, the New Atheists are not a politically homogeneous grouping, and neither can the New Atheism in any straightforward way be clearly demarcated from broader humanist, atheist and secularist currents. In his study, LeDrew suggests that the bulk of the contemporary atheist movement are more conciliatory towards religion, and hold more pluralistic views, than the leading New Atheist intellectuals. He distinguishes between humanist atheism – which understands religion as a product of social organisation, to be overcome by social transformation – and the atheism of the New Atheists – which in the tradition of Victorian scientific atheism sees religion as an organised delusion to be corrected by modernity and scientific rationality. He describes the various conflicts within secularist, humanist and rationalist organisations and societies between these conflicting visions. He notes, for example, the shift to the right at the Center for Inquiry in the US, from a philosophy of secular humanism, and a more conciliatory politics, under its founder Paul Kurtz, to a more confrontational approach under Ronald Linday, who brought it closer to a right-wing libertarian position and pioneered International Blasphemy Day (LeDrew, 2015: 195–7). LeDrew argues that this is symptomatic of the growing prominence of what he terms the Atheist Right, and suggests that the 'New Atheism's totalitarian and neoconservative streak is only one aspect of the growth of the right wing of the secular movement more broadly' (LeDrew, 2015: 188).

Similar conflicts over the politics of the atheist and secularist movement are evident in the UK. In 2013, the incoming editor of the *New Humanist*, Daniel Trilling, criticised Dawkins's remarks about Islam, arguing that some 'criticisms' of religion can be racist, and emphasising the need 'to find common ground between people of different religious beliefs and none' (Trilling, 2013).

Secularism, feminism and anti-racism

Similar arguments and disputes over the role of religion have animated the feminist movement and in particular led to one strand of black feminism which prioritised sexism and patriarchy within ethnic minority communities, as opposed to, or in addition to, anti-racist struggles. The particular current we discuss here has, we contend, ended up supporting Islamophobic positions and activities.

Southall Black Sisters

Southall Black Sisters emerged, ten years before the Rushdie Affair, in 1979 during a period of a wide variety of political struggles – including significant anti-racist struggles. During this time, there were mass campaigns against immigration controls, fascist violence, racist policing and widespread criminalisation of black communities. Black feminist organisations grew rapidly in this period, partly in response to racism within the feminist movement (Amos and Parmar, 1997; Carby, 1997).

In 1978 the Organisation of Women of Asian and African Descent (OWAAD) was founded as a national body with the overall aim of challenging the specific forms of oppression faced by the different categories of black women. Informed by the political blackness of the anti-racist movement, the commitment was to forge unity between African, Caribbean and Asian women and the aim was to stress common-alities as well as heterogeneity of experiences. The demise of OWAAD in 1982 came partly as a result of tensions amongst black feminists over the competing priorities of feminist and anti-racist struggles. According to Avtar Brah (1992) (a founding member of Southall Black Sisters), there were disagreements over the importance of racism in structuring oppression felt by black and minority women. For some within OWAAD the racist devaluation of black cultures meant the priority should be activities to 'reclaim' these cultural sites. Others placed greater emphasis on challenging aspects of minority cultures in which women's oppression was reproduced: the problem of male violence; the division of labour; dowry and forced marriages; clitorecdectomy; and heterosexism (Brah, 1992: 134–5).

Southall Black Sisters (SBS) and then later Women Against Funda-mentalism (WAF) emerged within this context. Although SBS arose initially in response to the death of Blair Peach – a teacher from New Zealand killed by police at a demonstration against a National Front rally in Southall – the organisation soon shifted its attention to supporting Asian women who had been victims of domestic violence. By Pragna Patel's (2014) account, the organisation had in fact started to dwindle by 1981. Patel then re-established SBS (later joined by Meena Patel and Hannana Siddiqui) to – in her own words – work 'against the grain' of existing anti-racist and feminist orthodoxies. The new incarnation of SBS sought to challenge patriarchy within ethnic minority groups while remaining committed to anti-racism. In short, their argument was that the official policies and funding arrangements of state multiculturalism produced a distinctly male 'community' leadership. This, they claimed, elevated conservative figures as 'community leaders' at the expense of more radical, secularist voices, and as a result worked against the interests of minority women (Patel, 1997: 263). While in some ways this aligned with the left critiques of a top-down state-sponsored multiculturalism (Sivanandan, 1990), the organisation ran into conflict with existing anti-racist organisations (Patel, 1997; Sahgal and Yuval-Davis, 1992).

The Rushdie Affair

The publication of Salman Rushdie's *Satanic Verses* at the end of the 1980s marked an important turning point in both expressions of Muslim political agency and liberal-left secularist politics in the UK. Following the publication of the book, Iranian leader Ayatollah Khomeini issued a fatwa (religious ruling) calling for the death of Rushdie, and there were mass mobilisations globally against the book for its portrayal of the Prophet Muhammad and other revered figures.

What followed from these mobilisations was a distinct form of political organisation of Muslim groups in Britain. Most notably, the UK Action Committee on Islamic Affairs (UKACIA), which later broadened into the Muslim Council of Britain (MCB), became the organisation accepted by the government and other bodies as the chosen interlocutor for addressing the concerns of British Muslims. The organisation focused on lobbying on four issues: a distinct Muslim religious voice; legislation on religious incitement to racial hatred; socio-economic policies addressing the severe disadvantage of Pakistani and Bangladeshi groups; and finally, state recognition and allocation of resources to Islamic schools (Modood, 2009: 492).

Many on the left were critical of such religiously oriented identity-based politics, which they considered a distraction from more radical, broad-based politics such as the Asian Youth Movement (Sivanandan, 1990). Although at the time of the Rushdie Affair the response of anti-racist and leftist organisations was formally in support of Muslims in their struggle against racism, there was a reluctance to support the full range of political demands being made – particularly the demands for censorship. Instead, the left campaigned on the basis of the slogans such as 'Fight racism, not Rushdie' (Modood, 2005: 103) or 'No to censorship; no to racism' (Jenkins, 2014). This orientation was critical of Muslim political agency, but saw the struggle against fascism as a clear area where unity against racism was important. Matters were not so clear for SBS.

Women Against Fundamentalism

A significant development in the post-Rushdie fallout was the formation of Women Against Fundamentalism (WAF). WAF was founded in London in spring 1989 following a meeting organised by SBS and the Southall Labour Party Women's section, in defence of Salman Rushdie. Formed on the basis of the founding statement: 'the separation of the state and religion in Britain as a precondition for defeating fundamentalism' (WAF, 1990), WAF's first major political action was to confront anti-Rushdie protestors at a demonstration in Parliament Square in May 1989 with the slogans: 'Our tradition: struggle not submission', 'Religious leaders don't speak for us', 'Blasphemy law polices dissent', 'Fear is your weapon/courage is ours'. Two separate groups of fascists were also marching that day against the Rushdie protestors, so anti-racists and leftist activists reportedly decided to support the anti-Rushdie protestors. WAF marched separately to all these groups. Their key demands were to support Salman Rushdie and free speech, to oppose representation by 'community leaders' and to abolish the blasphemy laws (Dhaliwal and Yuval-Davis, 2014: location 5905). Later, WAF expanded these to include disestablishment of the Church of England and an end to the funding of religious schools.

Women Against Fundamentalism and the 'War on Terror'

During the 1990s, WAF played a less active role, formally closing their offices in 1996 (Dhaliwal and Yuval-Davis, 2014: location 305). But following the events of 9/11 and the subsequent Iraq War, WAF began to revive its activities. By this time, however, they were operating in quite a different political environment. Firstly, unlike during the Rushdie

Affair, sections of the left and some Muslim groups had begun working in a closer political coalition. Also, in marked contrast to the Rushdie Affair (Asad, 1990), politically mobilised Muslims now had a plurality, or a majority, of public opinion behind them. The Muslim Association of Britain (MAB) began working closely with the Stop the War Coalition (StWC) and the Campaign for Nuclear Disarmament (CND) in organising protests against the US–UK Iraq War. The first joint demonstration was called on 28 September 2002, co-sponsored by StWC, MAB and the CND, mobilising an estimated 400,000 people.

The Iraq War shifted the relationship between the MCB and the government, with the MCB attacked and then sidelined for its opposition to the wars in Iraq and Afghanistan – part of a broader political attack on multiculturalism. In 2006, the New Labour Minister, Ruth Kelly, made a speech, which announced the government's intention to actively: 'develop relationships with a wider network of Muslim organisations' especially those involved in 'taking a proactive leadership role in tackling extremism and defending our shared values'. This 'wider network' included the a range of groups less critical of the war in Iraq than mainstream Muslim opinion, such as the Sufi Muslim Council, Al Khoei Foundation, British Muslims for a Secular Democracy and the Quilliam Foundation.

WAF found themselves in a difficult position in this environment; their criticisms of multiculturalism were now commonly heard from conservative, neoconservative and far-right sources. But despite this, WAF once again defined themselves against the existing positions of the left. They opposed StWC's relationship with the MAB. In language not dissimilar to that of the English Defence League and the counterjihad movement (see Chapter 8), they accused the StWC of an 'Islamisation of demonstrations' for allowing prayers to be led from the stage on one occasion. We can assume the incident they are referring to (as they do not elaborate) was the StWC-led demonstration against the Afghan War in November 2001. At this demonstration, which occurred during the month of Ramadan, there was a communal breaking of the fast, with a prayer led by an Imam. Since WAF claim to have no issue with religious observance, we would not expect them to object to allowing Muslims present at a demonstration to observe their religious practice. Yet, WAF criticised StWC on exactly this basis, part of a broader effort to incorporate opposition to religious fundamentalism into their campaigns. Their anti- (Iraq) war leaflet carried the slogan: 'No to imperialism – no to all religious fundamentalism', and stated:

> While condemning the 'War on Terror', which is fuelling increased anti-Muslim racism and the criminalisation of certain Muslims, we oppose the fundamentalists in the USA, in Iraq and across the world, who are using the conflict as an opportunity to promote reactionary, violent, discriminatory and divisive politics under the banner of religion. (cited in Dhaliwal and Yuval-Davis, 2014: location 5919)

WAF's position in this period did not sit comfortably with all members of the organisation. Some were concerned that they were not getting the balance right between addressing issues of anti-Muslim racism while staying committed to their secular feminist project (Al-Ali, 2014: location 3785). In fact, some members were becoming uncomfortable with some of the company WAF was beginning to keep. As Nadje Al-Ali (2014: location 3792) writes:

> I also started to get a bit worried about WAF's occasional working together with groups and individuals I perceive to be 'secular fundamentalists' – i.e. those who have a righteous, 'I have the only one truth' kind of attitude – and about whether WAF are being careful enough about disentangling religious fundamentalism and religion.

The strange political convergence between radical feminist anti-racists and various Islamophobic movements came to the fore very publicly in early 2010 when Gita Sahgal, a co-founder of SBS and WAF, publicly attacked CAGE's Moazzam Begg in the pages of the *Sunday Times*. In a relatively short article leading to an international media storm, Sahgal aired her objections to her then employer Amnesty International partnering with Begg and CAGE. Sahgal, who was head of Amnesty International's Gender Unit at the time, was quoted as saying: 'it was absolutely wrong to legitimise [Moazzam Begg] as a partner'. The article quoted an email she had sent to her bosses in which she described CAGE as a 'jihadi' organisation and Begg as 'Britain's most famous supporter of the Taliban'. The inflammatory accusations were repeated across the British and international media, putting Amnesty under intense pressure to sever its relationship with CAGE.

Gita Sahgal was suspended and later forced to resign from Amnesty, becoming something of a cause célèbre for neoconservatives, the pro-war left and similar groupings. She and her supporters then wrote a number of articles attacking both her former employer and Moazzam Begg. We have written extensively elsewhere about the unsubstantiated and inflammatory nature of the accusations Sahgal makes against Begg (Mills et al., 2015b). The whole affair led to a political crisis within WAF and subsequently led to its demise. It seems that some members – as anti-racist activists – were (in our view rightfully) uncomfortable with the direction in which the public debate had travelled and saw the focus on Moazzam Begg and CAGE as misplaced (Dhaliwal and Yuval-Davis, 2014: location 621).

What is religious fundamentalism?

While the term fundamentalism originally arose to describe literalist interpretations of the Bible by certain American Protestant sects in 1919, since the Iranian revolution (1979) it has become a commonplace derogatory term to indicate reactionary and conservative interpretations of Islam. According to WAF, fundamentalism:

> refers to modern political movements that use religion to gain or consolidate power, whether working within or in opposition to the state. We strictly differentiate fundamentalism from religious observance which we see as individual choice.

This wide-reaching definition of fundamentalism in principle includes a range of progressive social and political movements formed in the struggle for social, civic and political freedoms. The obvious example here is liberation theology, but the definition is so far-reaching it would even include the Quakers – pacifists who deploy their religion for purposes of peace, humanity and social justice.[3] The problem with this definition of fundamentalism is that it fails to account for the social processes involved in political mobilisations. Movements do not develop in a vacuum; they emerge through a process of political struggle within the society in which they are situated. Movements of oppressed groups engage in struggle against the terms of their oppression – this means that they rely on the existing resources available at the time. The black civil rights movement in the US, for example, came out of activities based within the black churches. The social, political and civic exclusion of black people at the time meant that the churches became centres of social and political life. Free from white control, the churches provided a space for the development of culture and lifestyle, as well as civic and social activities that laid the foundations for a more widespread movement (Morris, 1984, 1992). Black civil rights activism rested on the cultural, ideological and institutional resources offered by religion.

Furthermore, while WAF claim that they are targeting *all* religious fundamentalisms, in reality it is Islam, or as they understand it, Islamism, that is the primary target of their critique. Yet it is difficult to see within the secularist critique of what they call religious fundamentalism how they would allow for any distinction between Islam and Islamism. For a start, the secularist charge against religion is not applicable in the same way to all religions. In fact, secularism itself cannot be divorced from the particular social experience in which it emerged.

As Salman Sayyid (2014) argues, this conception of secularism relies on an epistemological foundation derived from the historical, political and cultural experience of Christianity. Secularism in this tradition emerged as a result of a number of shifts in European societies, which began in the fifteenth century and later consolidated around key events in the seventeenth century. These processes led to the decoupling of religious and scientific authority (e.g. the Renaissance and then later the Enlightenment), as well as religious and political authority (e.g. Peace of Westphalia ending the European imperial wars of religion). The lack of a centralised formal institution of religious authority within Islam – particularly Sunni Islam – makes such comparisons difficult and problematic.

Muslims should not have to prove their allegiance to a form of secularism that reflects a Christian experience – and in any case questions concerning religious epistemological foundations can be rather abstract. It is may be more fruitful to consider the sociological reality of Muslim socio-political participation, and whether this in fact poses a threat to democratic principles. There are numerous studies that show that even an overtly politicised adherence to Islam is not necessarily incompatible with democratic, or even leftist politics (Mandaville, 2009; O'Toole and Gale, 2010). The question then obviously requires careful analysis, yet SBS and WAF rarely identify the specific groups of 'fundamentalists' that allegedly pose a threat to progressive movements. Instead, they make sweeping references to 'religious fundamentalists' and 'Islamists' which rely on a baseline of common sense racism. Indeed, as Tariq Modood wrote in his criticisms of WAF back in 1996, in using the 'demonising term fundamentalism', WAF's terminology was 'located in the prejudices of most Britons'. An example of this is their anti-Iraq War leaflet, which said:

> WAF is alarmed that elements on the Left are colluding with funda-mentalist religious leaders who are attempting to undermine rights and freedoms, including in their own communities. WAF believes that the anti-war movement has been silent too long on the reactionary and destructive role of Christian and Muslim fundamentalism in the occupation of Iraq and in the 'War on Terror'.

There is, however, an elaboration on this in one of the more detailed passages of their book (Dhaliwal and Yuval-Davis, 2014: location 610):

> This [post 9/11] saw the emergence of new constellations of activists and organisations from many religions but with compatible fundamentalist world views; such groups were actively building alliances with both state institutions and civil society organisations in order to embed themselves within broader discussions about equality, civil liberties and human rights. For instance a number of Muslim Brotherhood, Jamaat-e-Islami, Salafist organisations and the Hizb-ut-Tahrir began working with each other across different forums and spaces. Moreover, these groups have been projecting themselves as 'moderate'. They have been critical of the anti-Muslim, anti-imperialist (sic) nature of the state, but at the same time have worked closely with the police and the state to attract PVE funding, which they have used to strengthen their own position and perpetuate their specific version of Islam.

The conflation here of a diverse set of traditions with no reference to context is telling. The source cited for this is Meredith Tax's Centre for Secular Space report *Double Bind: The Muslim Right, the Anglo-American Left and Universal Human Rights*. That report makes no such claims about the collaboration of these groups. It does, however, suggest that there is little distinction between violent and non-violent 'political Islamists' (Tax, 2012: 7) and implicitly applauds the revisions to the government's Prevent strategy in 2011 (Tax, 2012: 75), which switched from engagement with peaceful Muslim groups to the targeting of non-violent politically active Muslims, a move that led to a step change in attacks on the status of Muslims in public life. This political orientation echoes that of the neoconservatives, as do many of the other positions advanced in Tax's analysis, the first publication of Gita Sahgal's Centre for Secular Space. For instance, her argument against the use of the term Islamophobia follows that of the standard Islamophobia deniers from Fred Halliday through the secular movement and the neocons to the far right.

The assault on politically active Muslims

Throughout this book, we have discussed the role of the state and its sprawling counter-terrorism apparatus as the central pillar of Islamophobia. As described in Chapter 1, the Counter-terrorism and Security Act 2015 (CTSA) has extended these powers beyond the police and security agencies to other branches of the state: universities, libraries, schools, hospitals – even nurseries. This has involved, amongst other things, an attack on politically active Muslims, limiting the role Muslim organisations can play in public life (see Chapter 5). Meanwhile, there has been significant opposition to this – the National Union of Teachers (NUT), the University and College Union (UCU) and the National Union of Students (NUS) all have policies to boycott Prevent. The Students not Suspects campaign, initiated by the NUS black students campaign, has mobilised large sections of the student body in opposition to Prevent. In a testament to their success, Malia Bouattia – a leading figure in this campaign – was elected as the first female black (and Muslim) president of the NUS in the autumn of 2016.

As in the case of the anti-war movement and the Rushdie Affair before that, SBS and former WAF members have chosen to distance themselves from the opposition to Prevent. Rahila Gupta of SBS argues that Prevent is a 'noose that is both too tight and too loose'. It is 'too tight' in that it violates fundamental human rights and civil liberties; yet, it is also 'too loose' in that it does not adequately address the issue of religious fundamentalism. She goes on to criticise what she calls the 'anti-prevent lobby' – a term often used by counter-extremism group Quilliam and government-funded Prevent operatives to attack anti-racist campaigners. According to Gupta, religious fundamentalists populate the anti-Prevent lobby and close down the spaces for secular feminist dissent. She is referring to CAGE, the NGO that defends those accused of terrorism-related offences. As we have already noted, there are a diverse set of actors campaigning in opposition to Prevent, and while CAGE have played a significant role in initiating a number of petitions and campaigns, they are one amongst a growing number of organisations. But there is in any case no evidence that employees of CAGE have ever acted in any way to prevent secular feminists (or anyone else) from participating in any of the campaigns or activities that they have been involved in. What appears to us to underlie this argument, one that is made time and again by SBS, is that CAGE (and other politically active Muslims – who they call fundamentalists) either have a covert agenda to implement patriarchal and reactionary practices through their participation in human rights causes or that some members of staff at CAGE have private religious convictions that are reactionary.

If the latter is true, the secularist test is surely whether they bring these to bear on their human rights practice. It is pretty clear that this is not the case – that CAGE does not in fact do that. SBS have, on the other hand, teamed up with reactionaries and Islamophobes to pursue their attempt to help 'tighten the noose' of Prevent. In March 2016, the Feminist Society, Socialist Society, Islamic Society and Friends of Palestine Society at the University of Exeter organised a meeting on Prevent at which Moazzam Begg (the outreach director at CAGE) was amongst the speakers. SBS criticised the event in a letter sent to the Feminist Society urging them to withdraw their sponsorship of the event. It was signed by both Gita Sahgal (Centre for Secular Space) and Pragna Patel (Southall Black Sisters), but also by secularist activists Maryam Namazie (listed as One Law For All, Council of ex-Muslims) and Haydar Zaki (Quilliam Foundation) (Fuller, 2016). This example illustrates the alliances into which the SBS tradition have now entered, along with parts of the broader secularist movement – alliances that indicate their emergence as social movements from above. Moreover, the Quilliam Foundation, as we note elsewhere, is not a genuine expression of Muslim civil society, but a grouping whose creation was heavily subsidised by the British state and latterly funded by (amongst others) conservative foundations that also fund the Islamophobia network in the US. Perhaps we might end with the imagery of the tightening noose. What we see here, therefore, is a movement that purports to represent a radical anti-racist tradition that has not only sought to marginalise and defame Muslim civil society actors engaged in campaigning for human rights and civil liberties, but has done so in alliance with the racist counter-terrorism policy of the state.

The secularist movement

The curious peregrinations of one strand of the black feminist movement notwithstanding, is there any more general tendency suggestive of a movement in development? There is a strong clue in the names of the organisations listed above as signatories to the letter to Exeter Feminist Society. The arguments put forward by the New Atheists and advanced by SBS, and to some extent WAF, are echoed in the broader secularist movement. It should be noted, however, that as with the history of WAF the story here is very much one of contest and struggle over the meaning of secularism as Islamophobic ideas have spread across society. Just as with Zionism, the secularist movement is not entirely in the grip of Islamophobia, and the story we tell of the Islamophobic currents and their evolution is illustrated by details of the resistance to such ideas from within the movement.

We can see such conflicts in the politics of the National Secular Society in the UK and in a range of other similar organisations. As WAF began to fall apart, Sahgal worked in a 'subgroup' on Law discussing Sharia councils and tribunals. In this she felt her 'most useful contributions' were to 'the One Law for All campaign, where, after immense hard work Maryam Namazie and Anne Marie Waters built an important coalition' – a coalition with which some members of WAF did not want to affiliate (Sahgal, 2014: location 1877). This coalition illustrates very well the milieu in which Sahgal's faction from WAF operated in the period from 2011 onwards. It also neatly ties together the key secularist groups with the Christian right, the neoconservatives and the counterjihad movement, as we now discuss.

Let us start with One Law for All, the grouping cited by Sahgal, and then consider other elements of the coalition. One Law for All (OLFA) was created in 2008 to campaign against Sharia courts and tribunals. It was headed by Maryam Namazie and Anne Marie Waters. Namazie is an Iranian-born activist who became a director of OLFA in June 2012, along with Anne Marie Waters. Namazie is also associated with a range of other secularist groupings including the Council of Ex Muslims, and she is on the Central Committee of the Worker-Communist Party of Iran. In 2006 she joined Ayaan Hirsi Ali, Irshad Manji, Taslima Nasreen and a host of other neocon and counterjihad-connected activists in signing the 'Manifesto against Islamism', which affirmed that 'after having overcome fascism, Nazism, and Stalinism, the world now faces a new totalitarian global threat: Islamism'. In OLFA, the Manifesto and numerous other activities it is clear that the primary target is Islam. It is doubtful that any other religion would be described as exhibiting 'totalitarianism'. The orientation of OLFA towards the right is inadvertently illustrated by the title of its report on the far right, *Enemies, Not Allies* (One Law for All, 2011). The implication is that readers of the report might be in some doubt about the politics of the far right.

Also in the coalition on Sharia was an organisation called British Muslims for Secular Democracy, a group set up by the journalist Yasmin Alibhai-Brown amongst others. Its spokesperson, Tehmina Kazi, is listed as an expert on the website of the European Foundation on Democracy, a neoconservative outfit in Brussels that claims to be independent but which was in fact funded significantly by the hardline neocon Foundation for Defense of Democracies, based in Washington, DC (Cronin et al., 2016). Kazi also advised on the proposed bill that gave expression to the demands of the coalition on Sharia, the Arbitration and Mediation Services (Equality) Bill in January 2012, which sought to make it an offence for anyone to claim or imply that Sharia courts or councils have legal jurisdiction over family or criminal law in Britain.

The figurehead who introduced the bill was a member of the House of Lords, the ultra-conservative Christian, Baroness Caroline Cox. Cox is well known for her involvement with organisations often described as Christian fundamentalist, strange company for secularists. Cox has a career-long connection to the Christian right. She was involved with a series of conservative and Cold War pressure groups including the Freedom Association and the Committee for a Free Britain, as well as the early US-funded neoconservative group, the Institute for European Defence and Security Studies (Powerbase, 2016b). Cox was also a founder of One Jerusalem set up in 2000 to oppose the peace negotiations and to campaign for an undivided Jerusalem as the capital of Israel, a status that would require normalising the illegal occupation of East Jerusalem – a policy not in line with that of either the UK, US or Israeli governments. More recently, Cox was expelled from the Conservative Party in 2004 for urging a vote for UKIP, and with UKIP peer Lord Pearson invited Dutch anti-Islam politician Geert Wilders to show his film *Fitna* in Parliament (which has also received praise from Richard Dawkins). Wilders was banned by the Home Secretary when Cox was party to a subsequent attempt to invite him to the UK.

Baroness Cox had previously confirmed that Kazi was 'prepared to speak out in public and support my Bill' in a talk at David Horowitz's Restoration Weekend in Florida in November 2011. Kazi further contributed to a booklet seeking to provide evidence in support of Cox's bill.

Also contributing chapters were an organisation called Inspire and the Bristol counter-terror police officer, Kalsoom Bashir (who was by that stage already involved with Inspire and later appointed secretary and then director of the group (Miller and Massoumi, 2016)). It can be noted that Inspire is a very striking case of penetration of civil society by the state. Despite maintaining that it is an independent women's rights organisation, leaked internal Home Office documents record its flagship Makingastand campaign as a 'RICU product', that is, a covert product of the Home Office strategic communications department (Miller and Massoumi, 2016).

The National Secular Society

In this section we briefly examine the National Secular Society. This is the venerable and long established (since 1866) key secularist organisation in the UK. While it retains a significant number of liberal and left 'honorary associates', and is by no means straightforwardly an anti-Muslim organisation, the National Secular Society has provided a space for Islamophobic ideas and arguments. Gathered together as honorary associates are a number of those we have discussed in this chapter including from the New Atheist camp Dawkins, Hitchens and A.C. Grayling. In addition, the list includes Nick Cohen, Maryam Namazie, Pragna Patel, Gita Sahgal, as well as Maajid Nawaz of Quilliam and Taslima Nasrin (associated with both the Islamophobic Gatestone

Institute and the counterjihad grouping, the International Free Press Society) (Powerbase, 2017). It should be noted that others on the list of associates are not connected to these Islamophobic networks and we assume most would oppose this kind of activity.

The links with openly anti-Muslim organisations are underscored by the Islamophobia denial featured on the National Secular Society website, such as a piece by the National Secular Society Communication Officer Benjamin Jones titled, 'The "Islamophobia" delusion'. Amongst Jones's objections to the term Islamophobia was the familiar refrain that Islam is a religion not a race. He notes that 'ex-Muslims, non-devout Muslims, or even Sikhs – and others who are mistaken for Muslims' are often victims of Islamophobia. This is of course correct, but it is not at all clear to us in what sense this renders Islamophobia a 'delusion'. If anti-Semites target not only devout Jews visibly identifiable through their religious dress, but also liberal and secular Jews, or Gentiles wrongly assumed, for whatever reason, to be Jewish, that does not in any way minimise the problem of anti-Jewish racism. The same point applies to Islamophobia. A similar confusion over race and religion is evident later in the piece where Jones claims that we 'lazily use the phrase "anti-Muslim racism" – which,' he writes, 'makes as much sense as "anti-Christian racism": because in fact "Muslims are the most ethnically diverse" religion in England and Wales.'

We discussed the limitation of this argument in the Introduction of this book and will not go over it again here. Suffice it to say that Jones's argument about the diversity of both British Muslims and the victims of 'anti-Muslim bigotry' in Britain, while true, really has no bearing on the issues at hand. And it is also why we turn our attention to the state and powerful social movements 'from above'. It is largely the practices of the state and the activities of powerful political movements – whether driven by animus or expediency – that leads to violence and discrimination towards people of particular cultural, linguistic, ethnic and religious backgrounds; in this case Muslims.

In concluding on the National Secular Society, let us note that Companies House records that up until April 2014, Anne Marie Waters served as a director of the organisation (Companies House, 2017). This is the same individual who, as noted earlier, was a spokesperson for One Law For All alongside Maryam Namazie. Waters has since joined UKIP, started the anti-Islam groups, Sharia Watch and VOICE (Victims Of Islamic Cultural Extremism), consorted with Alan Ayling (strategist and sometime funder of the English Defence League (Aked, 2015b)) and was recorded by the *Daily Mirror* (Cortbus and Myers, 2015) saying: 'a lot of people need to be deported', 'many mosques need to be closed down' and 'immigration from Islamic countries has to stop entirely' (cited in Mills et al., 2015b). As far as we are aware, the National Secular Society has never condemned these comments, nor distanced itself from Waters, whereas another of her former organisations, One Law For All, has done so. Indeed, in its 2014 annual report published in October, the National Secular Society pictured and thanked Waters, and even promoted Sharia Watch's tendentious Learning Jihad 'report' in November (National Secular Society, 2014).

Social movements in the service of the state

The evidence we give above suggests that social movements from above are not only engaged in attempting to push the state to intensify discrimination and oppression (or limit the space for dissent and democratic participation), but are also engaged in trying to push through and implement state policies, whether or not they have campaigned or lobbied for them. Quilliam is an excellent example of such an organisation. In a way, though, Quilliam and a number of other counter-extremism groupings – such as Inspire – are not cleanly separable from the state. In fact, the state plays a strong role in managing and deploying such civil society groups as part of its counter-terrorism apparatus. As we have seen elsewhere in this book, Quilliam was set up with more than £3 million funding from the government in its first three years and is now funded by a range of non-government actors including foundations which also fund the Islamophobia network (Aked, 2015c). Amongst its other activities, Quilliam is attempting to drive through the government's Prevent policy in higher education in the UK through its 'right2debate' campaign and by forming Quilliam student societies. Right2debate is ironically named since its intention is to ensure either that pro-government speakers are added to the platform at meetings on Prevent, or Palestine, or British foreign policy, or to ensure that the events cannot take place. The organisational basis of Quilliam's campus groups is often the secular or humanist societies on campus, which is interesting given the attempt by Quilliam to present itself as a Muslim organisation.

Outcomes, as we have suggested, are a crucial delimiter, and notionally liberal or left social movements to some extent have to argue that they are not intending the kinds of outcomes that we are suggesting here. There seems to us to be only a limited number of responses to that. Either they are deliberately misleading their own supporters, and the world more generally, about the real intention and outcomes of their activities, or they are naive and mistaken about the geopolitical stakes of the struggles in which they engage, or perhaps some combination of the two.

Concluding comments

We have outlined here an array of political currents from the pro-war left to various stripes of secularism. We have noted the overlapping similarity of their ideas and the inter-organisational networks through with they work. We have tried to show that their disputes and developments have often been in the context of internal debate and dissent as well as in the context of a developing politics. It seems clear that while some of those in these groups did not start off as campaigners pushing for the oppressive conditions that are faced by Muslims in the West, many of them have ended up there. It is in this sense that we refer to the movements discussed here as becoming social movements from above – their trajectory putting them into de facto alliance with other Islamophobic currents, whether they intended this or not.

Notes

1. This applied not only to Hitchens's analysis of the 9/11 attacks, the Iraq War and its aftermath, but also, for example, to Northern Ireland, which he claimed was characterised by 'religious gangs' (Seymour, 2012: 65).
2. In an interview on the Russia Today programme, *Worlds Apart*, for example, Dawkins declined to attribute the violence of ISIS to religion, referring instead to a biological drive for selfish violence and vengeance (Russia Today, 2014).
3. In some places WAF seem to offer a contradictory account of this view and suggest that liberation theology must be differentiated from fundamentalism because 'they cooperate with, rather than subjugate, non-religious political struggles for freedom' (Sahgal and Yuval-Davis, 1992: 279; see also Conolly, 1990). However, by this definition organisations such as CAGE, MAB, MEMO, MEND and the Cordoba Foundation – that all work with a range of non-religious actors in political struggles for freedom – would need to also be differentiated from their definition of fundamentalism. Yet this is not consistent with WAF's view (Dhaliwal and Yuval-Davis, 2014: 347; Gupta, 2015).

Bibliography

Aked, H. (2015a), 'The lawyer, the Mohammed Cartoon Exhibition and the "Civil War" that wasn't', *Ceasefire*, 7 September. https://ceasefiremagazine. co.uk/lawyer-mohammed-cartoon-exhibition-civil-war-wasnt/. Accessed 13 February 2017.

—— (2015b), 'Sharia Watch UK and the metamorphosis of Anne Marie Waters', Institute for Race Relations, 21 January. www.irr.org.uk/news/sharia-watch-uk-and-the-metamorphosis-of-anne-marie-waters/. Accessed 10 February 2017.

—— (2015c), Questions for Quilliam: counter-extremism and Islamophobia, Al Araby, https://www.alaraby.co.uk/english/comment/2015/12/25/questions-for-quilliam-counter-extremism-and-islamophobia. Accessed 13 February 2017.

Al-Ali, N. (2014), 'From Germany to Iraq via WAF: a political journey', in S. Dhaliwal and Y. Yuval-Davis (eds), *Women Against Fundamentalism: Stories of Dissent and Solidarity.* London: Lawrence and Wishart, location 3556–806.

Amos, V. and Parmar, P. (1997), 'Challenging imperial feminism', in H.S. Mirza (ed.), *Black British Feminism.* London: Routledge, pp. 54–8.

Asad, T. (1990), 'Multiculturalism and British identity in the wake of the Rushdie Affair', *Politics & Society*, 18, 455–80.

Atran, S. (2006), 'The moral logic and growth of suicide terrorism', *Washington Quarterly*, 29 (2), 127–47.

Brah, A. (1992), 'Difference, diversity and differentiation', in J. Donald and A. Rattansi (eds), *'Race', Culture and Difference.* London: Sage, pp. 126–45.

Carby, H. (1997), 'White woman listen! Black feminism and the boundaries of sisterhood', in H.S. Mirza (ed.), *Black British Feminism.* London: Routledge, pp. 45–53.

Cohen, N. (2007), *What's Left?: How Liberals Lost Their Way.* London: HarperCollins.

Companies House (2017), 'Anne Marie Waters'. https://beta.companieshouse. gov.uk/officers/rFq09rMxreUc5-e7vuuQhaIVXoY/appointments. Accessed 15 February 2017.

Connolly, C. (1990), 'Splintered sisterhood: antiracism in a young women's project', *Feminist Review*, 36, 52–64.

Cortbus, C. and Myers, R. (2015), 'Watch UKIP candidates spouting vile anti-Islamic hate messages at a far-right rally', *Daily Mirror*, 15 April. www. mirror.co.uk/news/uk-news/watch-ukip-candidates-spouting-vile-5526503. Accessed 15 February 2017.

Cronin, D., Marusek, S. and Miller, D. (2016), *The Israel Lobby and the European Union*, Glasgow: Spinwatch and Europal.

Dawkins, R. (2001), 'Religion's misguided missiles', *Guardian*, 15 September. www.theguardian.com/world/2001/sep/15/september11.politicsphilosophy andsociety1. Accessed 10 February 2017.

—— (2016), *The God Delusion, 10th Anniversary Edition*. London: Black Swan.

Dennett, D. (2006), *Breaking the Spell*. New York: Penguin Books.

Dhaliwal, S. and Yuval-Davis, Y. (2014), 'Introduction', in S. Dhaliwal and Y. Yuval-Davis (eds), *Women Against Fundamentalism: Stories of Dissent and Solidarity*. London: Lawrence and Wishart, location 81–1035.

Fuller, H. (2016), 'Feminists ask students not to sponsor extremist speakers', Howie's Corner, 15 March. http://howiescorner.blogspot.co.uk/2016/03/feminists-ask-students-not-to-sponsor.html. Accessed 14 February 2017.

Geras, N. (2003a), 'The war in Iraq', normblog, 29 July. http://normangeras.blogspot.co.uk/2003_07_27_archive.html#105938911349286013#105938911349286013. Accessed 10 February 2017.

—— (2003b), 'Prehistory', normblog, 28 July. http://normangeras.blogspot.co.uk/2003_07_27_archive.html#105938911349286013#105938911349286013. Accessed 10 February 2017.

—— (2003c), 'Thanks', normblog, 28 July. http://normangeras.blogspot.co.uk/2003_07_27_archive.html#105938911349286013#105938911349286013. Accessed 10 February 2017.

—— (2006), 'Introducing the Euston Manifesto', *Guardian*, 13 April. www.theguardian.com/commentisfree/2006/apr/13/introducingtheeustonmanifes. Accessed 10 February 2017.

Gupta, R. (2015), 'Preventing violent extremism: a noose that is both too tight and too loose', Open Democracy, 26 October. www.opendemocracy.net/5050/rahila-gupta/preventing-violent-extremism-noose-both-too-tight-and-too-loose. Accessed 10 February 2017.

Harris, S. (2004), *The End of Faith*. London and New York: W.W. Norton & Company.

'Hatchet Harry' (2002), 'Welcome to Harry's Place', Harry's Place, 24 November. http://hurryupharry.org/2002/11/24/welcome-to-harrys-place/. Accessed 10 February 2017.

Hitchens, C. (2001), 'Images in a rearview mirror', *The Nation*, 15 November. www.thenation.com/article/images-rearview-mirror. Accessed 10 February 2017.

Institute for Economics and Peace (2015), *Global Terrorism Index 2015*. New York: Institute for Economics and Peace.

Jenkins, G. (2014), 'The tragedy of Salman Rushdie', *Socialist Review*, 374, November. http://socialistreview.org.uk/374/tragedy-salman-rushdie. Accessed 13 February 2017.

Johnson, A. (2006), 'No one left behind: Euston and the renewal of social democracy (by Alan Johnson)', normblog, 1 June. http://normblog.typepad.com/normblog/2006/06/no_one_left_beh.html. Accessed 10 February 2017.

—— (2008), 'The Euston moment', *Guardian*, 21 April. www.theguardian.com/commentisfree/2008/apr/21/theeustonmoment. Accessed 10 February 2017.

Krueger, A. (2007), *What Makes a Terrorist: Economics and the Roots of Terrorism*. Princeton, NJ: Princeton University Press.

LeDrew, S. (2015), *The Evolution of Atheism: The Politics of a Modern Movement.* Oxford: Oxford University Press.

Mandaville, P. (2009), 'Muslim transnational identity and state responses in Europe and the UK after 9/11: political community, ideology and authority', *Journal of Ethnic and Migration Studies,* 35 (3), 491–506.

Miller, D. and Massoumi, N. (2016), Briefing on the Home Office, RICU and Muslim Civil Society Groups, Submission to the Home Affairs Select Committee Countering Extremism Inquiry. CEX0062. 10 June. Ordered to be published on 14 June 2016.

Mills, T., Aked, H., Massoumi, N. and Miller, D. (2015a), 'Taking racism seriously: Islamophobia, civil liberties and the state', Open Democracy, 22 June. www.opendemocracy.net/ourkingdom/tom-mills-hilary-aked-narzanin-massoumi-david-miller/taking-racism-seriously-islamophobia. Accessed 15 February 2017.

Mills, T., Massoumi, N. and Miller, D. (2015b), 'Apologists for terror or defenders of human rights? The Cage controversy in context', Open Democracy, 31 July. www.opendemocracy.net/ourkingdom/tom-mills-narzanin-massoumi-david-miller/apologists-for-terror-or-defenders-of-human-righ. Accessed 10 February 2017.

Modood, T. (2005), *Multicultural Politics: Racism, Ethnicity and Muslims in Britain.* Edinburgh: Edinburgh University Press.

—— (2009), 'Ethnicity and religion', in M. Flinders, A. Gamble, C. Hay and M. Kenny (eds), *The Oxford Handbook of British Politics.* Oxford: Oxford University Press, pp. 484–99.

Molyneux, J. (2016), 'Secularism, Islamophobia and the politics of religion'. *Irish Marxist Review,* 16, 5 December. http://johnmolyneux.blogspot.co.uk/2016/12/secularism-islamophobia-and-politics-of.html. Accessed 13 February 2017.

Morris, A. (1984), *The Origins of the Civil Rights Movement.* New York: Free Press.

—— (1992), 'Political consciousness and collective action', in A.D. Morris and M. Mueller (eds), *Frontiers of Social Movement Theory.* New Haven, CT: Yale University Press, 351–73.

National Secular Society (2014), '"Learning jihad": new report on campus extremism has launch event cancelled by the University of West London', 11 November. www.secularism.org.uk/news/2014/11/learning-jihad--new-report-on-campus-extremism-has-launch-event-cancelled-by-the-university-of-west-london. Accessed 15 February 2017.

O'Toole, T. and Gale, R. (2010), 'Contemporary grammars of political action among ethnic minority young activists', *Ethnic and Racial Studies,* 33 (1), 126–43.

One Law for All (2011), *Enemies Not Allies: The Far Right,* August. www.onelawforall.org.uk/wp-content/uploads/Enemies-not-Allies-web-version1.pdf. Accessed 14 February 2017.

Pape, R (2003), 'The strategic logic of suicide terrorism', *American Political Science Review*, 97 (3), 343–61.

—— (2005), *Dying to Win: The Strategic Logic of Suicide Terrorism*. New York: Random House.

Patel, P. (1997), 'Third wave feminism and black women's activism', in H.S Mirza (ed.), *Black British Feminism: A Reader*. London: Routledge, pp. 255–67.

—— (2014), 'Flying by the nets of racism, patriarchy and religion', in S. Dhaliwal and N. Yuval-Davis (eds), *Women Against Fundamentalism: Stories of Dissent and Solidarity*. London: Lawrence and Wishart, location 1045–308.

Powerbase (2010), 'Harry Hatchet', Page modified 15 July. http://powerbase.info/index.php/Harry_Hatchet. Accessed 13 February 2017.

—— (2016a), 'Euston Manifesto', Page modified 10 June. http://powerbase.info/index.php/Euston_Manifesto. Accessed 13 February 2017.

—— (2016b), 'Caroline Cox', Page modified 7 October. http://powerbase.info/index.php/Caroline_Cox. Accessed 14 February 2017.

—— (2017), 'Taslima Nasreen', Page modified 15 February. http://powerbase.info/index.php/Taslima_Nasreen. Accessed 15 February 2017.

Russia Today (2014), 'Faith in reason', Russia Today, 25 September. www.rt.com/shows/worlds-apart-oksana-boyko/190352-religion-isis-violencia-politics/. Accessed 10 February 2017.

Sahgal, G. (2015), 'Knowing my place – the secular tradition and universal values', in S. Dhaliwal and N. Yuval-Davis (eds), *Women Against Fundamentalism: Stories of Dissent and Solidarity*. London: Lawrence and Wishart, Chapter 3.

Sahgal, G. and Yuval-Davis, N. (1992), 'Introduction: fundamentalism, multiculturalism and women in Britain', in G. Sahgal and N. Yuval-Davis (eds), *Refusing Holy Orders: Women and Fundamentalism in Britain*. London: Virago, pp. 1–25.

Sayyid, S. (2014), *Recalling the Caliphate: Decolonisation and World Order*. London: Hurst and Co.

Seymour, R. (2005), 'The genocidal imagination of Christopher Hitchens', *Monthly Review*, 26 November. http://mrzine.monthlyreview.org/2005/seymour261105.html. Accessed 10 February 2017.

—— (2012), *Unhitched: The Trial of Christopher Hitchens*. London and New York: Verso.

Sivanandan, A. (1990), *Communities of Resistance: Writings on Black Struggles for Socialism*. London: Verso.

Sylvester, R. (2016), 'We're too stupid to decide on EU (that includes me)', *The Times*, 23 May.

Tax, M. (2012), *Double Bind: The Muslim Right, the Anglo-American Left and Universal Human Rights*. New York: Centre for Secular Space

Trilling, D. (2013), 'Beyond Dawkins', *New Humanist*, 16 August. https://newhumanist.org.uk/articles/4271/beyond-dawkins. Accessed 10 February 2017.

WAF (1990), 'Women against fundamentalism', Newsletter, No. 1, November.

PART 4

Fighting Back

12

Fighting Back: Challenging the State and Social Movements from Above

Narzanin Massoumi, Tom Mills and David Miller

In this short concluding chapter, we draw on the analysis in the preceding chapters to suggest how anti-racists can most effectively fight back against Islamophobic ideas, policies and movements and ask what can be done in the face of the very serious onslaught on the status of Muslims in public life.

The first point to make is that an effective political response to Islamophobia must go further than limited ideas-based approaches. A number of attempts to address rising Islamophobia have sought to challenge negative stereotypes, hoping to reassure a hostile or suspicious public that Muslims are not all dangerous extremists or terrorists; that they do not in fact represent a threat to British culture or values; and that Islam is a religion of peace. Naturally, we sympathise with such initiatives. Any organised efforts to challenge racism should be welcomed. But in our view the effectiveness of such approaches will at best be limited since they direct anti-racist action away from where Islamophobia emanates: the institutions of the state and 'movements from above'.

Well-intentioned PR campaigns and educative initiatives seeking to rehabilitate the reputation of Muslims and Islam will likely face less powerful opposition than more overtly 'political' approaches, and if successful, they may insulate some sections of the public from Islamophobic ideas and thereby contribute towards a less hostile atmosphere for Muslims. But even assuming such campaigns are effective in stemming the spread of racist ideas – and this is very difficult to assess – they will at best be ameliorating the effects of Islamophobia, rather than addressing its causes. Ultimately, Islamophobia is not, as liberals tend to assume, rooted in ignorance or bigotry, and the challenge for anti-racists is not only to confront wrong ideas, but also the powerful actors and movements mobilising such ideas *in pursuit of certain interests*.

In concrete terms this of course means mobilising against the most obnoxious racist movements in society. But not only that. An effective anti-racist strategy must do more than challenge the far right. As should be clear from preceding chapters, we consider fascists, the 'alt-right' and other far-right Islamophobic movements to be a significant part of the overall picture. Such movements interact with more elite political actors in ways which are not always appreciated, and there are moreover worrying signs that they are themselves beginning to make inroads into state power. But at present they remain amongst the more marginal of the political forces driving Islamophobia, and they often circulate political ideas within their own organisational networks that are essentially more extreme versions of 'mainstream' ideas and policy positions. An exclusive focus on the activities of the far right, therefore, can serve to distract from apparently more respectable, and powerful, political actors. The fascists then must be politically opposed, without quarter, but always as part of a broader anti-racist strategy.

For now at least, the far right remains somewhat marginal. The state, however, has been absolutely central to contemporary Islamophobia, and it follows rather straightforwardly that any movement against Islamophobia must focus not on public prejudice, nor exclusively on the far right, but first and foremost on the excessive powers of the state counter-terrorism apparatus, campaigning for the reform of racist laws and practices. This means first of all defending to the utmost the basic human rights and legal processes that are abused and eroded with appeals to 'counter-terrorism' and 'counter-extremism' – hardly a controversial position to take. But in our view, it also means challenging a militaristic and anti-democratic geopolitics that is deeply embedded in state institutions and elite policy making, and which similarly offends against basic liberal and democratic principles. An effective movement against Islamophobia then, in our view, should also be a movement for peace, democracy and human rights.

There are also consequences here in terms of how an anti-racist movement should organise. In a situation in which the state has not only supported or participated in the most egregious abuses of human rights, but domestically has sought to coerce and co-opt social movements and civil society organisations into compliance with its policy agendas, no anti-racist group, whether 'Muslim' or 'left', can support, still less actively participate in, state 'counter-extremism' initiatives and expect to emerge with any credibility. Anti-racists should maintain complete independence from the counter-terrorism apparatus; they should defend civil society from all state incursions; and under no circumstances should offer support, whether overt or tacit, to racist policies and practices.

To be clear, this does not mean that anti-racists should refuse to engage with politicians and other state actors. On the contrary, an effective anti-racist movement should be open to alliances with 'elite' critics of racist policies and excessive executive powers. As emphasised in previous chapters, we do not regard the state as an undifferentiated set of institutions, and neither do we regard the policy elite that operates in and around state institutions as a homogeneous group with a unified set of ideas and interests. Indeed, one of the great advantages of the sort of analytical framework we propose is that since it recognises political structures as a product of social action, and elite networks as contingent and to some extent fluid, it allows us to identify weaknesses in what can otherwise seem 'from below' to be an unassailable apparatus of oppression. As we have argued, this is in fact one of the problems with many radical accounts of racism. While offering an uncompromising response to the complacency of liberalism on the question of racism, radicals have too often failed to then convincingly account for how racism is in fact produced and reproduced, thus risking falling into a fatalistic hyper-critical mode and ultimately political paralysis. History though clearly shows that elites do not always get what they want; that behind closed doors they do not necessarily agree on priorities, strategies and tactics; that they can buckle under pressure; and that racist structures, policies and movements can be defeated by movements from below. In our view, such victories will be most likely in the fight against Islamophobia if anti-racists can build broad social coalitions within and without institutions, appealing to basic human rights, the professional values and integrity of workers and their representative organisations, while targeting and exposing racist institutions and policies and their advocates.

Effectively opposing racist state policies also requires that we show active solidarity with the victims of racism. It is not enough to defend liberal principles in the abstract, nor to campaign for the reform of racist laws and policies. Solidarity with the Muslim 'community', and especially Muslim civil society groups, should be a central principle of contemporary anti-racism. As a result of years of Islamophobic action by the institutions and movements we have detailed here, an air of permanent suspicion hangs over any Muslim or Muslim organisation. In such a context, where racist ideas have been thoroughly mainstreamed, politics and public life are heavily weighted against politically active Muslims and even completely baseless accusations, insinuations and smears can do a great deal of political damage. It is ethically incumbent on all non-Muslims who hold to principles of equality to never abuse the relative political advantages this situation affords them, and moreover to stand in active solidarity with those whom it disadvantages.

These seem to us to be straightforward principles that all liberals and leftists should uphold. But as we have detailed in Chapter 11, the waters have been muddied by certain sections of the left which have adopted de facto racist positions; and in a broader climate of pervasive Islamophobia, the arguments they have mobilised have wrong-footed many on the left, diminishing anti-racist mobilisations. An important aspect of anti-racist strategy, therefore, must also be to confront those on the left who give cover to Islamophobia; to win the arguments through reasoned appeals to anti-racist principles; and to thereby foster an effective form of anti-racism that engages in a clear-sighted way with contemporary politics.

Contributors

Hilary Aked is a PhD candidate at the University of Bath. Her thesis investigates Israel and the Zionist movement's response to the Boycott, Divestment and Sanctions (BDS) movement in the UK. She is co-author of *The Britain Israel Communications and Research Centre: Giving Peace a Chance?* (2013) and *The Henry Jackson Society and the Degeneration of British Neoconservatism* (2015) and has worked on an Open Society-funded Public Interest Investigations project on the counterjihad network.

Linda Briskman holds the Margaret Whitlam Chair of Social Work at Western Sydney University. Her areas of research and advocacy include asylum seeker rights, Indigenous rights and Islamophobia. Her extensive publications include the award-winning co-authored *Human Rights Overboard* (2008). She is a convenor of Voices Against Bigotry.

Tom Griffin is a freelance researcher and journalist. He is co-author of the Spinwatch report *The Cold War on British Muslims* (2011). He has worked with organisations including the Pat Finucane Centre and Justice for the Forgotten on documentary research into the Irish Troubles and is a former managing editor and Political Correspondent of the *Irish World* newspaper.

Deepa Kumar is Associate Professor of Media Studies at Rutgers University. Her work is driven by an active engagement with the key issues that characterise our era – neoliberalism and imperialism. Kumar began her research into the politics of empire shortly after the tumultuous events of 9/11. Her book titled *Islamophobia and the Politics of Empire* (2012) looks at how the 'Muslim enemy' has historically been mobilised to suit the goals of empire.

Arun Kundnani is an activist, academic and author who has written extensively about race, Islamophobia, political violence and surveillance. He is the former editor of the journal *Race & Class*, received his PhD from London Metropolitan University and now teaches at New York University. His books include *The Muslims are Coming! Islamophobia, Extremism, and the Domestic War on Terror* (2014) and *The End of Tolerance: Racism in 21st Century Britain*, which was selected as a *New Statesman* book of the year in 2007.

Nathan Lean is a writer and researcher whose work focuses on Muslim-Christian relations and anti-Muslim prejudice. He holds a Master's degree in

International Studies from East Carolina University and a Master of Arts in Arab Studies from Georgetown University, where he is currently pursuing a PhD in Theology and Religious Studies. Nathan is the author of three books, including the award-winning *The Islamophobia Industry* (2012). His writing has been featured in the *Los Angeles Times*, *Washington Post*, *New York Daily News*, CNN, Salon, *The New Republic* and the *Christian Science Monitor* among others.

Sarah Marusek is a postdoctoral research fellow in Religion Studies at the University of Johannesburg, researching Islam, Islamophobia, decolonial frameworks and theologies of liberation. Her doctoral research focused on Shi'i Islamic activism in Lebanon and her fieldwork was funded by the generous support of the Mellon Foundation. A manuscript of this research, entitled *Faith and Resistance: The Politics of Love and War in Lebanon*, will be published by Pluto Press in 2018. Marusek also undertook fieldwork in Iran and Senegal during her graduate studies. She holds a PhD in Social Science from the Maxwell School of Syracuse University and a Master's in International Affairs from the New School, New York. She is co-author of *The Israel Lobby in Europe* (2015); *The Henry Jackson Society and the Degeneration of British Neoconservatism: Liberal Interventionism, Islamophobia and the 'War on Terror'* (2015); and *How Israel Attempts to Mislead the United Nations: Deconstructing Israel's Campaign Against the Palestinian Return Centre* (2015).

Narzanin Massoumi is a British Academy postdoctoral fellow (2016–19) in the Department of Social and Policy Sciences at the University of Bath. She is co-convenor of the British Sociological Association Race and Ethnicity Study Group and the author of *Muslim Women, Social Movements and the 'War on Terror'* (2015).

David Miller is Professor of Sociology in the Department of Social and Policy Sciences at the University of Bath. He was RCUK Global Uncertainties leadership fellow (2013–16) conducting a project to examine the construction, use and impact of expertise on 'terrorism'. He has written widely on propaganda, spin and lobbying and was co-founder of Public Interest Investigations, a non-profit company of which Spinwatch and Powerbase are projects. Recent publications include: *A Century of Spin: How Public Relations Became the Cutting Edge of Corporate Power* (co-author, Pluto Press, 2008); *The Britain Israel Communications and Research Centre: Giving Peace a Chance?* (co-author, 2013); *Critical Terrorism Studies since 11 September 2001: What has been Learned?* (co-editor, 2014); *Stretching the Sociological Imagination: Essays in Honour of John Eldridge* (co-editor, 2015); *The Henry Jackson Society and the Degeneration of British Neoconservatism* (co-author,

2015); *The Israel Lobby and the European Union* (co-author, 2016); *The New Governance of Addictive Substances and Behaviours* (co-author, 2017); *Impact of Market Forces on Addictive Substances and Behaviours: The Web of Influence of Addictive Industries* (co-author, 2017).

Tom Mills is Lecturer in Sociology at Aston University. His doctoral research examined how the end of social democracy and the rise of neoliberalism impacted on the BBC, and is the basis of his book, *The BBC: The Myth of a Public Service* (2016). He is the co-author of *The Cold War on British Muslims* (2011) and *The Britain Israel Communications and Research Centre: Giving Peace a Chance?* (2013) and a former co-editor of the political website, New Left Project.

Scott Poynting is Adjunct Professor in the School of Justice at Queensland University of Technology, and in the School of Social Sciences and Psychology at Western Sydney University. He researches on state crime, ethnic targeting and 'racial' profiling. He is co-editor (with David Whyte) of *Counter-terrorism and State Political Violence: The War on Terror as Terror* (2012) and (with George Morgan) *Global Islamophobia: Muslims and Moral Panic in the West* (2012). He is co-author of *Bin Laden in the Suburbs* (2004).

Asim Qureshi graduated in Law (LLB Hons) LLM, specialising in International Law and Islamic Law. He is the Research Director at CAGE, and since 2003 has investigated the impact of counter-terrorism practices worldwide, having published a wide range of NGO reports, academic journals and articles. In 2009 he authored the book, *Rules of the Game: Detention, Deportation, Disappearance*. In 2010, he began advising the legal teams involved in defending terrorism trials in the USA and at Guantánamo Bay, Cuba.

Shenaz Bunglawala is former head of research at Mend where she led research into Islamophobia, racial and religious equality and the impact of counter-terrorism legislation on British Muslim communities. Before that she was head of research at ENGAGE, an initiative designed to improve British Muslim representation and participation in British media and politics.

She taught undergraduate courses in political science at the LSE and King's College, London while studying for her doctoral degree. She sat on the Research Excellence Framework 2014 expert sub-panel for Theology and Religious Studies and has advised on various AHRC/ESRC research projects. She is a director of the Byline Festival Foundation for independent journalism.

Index

Bashir, Kalsoom, 260
Bawer, Bruce, 180
Bayoumi, 37
BBC, 115, 224
Becker, Newton and Rochelle, 205
Beckert, Sven, 66
Begg, Moazzam, 252–3, 257
Bender, Thomas, 51
Bernard Lewis Family Charitable
    Trust, 228–9
Bernardi, Cory, 145
Bernstein, Zalman, 206
BICOM, 240
Birthright Israel, 202
Bishop, Julie, 145
Blackburn, Robin, 66, 217
Blair government, 8, 220, 236, 239
Blazing Cat Fur, 126
Bloc Against Islam, 2015 rally, 178
Blumenthal, Max, 194, 217
Boies and Pichardo, 18
Bolton, John, 177, 191
Bonazzi, Roberta, 191
Bouattia, Malia, 256
Boucher, Miguel Papi, 191
Boykin, William, 194
Brah, Avtar, 248
Brandis, George, 144
Breakthrough Media, 109
Breitbart, media enterprise, 124, 131,
    178, 207
Breivik, Anders Behring, 165
Bridge Initiative, 127
Britain First, 172
British Muslims for Secular
    Democracy, 22, 251, 259
British National Party, 77
Burgerbewegung Pax Europa, 165,
    176
Burnham, Andy, 112
Bush administration, 216, 220–1, 244

CAGE, 12, 74, 97, 106–8, 110–11,
    114–15, 252, 257

Cameron, David, 12, 105–6, 169, 223,
    225, 228
Camp, Jordan, 69
Campaign for Nuclear Disarmament
    (CND), 235, 251
Campus Watch, 192
Camus, Renaud, 174, 177
Carmon, Ayre, 204
Carmon, Yigal, 192
Carson, Ben, 130
Casuals United, 172
Catherine Lewis Foundation, 228
Center for American Progress, 189,
    206
Center for Inquiry, 247
Center for Security Policy, 22, 24, 124,
    130, 178, 189–90, 219, 230
Center for Vigilant Freedom, 22
Central Fund of Israel, 202
Centre for Social and Economic
    Progress, 228
Centre for Social Cohesion, 167,
    221–2, 227
Centre for Social Justice, 228
Channel programme, 10–12, 169
Charities Commission, 114–15
Charlie Hebdo, event, 143, 147, 191
Choudary, Anjem, 175, 239
Christians United for Israel, 202
Christine Brim, 22
Ciobo, Steve, 153
Civitas, 222, 229
Clarion Fund, The, 24, 189–90
clash of civilisations, 38, 54, 65, 139,
    155
Coalition government 2010, 103
Cohen, Adrian, 239
Cohen, Nick, 236–7, 239, 260
Cohen, Stan, 138
Collier, Peter, 191
colonialism, 36, 40, 54, 58–9, 63, 137
Commentary magazine, 22, 218–19,
    221, 229